Ninety-Nine Chances

THE NINETY-NINE SERIES
BOOK FOUR

ELISHEBA HAXBY

JESSE VINCENT

ABOVE THE
SUN

Contents

CHAPTER 1

January 20, 7:39 p.m.

DAKOTA

As I walked out of the weekly Narcotics Anonymous meeting, my muscles tightened and unease crept into my chest. The creepiest sensation of being watched settled heavily into my nerves, putting me on edge. I scanned the parking lot, but nothing was out of the ordinary—just a handful of people walking toward their cars.

Fumbling through my purse for my keys, I tried to push aside the disturbing sensation.

What was wrong with me lately? Why couldn't I just enjoy this newfound happiness I had worked so hard for?

For years, my life had been consumed by addiction and struggle. But now, I was finally starting to feel like my feet were firmly planted on solid ground. My relationship with Tim was stronger than ever, and it had been over a year since my last relapse. Yet there was still a lingering fear that this happiness could all come crashing down at any moment—that somehow, despite everything, I'd manage to screw it all up again. The sickening feeling gnawed at my gut and refused to let go, no matter how much I tried to push it aside.

Keys clutched tightly in my hand, I rushed to my car. My hand shook as I clumsily unlocked my 1993 Honda Civic. *Calm down, Dakota. You're being ridiculous. Ryan's dead.* No one was coming for me. It had been over two years ...

I sank into my seat and turned the car on before scanning the parking lot for the final time. A deep blue Mustang with tinted windows sat off to the left on the far side of the lot. Had I seen that car before? It didn't matter. My nerves were getting the best of me.

These were the moments I had learned to be extra careful. When my mind started playing tricks on me. It meant the addict was close to the surface, begging to get out. Cranking the radio, I took a deep breath and counted backward from ten. The Serenity Prayer flitted through my head. It was still hard for me to say out loud. I'd come a long way with the Higher Power thing, but there were still places of resistance.

I gave the Mustang one last look, then backed out of the parking spot and peeled out of the parking lot, desperate to put the meeting and my unease behind me. My tires squealed as I made the turn onto the main road, and my heart pounded in rhythm with the beat of the music flooding from the speakers. "Unwell" by Matchbox Twenty played on the radio. Rob Thomas' voice, laden with melancholy and regret, echoed my own emotions.

A quick glance in the rearview mirror sent my pulse racing. A few cars back, the Mustang followed, gliding smoothly around the corner like a predator stalking its prey. What the freak? Were they following me?

Old memories flooded back like a tsunami. Ryan's cruel laughter, the harsh whisper of his threats against the thunderous backdrop of pounding music. The metallic taste of fear. I couldn't breathe. Couldn't think straight.

My fingers gripped the steering wheel tightly as I made a sharp turn onto a old road leading to my house. In the mirror, I could see the car continuing on the previous road.

Wow. I was seriously losing it. Nobody was following me. No one was watching me. I was just a complete paranoid mess. I changed the radio station and ignored my anxious thoughts. One of these days, the demons that tried to torment me would fully be gone. Until then, I needed to fake it. To pretend that everything was okay.

I pulled into the driveway at the home Tim had purchased earlier this year and breathed in deep. He had sold his home on Quilcene and purchased this one in Port Hadlock, wanting to give us a fresh start in a new town. Not to mention it was closer to his job at the Jefferson County Police Department. Some days, though, twenty minutes away from my hometown didn't feel like far enough. Memories lurked around every corner, and I still ran into people I used to party with on a regular basis.

I opened the car door and stepped out, and made my way into the house. When I walked in, Barenaked Ladies' "One Week" was playing, and the smell of popcorn wafted in the air. Tim stood in the kitchen, his back to me, shaking a cast iron pan over the stove.

A smile formed on my lips at the sight of him—Tim, in his faded jeans and police academy sweatshirt, cooking popcorn. He was so ordinary, so domestic, so unlike the life I knew before.

As quietly as possible, I tiptoed toward him, suppressing the giggle that wanted to rise. I jabbed his sides with a sudden "Boo!"

He screamed like a girl and spun around. "Uh! You are so paying for that!"

Smiling broadly, I backed away. He lunged for me, grabbing my sides and tickling me.

I squirmed and fought against him as laughter erupted from my mouth. "Stop! You're gonna burn the popcorn!"

"Oh well." He laughed, tickling harder. "There's plenty where that came from!"

I fought back for a while but soon we were both laughing so hard we could barely catch our breath. Tim's eyes locked on mine, his gaze warm and loving. His laughter faded into a soft smile as he moved closer, his hands still resting on my sides.

This was the man I'd known since childhood, the one who never ceased to amaze me with his kindness and dedication. His expression held a gentleness and heat that melted away all of my worries.

He kissed me softly yet passionately as he drew me in. My hands found their way around his shoulders as his encircled my waist. And just like that, between his playfulness and then his love, the fear that had weighed heavy on me five minutes ago vanished, replaced with this safe feeling of being loved. Only Tim could reach these places inside me.

Smells of burnt popcorn filled the air. "Oh crap." Tim pulled away from me and rushed to the stove.

"Told you!"

He pulled the burning popcorn off the heat. "And I told you we could make more." He leaned toward me and kissed me again, sweet and slow, before pulling away, searching my face. "And I'd say it was worth it."

There was so much emotion behind his expression that, after all this time, I still wasn't sure how to handle it. I looked at the floor to break the intensity. "You better make that popcorn, or we'll never get to our movie."

He hesitated and then turned to the popcorn mess.

"I'm going to change into something more comfortable for the movie." I walked to our bedroom, dug through my dresser, pulled out some sweats, then headed to the bathroom.

As the door clicked shut behind me, I caught a glimpse of myself in the mirror. My face was flushed with laughter and warmth as I reached up to touch my lips, still tingling from his kiss. The girl in the mirror didn't look haunted anymore, not like she used to. There was still an echo of the old fear, a shadow in the depths of my eyes, but being with Tim seemed to chase away those ghosts.

I sighed, my chest rising and falling steadily in the mirror. Was I worthy of this? This love, this warmth, this peace? After all that I had done in my addiction, the lying, the stealing—Gabriel's death... I wasn't sure. I swallowed the doubt that rose with these questions, the doubt that had always been a part of me, intertwining itself with every thought and action.

Turning on the water, I tried to push away the thoughts that pestered me.

I rinsed my face, the cool water seeping into my skin, washing away the residual traces of the day. I pulled on my sweats, and the comfort they brought was palpable.

On the way back to the living room, I snagged one of Tim's oversized hoodies and slipped it over my head. I breathed in through my nose, inhaling his musky, earthy scent. It smelled like home.

I stepped into the living room, and Tim was standing there, holding a large bowl of popcorn.

"You ready for this?" He threw a piece of popcorn in the air, and caught it with his mouth before grabbing the remote. We had been talking about doing this for weeks, but both of us had been busy.

"As I'll ever be," I smirked at him and then settled into the couch. Because you're about to finally be proven wrong."

"Whatever." He said and flicked on the television.

Ever since we were kids, we've had the same disagreement about which *Star Wars* episode was the best. Episode Three was my favorite, yet he swore Episode Five was the best movie of all time.

Tim sank into the couch next to me, placing the popcorn on his leg so we could both reach it. "There's no way for you to prove me wrong with this. It's strictly opinion. You have yours, and I have mine. We're just going to have to agree to disagree."

"Yeah, right," I scoffed. Twelve years of this ridiculous argument, and now he wanted me to agree to disagree? No freaking way.

"Most people on the planet, myself included, disagree with you on this."

"And you made my point for me. Most people are idiots." I reached into the popcorn and grabbed a handful.

"Touché," he said with a chuckle, then lifted the remote and pressed play.

When I first met Tim, I was probably one of six people on the planet who hadn't seen *Star Wars*. He would throw out references all the time because he thought it was cool or something. When I told him I had never even watched one episode, he was dumbfounded. How was it even possible to grow up in America and not have seen *Star Wars?*

The following weekend, he begged me to come over for a movie marathon. It was a rainy Saturday, and my parents were fighting anyway, so I accepted.

He gathered a bunch of pillows and blankets in his house and made us a comfy spot in front of the television. We binged all six episodes, starting from Episode One. And this is what began our playful feud.

To this day, Tim regretted showing me them in what I would say was the correct order.

Tim's arm slipped around my shoulders, pulling me closer to him. As the story began, a sense of contentment and belonging settled around me.

The opening crawl filled the screen, and sounds of John Williams' iconic music swelled as I leaned into Tim. For the moment, I let go of our silly banter and got lost in a galaxy far, far away.

Sometimes I wished I could be with Tim like this all the time and never have to leave the house. Being with him had always been the place I felt safe.

The popcorn bowl slowly emptied as the movie progressed. For a while, I was completely immersed in the world of Jedi and Sith, lightsabers and epic duels. But somewhere in the middle of the movie, a line spoken by Yoda turned anxiety in my guts once more. "Fear is the path to the dark side. Fear leads to anger. Anger leads to hate. Hate leads to suffering."

A sudden chill swept over me, making my skin prickle. It was something I had heard a thousand times, yet this time it hit differently. It was like Yoda was speaking directly to me, his words echoing my own fears.

I could practically feel Ryan's cold, menacing glare on me, his hands choking the life out of me. *Stop it, Dakota.* Ryan was dead. Yet his memory was as alive as ever, a ghost that refused to be laid to rest.

Fear is the path to the dark side.

So many years of my life had been stolen by fear. My fear had truly led to my dark side. And to so much suffering.

Thoughts of earlier that day intruded into the moment, and trepidation settled into my chest. That deep blue Mustang... it had seriously seemed like it was following me. Should I tell Tim about it? No. I shook off the thought and tried to refocus on the movie.

Was this fear trying to lead me into the darkness once more? Damn it! I couldn't let that happen. I had too much to lose now.

"You okay, Dakota?" Tim's voice broke through my spiraling thoughts, and I turned to look at him. His gentle gaze was filled with concern, his warm brown eyes flickering in the soft light from the TV.

I shook my head. "Yeah, I'm good," I lied, not wanting to go there. This was something I needed to process by myself for a while.

"Have you finally realized how wrong you've actually been?" he asked with a grin, leaning in for a kiss.

"You wish," I teased, but inwardly there was a gnawing ache in my guts.

His lips met mine, and the pain eased a bit. Tamara told me once that love was the antidote for fear. Sometimes when I was with Tim like this, I actually believed her. Sliding my arms around his neck, I invited his kiss to become deeper. For a moment, I allowed myself to forget about Ryan, about the Mustang, about everything. There was only Tim and me. His arms were my haven, his warmth a welcome respite from the demons that often haunted me.

His hand cradled my face, and he whispered "I love you" again and again between kisses. Tim had been my guiding light since we were kids. His love had never given up on me, even when I pushed him away so many times.

"Remember what tomorrow is," he said softly, kissing me near my ear. I smiled, though I wondered if this was the reason for the fear, the reason my mind was playing tricks on me. Tomorrow was our two-year anniversary when we officially got together. The day he met me in Ocean Shores for Tamara's wedding. It was kinda weird that our anniversary was the same as my sister's wedding day, but it felt right in a way. Tamara's love, just like Tim's, never faltered, and so it was fitting that the two occasions were etched in time together.

Two years though... It was a big deal for me. I'd never done anything for two years straight except for meth. Were these darker sides of who I was working to sabotage this? I couldn't let my darkness win. I could not let this happen.

Over the last few years, Tim had become everything to me. He was my new addiction. I needed him like I used to need that next hit of meth. Damn. I hated myself for thinking of Tim like that. He was so much more than an addiction.

"Coda," he whispered, his brow furrowing as he cupped my cheek, his thumb brushing against my lower lip. "What's wrong?"

"Absolutely nothing," I said, pulling his face to mine once more. He didn't need to know about my internal struggle. All I wanted him to know at that moment was that he was enough to quiet my demons. I crushed my lips against his and let his love consume me until I forgot every awful thing my dark side had done.

CHAPTER 2

January 21, 1:56 p.m.

DAKOTA

I grabbed the bag of garbage and hurried through the back door of the Chevron station where I worked. This was the final task on my list for the day, and I couldn't wait to finish so I could get ready for my date with Tim. The thought of a three-hour drive wasn't exactly thrilling, but he had insisted we meet at the same spot where our relationship began, in Ocean Shores. I had already clocked out and was about to toss the bag into the dumpster when I heard a motor rev.

My head jerked through the noise, and my heart pounded against my ribs like a hammer on an anvil. The Mustang from the night before sat there, its engine purring like a panther preparing to pounce. Justin, one of Ryan's former henchmen, stepped out of the back driver's-side door before Avery emerged from the other side. His cold stare locked onto me as he approached.

Memories from that terrifying night behind the casino flooded through me, when they were sent by Ryan to collect my debt. Fighting the urge to scream, I glanced around, planning an escape. Why were they here? What would they want from me after so much time?

"Hey, sugar," Avery said, his voice dripping with a sickening sweetness that made my stomach churn. "Where you been? I never see you around anymore."

Sugar? Barf. I couldn't stand this guy. "That's because I don't hang around the rodent holes you do anymore." I wanted to say so much more, but pissing him off wasn't a good idea.

He stepped closer and grabbed my shoulder, his grip iron-tight. "That's because you prefer hanging with the pigs."

Pulling away from his grasp, I glared at him and spoke through clenched teeth. "Pigs are an upgrade from snakes."

Avery's expression turned menacing as he stepped even closer. "Watch your mouth, Dakota, or you may not have one for much longer."

Taking in a deep breath, I mentally counted to five in a vain effort to calm myself. My skin crawled with a desperate need to escape. To run far away from this place. For the last few years, I'd tried so damn hard to forget the past, but it was seared inside my soul. Moments like this reminded me that I would never really be free, no matter how hard I tried.

"Why are you guys here?"

"We're calling in a debt," Justin said, stepping forward.

"What? No way." It didn't make sense. I had been out of the scene for two years. Why now?

"Yes, way, Dakota," Avery interjected harshly. "The way Victor sees it, you owe him." They were circling me now like vultures eyeing a carcass.

I could feel the icy pressure of their gazes, each eye like a serrated blade scraping over my fragile bravado.

"For what?" Flashes of that other life sent my mind reeling. Victor had been Ryan's boss, and from what I knew of him, he was ten shades darker than Ryan, with far more money and power. What could I possibly owe him?

"For Ryan's death." Avery scowled, his dark eyes gleaming with an unspeakable hatred.

Bile rose in my throat at the mention of his name. "What?"

Avery grabbed my shirt and slammed me against the dumpster. "His involvement with you got him killed."

I glared at him, the cold metal of the dumpster biting into my back. "Or it could have been that he shot a police officer."

Avery snarled, his grip tight around my collar. "Spoken like a true pig lover."

A car door slammed behind us. "That's enough!" a man yelled, his voice like a whip cutting through the tense atmosphere.

Avery immediately let go of my shirt and stepped away. I glanced around him to see my rescuer.

Ricky? Ryan's cousin? What was he doing here? Last I'd seen him was about two and a half years ago on his way to treatment. Now he was running with these guys? And he seemed to have some sort of authority over them.

"Hey, Dakota, sorry about all this. We just need you to run a package for us," Ricky said, his tone almost apologetic as he approached me, hands raised in a harmless gesture.

"What? Ricky, no!" I shook my head fervently, backing away from him.

"The hell you won't." Justin thrust his pointer finger toward me. "You owe us."

"Shut up, Justin!" Ricky snapped, then turned to me and spoke gently. "Listen, Dakota, it's not a big deal, okay? All you have to do is take a small package to a guy in Brinnon."

I stared at Ricky, disbelief clouding my mind. "It is a big deal."

I forced myself to keep my voice steady despite the quickening of my pulse. "Do you not know who I've been dating for the last two years? I couldn't do that to him."

Justin let out a sarcastic laugh, his expresion flashing with cruel humor. "You don't want to see what Victor will have us do to your precious cop boyfriend if you don't."

His words hit the center of my chest, knocking the air from my lungs. It was one thing to mess with my life—I probably deserved it—but Tim's life was worth so much more than mine. I looked at Ricky. Regret flickered in his eyes before he averted them. My stomach clenched. If Justin were blowing smoke, Ricky would have shut him up.

I took in another long breath and stared at the ground. "When is the package due?" How in the world was this happening?

"The sooner, the better," Ricky said, stepping away, turning back to the car with Justin and Avery in tow. "We'll be in touch."

"Don't you dare tell your boyfriend about this visit or he'll pay." Avery seethed as he walked away.

My eyes pricked with tears as I watched Ricky climb into the drivers seat of the Mustang, while Justing and Avery got in the back. For a moment, I was wrapped in a cocoon of silence and disbelief, my mind spinning chaotically. What the hell had just happened?

I looked around the empty parking lot and then trudged toward my car. My hands were shaking as I fumbled with the keys, dropping them onto the hard asphalt. Cursing under my breath, I bent to pick them up, my knees weak and wobbly. After a few futile attempts, I finally managed to unlock my car and slide into the driver's seat. I stared blankly at the windshield, my thoughts spiraling into a whirlwind of panic. This couldn't be happening. And yet it was. The chilling reality came crashing around me like a house of cards in a storm, and I wrapped my arms around my stomach, trying to quell the nausea that rose in waves.

My phone pinged, pulling me from my thoughts. A text from Tim. *So looking forward to our date. Happy anniversary.*

Tears welled up, blurring my vision as I read his message—our anniversary.

I glanced at the time and cursed under my breath. It was fifteen minutes past two, and I was supposed to be meeting Tim in Ocean Shores by six, before sunset. I had to go. Swallowing my tears, I shoved the phone into my purse and gripped the wheel tightly.

The sound of my tires screeching against the pavement echoed in my ears as I sped towards my house, music blaring to drown out my racing thoughts. If I could just pretend this was all a bad dream, I could make it through this night with Tim. Anger seethed under the layers of my fear, knotting my stomach tighter. How was it that Ryan, though dead, was still stealing my life from me? Sirens screamed in my mind as I turned the corner onto my street, a chorus of warning and dread. I pounded the steering wheel in frustration, biting back the scream that threatened to break free.

I parked haphazardly in my driveway, my hands still trembling as I yanked at the door handle. Once inside, I ran to the bathroom and quickly showered. As I stood in the hot stream, I erected a barrier in my mind. Today was my two-year anniversary with Tim. I should be proud of that. This was a day meant for celebration, not for fear, not for secrets. I had to compartmentalize this new threat and tuck it away neatly for later. For a moment, I allowed myself to imagine a world where monsters like Victor didn't exist. Where Ryan was just a name on an old-school roster, not a specter haunting my every waking moment.

Today I would celebrate my love for Tim. But how? The only way I knew how to celebrate was with a line of dope and a fifth of vodka.

I blinked, immediately shaking off the lingering memories of my old habits. No, that wasn't me anymore. I was better, stronger —for Tim, for myself.

I turned off the shower and quickly dried myself before heading to my closet to find something to wear. Tim had suggested dressing up for the evening, but I didn't have many options in that category. After some rummaging, I settled on a pair of black jeggings and a maroon sweater with a scoop neck that Tamara had given me for my birthday. It wasn't exactly my usual style—I preferred jeans and a hoodie—but I was willing to make an effort for Tim tonight. After applying some mascara and lip gloss, I headed to my car. The thoughts of Justin's threat lingered in my mind as I started the engine, causing waves of nausea to wash over me.

You don't want to see what Victor will have us do to your precious cop boyfriend if you don't.

I thought of all the terrible things Victor could do to Tim if given the chance. Sucking in a sharp breath, I blasted the radio to drown out the images. I had to be strong and find a way to protect Tim, protect us both, from the looming danger. I would get through the next few days, do the stupid delivery, then it would all be over.

CHAPTER 3
January 21, 5:06 p.m.
TIM

The evening was beautiful—almost perfect. As the sun began to set, the sky shifted from a brilliant shade of blue with big fluffy clouds here and there to a soft pink with orange hues. Cold as it was, the setting sun still bathed my face with golden light. Taking a deep breath, I took a step toward the bed and breakfast.

The two-story building, with its curved edges and thatched roof, stood out against the ocean's backdrop. As I walked, I inhaled the salty scent of the ocean to calm my nerves.

This had been my plan for months, and with the help of Joe and Tamara, I'd been able to make it a reality. I invited Dakota here to surprise her with a romantic evening, and in a little over half an hour, she'd be here.

I opened the door, and the scent of garlic and steak wafted in the air. Marie greeted me with a smile. "Good evening, Mr. Moore." She held out a room key with a grin. "Let me show you to your room."

I followed her up the stairs and watched her unlock the door to our suite. Dark mahogany furniture, a crackling fireplace, and a bed draped in lush crimson velvet greeted me. It was all so formal. I wasn't sure how Dakota would feel about that. She'd probably hate it. She was more of a hamburger and milkshake kind of girl, but tonight would be different. Tonight was about stepping out of what was comfortable and predictable.

"I'm going to tell Mr. Phillips you're here." With a tilt of her head, she turned and walked away.

With Marie gone, I took a few minutes to soak it all in. Despite its grandeur, the ornate bedroom was cozy. The walls were decorated with art from local artists, and candles flickered warmly on the marble mantelpiece.

On the bedside table was a bouquet of roses, meant to be a special gift for Dakota. Knowing her, she'd probably think it was all way too over the top, but it didn't matter. If things went well tonight, we would be engaged, and I wanted it to be a night she would never forget. I thought about the way she felt in my arms last night after watching the movie and making out. The softness of her lips against mine and the way she melted into my touch. There were no more walls between us.

I surveyed the room one more time before venturing downstairs. As I descended the staircase, the clinking of silverware, the low hum of conversation, and the savory scent of sizzling steaks wafting from the kitchen filled my senses. Joe and Lillie, his two-year-old daughter, arrived hand-in-hand and spotted me immediately. Lillie's cherubic face lit up, her dark curls bouncing as she broke free from Joe's grasp and toddled towards me. I scooped Lillie into my arms and twirled her around. She giggled, her innocent laughter filling the room. Her unbridled joy and carefree spirit warmed my heart and made me think of Dakota. Would she ever be ready to have children?

Joe chuckled at our interaction. "She sure does love her soon-to-be Uncle Tim. You ready for tonight?"

His question hit me in the nervous places of my gut. "Sure, sure." I threw Lily in the air and ignored the raw feeling. Lillie giggled with delight again as she landed in my arms. I set her down, and she ran back to Joe, babbling away in toddler-speak while tugging on Joe's pants leg.

"Let's go check out the room." He grabbed Lillie's hand and led her toward the room.

Shoving my hand into my pocket, I followed after him. I caressed the small velvet box, nerves dancing in my stomach, thinking about Dakota. I was more than ready for this. I just hoped she was too.

Joe led me into the grand room, and I was immediately awed by its beauty. A large window illuminated the space with a stunning view of the ocean, and twinkle lights adorned the ceiling, forming an intimate atmosphere. In the center of the chamber sat a solitary table covered in a white tablecloth. This was the room Joe and Tamara were married in two years ago, and this was the room where Dakota and I had our technical first date.

"Purrrdy, Dada," Lillie squealed and raced towards the table.

Joe chuckled, swooping her into his arms before she could reach the precarious crystal centerpiece. "Easy there, sweetheart," he cooed at her.

"Well?" Joe glanced at me with a grin. "What do you think?"

I looked around with amazement and nodded in approval. It was everything I imagined for this night—intimate, serene, beautiful. "You've really gone above and beyond, Phillips."

Joe chuckled and shrugged modestly. "Anything for family." His words eased the tight knot of nervousness that was making a nest in my stomach.

"So, are you ready for the big moment?" he asked with a raised eyebrow, his voice taking on a teasing note.

"Fingers crossed," I said with a laugh, running my hand through my hair. "Do you have an audio system that I can plug my phone in? I made a playlist."

"Absolutely! Right this way." He directed me towards a closet on the opposite side of the room. With a flourish, he opened the doors to reveal a top-of-the-line Bose setup.

"Huner, Dada, huner," Lillie said in a whiny voice, patting her stomach.

Joe tapped her playfully on the nose, and she giggled in

response. "Just a few more minutes, sweetie." Then he focused on me again and showed me how to sync my iPhone to the sound system.

Lillie began to fuss and squirm in Joe's arms. "It's okay, sweetie. We'll get you fed." Turning his attention to me, he said. "I better go. Is there anything else you need before I do?"

"Naw, I think I'm good. Thank you for everything."

"Alright." He headed toward the door. "Well, you got my number if that changes."

As the door shut behind Joe, I whispered a prayer for help. It wasn't something I did much. But tonight, I felt a greater need for some sort of divine guidance. My mind pictured Dakota's face, filling with the deep unshakable love I held for her. They say love is blind, but for me, the opposite is true. My love saw Dakota completely. I saw her pain and scars, but I also saw her fight. The spark in her that couldn't be quenched no matter what kind of trial had been thrown at her. Dakota had known pain deeper than most, yet she was still standing, still fighting through her shadows. I didn't fully understand it, but I loved her for it. Some days I wondered what she would have been like if she hadn't been raised in the family she had been; if she hadn't walked through the suffering she had, would she still carry the kind of tenacity that took my breath away? I guess it didn't matter. It didn't do me any good to think about such things.

I pulled out the ring and stared at it. The small white gold band in my hand encased a half-carat, star-shaped diamond, the symbol of our pact when we were only eleven—allies forever. Even back then, I had an inkling that Dakota would be the one I would marry. The one I would pledge my life to. It's funny how a single pact made between fifth graders could affect one's life.

When she turned thirteen and started doing drugs and pushing me away, I had tried so hard to let her go. I had been so angry at her for throwing away her life when I knew the potential that she carried. Truth be told, though, I understood it. I'd witnessed the abuse she grew up with, and I knew the secret that darkened her soul—the torment she was trying to numb. But I also knew who she really was. I knew her sarcastic humor, her quick wit, her fire, her tenacity. My heart had broken a thousand times as I watched my best friend self-destruct, as she chose to let her secret implode from the inside out.

Over the years, I tried to date other women, to find love with someone that didn't hurt so much, but for some reason when I'd close my eyes at night, I'd always see Dakota. I stared at the ring, so many emotions coursing through me. I loved this woman so much it hurt. I was ready to pledge my whole life to her. The only question that remained was whether she was ready to do the same. I was almost positive she was. But there was a tiny shred of doubt inside that left me cold on the inside.

CHAPTER 4

January 21, 5:26 p.m.

DAKOTA

I rolled down the window and lit a smoke as I drove. Despite the beauty of the Washington landscape, the three-hour drive to Ocean Shores had been exhausting. Every few minutes, my mind would circle back to Justin and Avery and then to Ricky. What was his involvement in all of this? Ricky was Ryan's cousin, but he wasn't anything like him. There were several times Ricky had bailed me out of bad situations when we were younger. He even defended me to Ryan a few times. Nobody had the guts to stand up to Ryan.

My mind flashed to Gabriel for a moment. He had stood up to Ryan, and it had cost him his life. Guilt swam in my stomach the same way it always did when I thought of Gabriel. Even though Ryan had been the one who killed him, he wouldn't have been there that night if it wasn't for me. Maybe this was karma coming for me.

I shook my head and refocused my mind on Ricky. When he left to rehab, I was truly happy for him. Like maybe he would do better than his creep show of a family. But now he was barking orders to Justin and Avery, and they instantly obeyed like he had something over them. Maybe it was better that I didn't have the answers to these questions. The less I knew, the better.

My phone rang, jolting me out of my thoughts. My mom's number flashed on the screen, but I ignored it, taking a long drag from my cigarette instead. I wasn't in the mood for talking to anyone right now. As I mindlessly flicked through radio stations, searching for a song to distract me from my current reality, my phone rang again.

My phone rang a third time.

Mom? Why hadn't she just left a message? Nausea twisted my stomach. I answered the phone with a distant tone. "Hello." Our relationship had come a long way over the last few years, but I still had walls toward my parents. I wasn't sure that would ever change.

"Hi, sweetheart. You got a minute?" I could hear her hesitation, a thin veer from her usual warm tone that did nothing to ease the unease coiling in my stomach.

I flung my cigarette out of the window and braced myself. Nothing could be as bad as earlier today, right? "Sure," I said. I still had about ten minutes until I pulled into Ocean Shores.

She sighed heavily before she spoke. "We got your father's tests results today, and things don't look great."

A dart of fear shot through my chest as her words sank in. "What kind of tests, Mom?"

"It's his liver, honey. He has the beginning stage of cirrhosis."

"Okay ... and what does that mean exactly?" Breathing in deeply, I fought back the frustration that was growing inside me. "If it's the beginning stages, isn't it treatable?"

"Well—" Her voice broke on that one word. "It can be if he quits drinking and does what the doctor tells him, but you know how your father is."

I nodded and reached for another smoke, hand trembling as I lit the thin cylinder, the familiar burn of smoke in my lungs offering some undeserved solace. I couldn't change my dad. The last few years, he'd taken steps to work on his anger issues, but he hadn't stopped drinking, and I wasn't sure he ever would.

This could be bad... really bad. "Have you talked to Tamara?"

Of all of us kids, this news would hit her the hardest. She was the one who cared the most.

"Yes, she was the first person I called. I asked her to put your dad on the prayer chain at her church."

For a fleeting moment, I wished I had faith like my sister. On a day like today, I certainly needed it. "I'll say a prayer for him too," I said, though I wasn't sure how much good it would do. Most of the time, my connection with my Higher Power was a bit sketchy.

"Thank you. That means a lot." There were a few moments of silence before she spoke again. "I better go. I still need to call Josiah."

Desperation engulfed me as I ended the call. My veins pulsed —the addict in me feeling more alive than it had been in months. I longed for anything that could alleviate this overwhelming sensation.

If there was a line in front of me, I couldn't say I wouldn't do it. Steering into the parking lot of the bed and breakfast, I shut off the engine. In an attempt to calm myself, I stared at the charming yet quaint establishment my sister bought a year and a half ago. Taking deep breaths, I sat there reeling, striving to suppress the addict within.

After taking a final pull from my cigarette, I smashed it in the ashtray and popped a breath mint in my mouth. For Tim's sake, I had to pull it together. He was waiting for me to come in to celebrate our relationship. I couldn't arrive to our date in crisis mode. I needed to be strong for him. I could deal with the tumultuous emotions later.

With determined steps, I exited my car and ascended the steps to the grand entrance. Maria, the ever-charming event coordinator, greeted me with a bright smile as I entered. "Ms. Dakota, so great to see you this evening."

I suppressed an eye roll and forced a fake smile in return. "Good evening," I responded, though there was little that seemed good about it so far.

"Right this way." She gestured with a sweep of her arm and led me toward the room where Tamara and Joe had been married.

As she opened the double doors, I spotted Tim seated at an elegantly set table. He stood immediately upon seeing me and took a few strides in my direction. Despite this day, the sight of him made something spark inside my stomach—that raw sting of attraction that never seemed to fade.

Tim was dressed in a midnight blue Oxford shirt with his sleeves rolled up and gray slacks. A five o'clock shadow shaded his perfect jawline. The early evening sunbathed him in a warm glow as he stood upon seeing me.

As he approached me, the endless ocean provided a stunning backdrop, and the sun slowly sank towards the horizon. His chocolate brown eyes sparkled as he wrapped his arms around me, emanating a comforting mix of citrus and musk. I leaned into him, taking a deep breath to fully embrace his presence.

In that fleeting moment, the rest of the world faded away. All that mattered was Tim and me, our bodies pressed together in an embrace that felt like home. His lips found mine in a gentle, knowing kiss that had the power to momentarily erase my anxiety. His hand cupped my cheek tenderly, thumb gently brushing over the sharp edge of my cheekbone. His touch was tender, filled with an intensity that left me breathless.

Pulling away slightly, he brushed a stray hair from my face. "Happy anniversary."

"Ditto." If only things were as simple as they seemed right now. If only I could let myself fully embrace this moment without the shadow of my past looming over us.

Tim weaved his fingers through mine and led me to the table. I took in the whole scene, feeling overwhelmed and unworthy, especially given the day's events.

Over the last few years, I'd done so much work to put the past behind me. I'd found a sponsor in Narcotics Anonymous and worked through the steps. I'd even made attempts toward making peace with a Higher Power, and it was working. Some days I actually felt happy, mostly because of Tim. But in so many ways I couldn't help but believe that he could do better than me, that he deserved better than me.

Tim slipped his arm around my waist and whispered, "I love you."

His words weighed on me with a blend of love and guilt. I leaned into him, soaking in his presence. "I love you too," I responded, and despite my past and my broken, marred heart, the words were from the most sincere part of myself.

With a broad smile, he pulled away and scooted out of my chair for me.

"This is all way over the top. You know that." I sat down at the elegant table decorated with a white tablecloth, a centerpiece made of tiger lilies and roses, with two tapered candles on each side of it.

"I beg to differ." He shot me a grin and slid into the spot across from me. "It's just the right amount for the two-year anniversary with the love of my life."

Thoughts of Justin's threat of violence toward him pummeled my stomach, and I sucked in a sharp breath.

"Dakota?" Concern shaded Tim's brow, and he reached for my hand. "Did I say something wrong?"

Shaking my head, I reached for a glass of water and took a drink. "No, I'm okay."

"You sure?" He traced my fingers with his.

I nodded with a slight smile, trying to put him at ease. I would not let my old life steal this night from Tim.

The doors opened, and a male server pushed a cart loaded with food through the door.

I threw Tim a look. "What's this?"

He shrugged with a grin that spread across his face. "I wasn't sure which appetizer you would enjoy the most, so I got one of each."

The server delicately arranged an assortment of mouth-watering appetizers in front of us. The baked brie drizzled with pesto sauce and served with a warm sliced baguette immediately caught my attention. Next to it were plump crab-stuffed mushrooms, their rich aroma wafting toward me. My focus settled on the bacon-wrapped jalapeños, perfectly crispy and oozing with cheese. Nearby were deep-fried bites of cauliflower coated in a crunchy batter and paired with a tangy dipping sauce. And lastly, there were fried pickles, their golden skin glistening under the dim restaurant lights.

"Seriously, babe, this is out of control." I guess this was the sober way of celebrating, though: food, food, and more food.

"What? I was hungry." He grabbed a cauliflower bit and dipped it in blue cheese dressing before popping it in his mouth.

I rolled my eyes. Tim was always hungry and constantly trying to make me eat with him, but he never gained weight. I, however, gained about fifteen pounds when we first got together until I slowed my eating, started jogging every morning, and joined a kickboxing class twice a week.

"These are so good." He snagged another cauliflower bite, dipped it, and brought it to my mouth.

"And probably ten thousand calories per serving. I'll pass," I said, gently pushing his hand away.

"Babe, it's cauliflower, for goodness sake," he said with a laugh.

"Breaded, cheesy, deep-fried cauliflower," I countered, trying to stifle my grin.

He tilted his head to the side with an enticing grin. "Come on, Dakota. We're celebrating."

"Fine." I opened my mouth, and he gently put the food in. "Mmmm." It was really good. The crispy batter had a nice crunch, and the cauliflower was soft and sweet inside. I chewed and swallowed, the flavors exploding on my tongue.

He leaned back with a gleam in his eye. "You're welcome."

I swallowed my bite and then stuck out my tongue at him.

"Hey, babe, I actually was going to ask you something." He

reached for the bacon-wrapped jalapeño and took a bite, chewing slowly.

"Oh yeah? What's that?"

He gave a broad goofy smile. "Do I have something in my teeth?" he asked with his best Jim Carrey impersonation.

I busted out laughing at the large chunks of jalapeño stuck in his front teeth, then reached for a jalapeño and stuffed it in my mouth, trying to outdo him. The next ten minutes or so were spent laughing and trying to one-up each other's jokes. These were my favorite moments with Tim. The moments that took us back to our childhood—the moments that made me forget everything else but us. Our silliness was interrupted by the server wheeling in another round of food.

This time there were two plates covered with a metal dome. The server uncovered Tim's first. Smells of flame-broiled steak and garlic swirled in the air.

Tim's face grew serious, almost as if he were scared. The server lifted the metal lid off of the plate closest to me, set it before me, and quickly turned away. The plate contained a little velvet black box. I swallowed hard and looked at Tim. Were those tears in his eyes?

I bit my lower lip and waited for Tim to speak. A few moments of silence passed as he searched my face.

"Dakota." Tim's voice trembled, and he reached across the table to take my hand. Trapped butterflies inside me fluttered madly as I felt his touch. It was as if time had slowed, his fingers intertwining with mine—so familiar yet so foreign in this moment. "These last few years with you have been some of the happiest of my life."

He hesitated, then stood, stepped around the table and knelt before me. "I know it hasn't always been easy, with you working through the steps of recovery and me studying all the time, but Dakota, I'm more confident than ever that I want to spend the rest of my life with you."

All the air was sucked out of my lungs. This was the moment

that most women dreamt about—to have the man of their dreams kneeling before them, proposing marriage. But at that moment, staring into Tim's eyes, thoughts of this afternoon rushed over me, filling me with dread.

His hand trembled as he reached for the small black box, opening it to reveal a stunning diamond ring. "Dakota Marie Jensen."

No, Tim, don't do this. Not today. Not when I was holding this secret that could tear us apart.

"Would you do the honor of becoming my wife?" Tim asked, his voice choked with emotion as he held out the ring towards me. His features shone with hope and apprehension. The ring sparkled under the restaurant lights, enchanting and terrifying all at once.

My insides were imploding, feeling like they were being ripped to shreds. I wanted to say yes. So bad. In the last couple of years, Tim had become my whole world. I trusted him with heart, soul and mind.

You don't want to see what Victor will have us do to your precious cop boyfriend if you don't.

How could I say yes, with this awful thing hovering over our heads? I loved him with everything in me, a love so deep it consumed me. He was one of the few people who showed me what love was. But to say yes now would feel like a lie. But to say no would crush him.

"Dakota?" Tim's voice trembled, the uncertainty in his eyes mirroring the conflict within me.

I held up a finger and then slipped out of my chair. "Hold on. I need a minute." The cold, hard floor beneath me felt like a solid reminder of the reality I was in, not some dream with a man who loved me enough to want me as his wife. "I'm so sorry, I just— I." I stammered and then bolted toward the door.

CHAPTER 5

January 21, 6:10 p.m.

TIM

Sitting at the table, I stared at the empty space where Dakota had sat just moments ago, a sense of dread pummeling me. She had owned every bit of my heart since childhood, and now this. The moment I found the guts to ask her to marry me, she literally ran away from me.

What did it mean? Were we over? Had I ruined our relationship with my presumption? I grabbed the velvet box from the table and slid it into my pocket. What was I thinking?

After all we'd been through, I thought everything between us was great. We'd had a few rough patches here and there, but after her relapse a year and a half ago, things had changed. She had immersed herself into her NA program, moved into my home, and began to build a life with me. It hadn't been perfect, but it was good—really good. How had I deluded myself into believing she was ready for marriage?

"Calm down," I whispered to myself. "It will be okay." But the words seemed empty as if they were vanishing into the void.

Throughout the entire day, my mind had been consumed with visions of Dakota saying yes. I could see her face lighting with joy, and I imagined us sharing an intimate moment—the beginning of our lifelong journey together. But as I sat there now, ring in hand, I couldn't help but wonder if I had been blinded by love and optimism. Had I been foolish to think that proposing was the natural next step in our relationship? I couldn't picture a future without her, yet that's exactly what she seemed to be implying with her flight. She said she had needed a minute, but it had now been fifteen. Should I go after her? Or would that make things worse? I caressed the velvet box in my pocket. This ring, the symbol of my love and commitment, felt heavy, weighing on my heart like a stone. I could barely breathe.

I reached for my cell phone, my shaky fingers finding Sage's number. I hit the send button and held the phone to my ear, listening to the ringing tone as I waited for Sage to pick up.

"Hey, Sage, it's Tim." I struggled to speak, my mind still reeling from the shock of Dakota's reaction.

"Tim?" After a half minute of silence. "Is everything okay?"

My eyes burned with tears threatening to come, but I brushed off the emotion. "Well, considering I just asked Dakota to marry me, and she got all weird and just took off, no, everything is not okay."

Silence on the other end of the line as Sage processed my words. "Tim, I'm so sorry," she finally replied.

"Yeah, me too," I said and took a drink of water to help swallow the knot in my throat. I stood and walked the length of the room, keeping my focus on the ocean as the last of the sun disappeared over the horizon. "I just don't understand why she reacted this way. We've come so far, and she's been making so much progress. She seemed ready, and I love her more than anything." My voice broke, and I hated myself for it. I couldn't let my emotions get to me like this. I needed to be strong for whatever this night might bring.

"Tim, we've all seen the progress she's made, but we both know that addiction is a lifelong battle. It's possible that Dakota still has a lot of work to do before she's ready for marriage. It doesn't mean she doesn't love you." Sage's voice was calm, attempting to offer solace in the midst of my confusion.

I thought of the way Dakota and I were last night. Sage was right, Dakota did love me. I could feel that. But would she ever be ready for marriage? Would she ever want to start a family with me? These were things I wanted so badly. And I wanted them with her. I was well aware that the journey of sobriety was one that extended a lifetime, but it didn't make it any easier. "I hear what you're saying, but what if she never fully recovers? What if I'm stuck in this cycle with her forever?"

"You can't think like that. I told you, you have to be patient with her."

A tear rolled down my cheek, and I quickly wiped it away, embarrassed by my own emotion. I just didn't want to lose her. As many times as I thought I had lost her, I could never imagine my life without her. Especially now that she had finally let me in.

"You just need to give her some space," Sage said, interrupting my thoughts. "Let her come to you when she's ready."

I nodded, although my body screamed at me to go after her.

"Thanks, Sage. I appreciate it." I hung up the phone and stared out into the dusk-covered ocean. What was I supposed to do now? Doubt pressed hard against my stomach, churning like a storm within me. I slowly pulled the velvet box out of my pocket and opened it, revealing the glistening diamond ring inside. As I held the ring in my hand, the shimmering diamond seemed to mock my uncertainty. Should I go after her? Sage's words replayed in my head. I needed to give her space. I needed to be patient with her. That was so much easier said than done. I closed the box and placed it in my pocket. This symbol of my love and commitment to her felt heavy in my chest—a noose around my neck, making it hard to breathe. This wasn't the way this night was supposed to go.

I cracked my knuckles as hopelessness settled inside my bones.

My love for Dakota was like a raging typhoon; it was a force I couldn't deny, but sometimes it felt like that very storm was tearing me piece by piece. I'd been going through these crazy cycles of addiction with her since we were teens. She'd come so far, but in moments like these, I wasn't sure how much more I could take.

CHAPTER 6
January 21, 6:14 p.m.
DAKOTA

I drove through the small town of Ocean Shores, veins pulsing, the addict screaming at me. This was too much! My past with Ryan rearing its ugly head, my dad possibly dying, and now this?

What in the hell, Higher Power?

What did I do to set off this crap storm?

Over the last year, I had walked the line. I had done everything they told me to make myself better. I'd done the steps. I'd made my amends. I'd clawed my way out of the darkness. I'd even done my best to surrender my life to a Higher Power. But maybe this nightmare would never really be over. Maybe there was no making amends for what I'd done. How does one atone for getting their brother killed? Fear coursed through my veins like a blowtorch on high octane.

I pounded the steering wheel and swore again and again. "What the hell am I supposed to do? What kind of person hurts the person they love like that?" I drove faster, the lights of the town blurring past me like scattered stars against the night.

An effing damaged, ex-addict whose demons were seeking retribution. That was who. I was being ripped in half, torn from limb to limb. I thought about Tim kneeling before me, features expectant, and then me running out of the room.

33

I sped down Point Brown Ave, driving as fast as I could, the addict in me screaming for a line. A hit. A pill. Anything that would take away the burning pain and the aching regret, if only for a moment. There was no way in hell I'd ever be free.

Tim... Thinking his name brought tears to my eyes, cutting through anger, bringing a greater depth of sorrow. I was so, so sorry. I didn't want to hurt him. He was the one thing that mattered most. But how could I say yes to him and keep him safe? How could I say no to him and break his heart? How could I allow the love of my life to be tethered to the wreckage of my past when I clearly would never be free of it?

The thought of him suffering because of me was unbearable. The demons that once haunted me were still lurking in the shadows, seeking retribution for the things I had done. There was no way out. My stomach clenched as self-hatred mangled my insides, stabbing my guts again and again with a dull serrated knife.

Tears spilled down my face as anger gave way to desperation and a pain that wouldn't stop. I found my way to the side of the road and leaned my head against the steering wheel as sobs made their way up my throat. "God!" I cried, desperate for the anguish to relent. I sucked in three sharp breaths and choked out the Serenity Prayer. I sat waiting for a moment of clarity or some sort of miracle, but the only thing that came to mind was my sister. Reaching for my phone with shaking hands, I searched for Tamara's name. I probably shouldn't bug her now, but she was the one person I knew could possibly help.

CHAPTER 7

January 21, 6:45 p.m.

TAMARA

I was snuggled in a blanket on the couch in our living room when Joe entered, carrying a sleeping Lillie. After a sweet afternoon walk, Joe had taken Lillie back to the restaurant earlier so I could have some time alone to process the news about my dad's illness.

This morning Joe brought me breakfast in bed for our anniversary, showering me with gifts and whispered words of love. But things had taken a hard turn for the worst when my mom called and told me about my dad's declining health. It had been nice to have some time to surrender my emotions to God concerning him.

God had proven to me a thousand times that he was trustworthy. But the news of my dad's liver disease had shaken me to the core. It had only been a few short years since we reconnected after what felt like a lifetime of estrangement. I wasn't ready to lose him again.

Brushing off the painful thought, I turned my attention to Joe. "Did she eat?"

"Did she ever," he said, walking toward me. "Matt made her chicken fingers, macaroni and cheese, and grapes—and she ate almost all of it."

I hadn't expected anything less. She seemed to be going through a growth spurt lately.

Joe slowly lowered himself next to me, adjusting Lillie's sleeping body so he could put his free hand on my swollen stomach.

"Is it wrong for me to want her to stay small forever?" I asked, tenderly running my hand along the top of her head.

"No, I know exactly what you mean," Joe replied with a fondness in his voice. "How was your time alone? Did it help?"

I leaned my head against his shoulder, and a swell of love for my family overwhelmed me. "It was good. I feel less... anxious. I mean, I know it's going to be a battle, but I feel peace."

Joe nodded and gently caressed my stomach, conveying his support without words. Part of me wished he'd tell me everything would be okay, but I knew that wouldn't help.

The baby kicked against Joe's hand, and he let out a soft chuckle. "Hey there, little man," he said softly as he bent closer to my stomach and spoke directly to our unborn child. "How are you doing today? Your daddy loves you very much."

Two quick kicks followed in response to his affectionate words, like an excited heartbeat echoing through my body. It brought a smile to both our faces, momentarily pushing my worries away.

"I think that means he loves you too,"

Joe asked with a sweet smile spread across his face, "So, you think he's a boy too?"

I put my hand over my mouth, surprised by my slip. "That was an accident! You must be getting into my head with your dreams, Mr. Phillips."

Ever since we found out I was pregnant, Joe had been convinced it was a boy. At this point, there was no way to be sure. Not that we didn't want to know, but when we went in for the ultrasound, the little guy had their legs closed tight.

"That's because you know I'm right." His grin widened as he stroked my belly.

I rolled my eyes, but inwardly I thought my chest might burst with the love I had for this man.

Beside me, my phone buzzed, interrupting the intimate moment. I glanced at the screen. Dakota? Was she calling me with news of her engagement or of our dad's condition? It is never easy to have news like that dropped on you, but I prayed that it did not ruin her engagement dinner.

I took a breath and answered. "Hey, Dakota, how's your night going?" I asked, voice bright.

Silence.

"Dakota?" I frowned, pressing the phone tighter against my ear. "Can you hear me?"

A hitchy breath came through the line and then a small sob.

My heart raced in my chest as a wave of panic washed over me. "Dakota, what's wrong?" My hand instinctively moved to my stomach as if I could somehow wrap our unborn child in a protective bubble.

She unleashed a string of swear words, throwing out f-bombs between, taking the Lord's name in vain.

Joe looked over with concern knitted onto his brows, his hand reaching out and intertwining with mine. I squeezed reassuringly but didn't meet his gaze, my focus solely on Dakota, feeling breathless.

Joe's phone vibrated then, sending out a low rumbling sound that echoed in the quiet room. He flashed me the screen to show me Tim's name lighting the screen.

What could have happened? Joe slowly stood, careful not to disturb Lillie's sleep, and quietly answered the phone before walking out of the room.

"Why in the hell is my life so freaking effed up, Tamara?" Dakota asked before choking out another string of expletives.

Inwardly, I prayed an earnest prayer for wisdom.

Dakota grew quiet, and another sob came through the phone. I took a long breath, steeling myself with courage and strength before I asked her again what was happening.

A few seconds of silence passed before she responded in a quiet voice. "Tim asked me to marry him..."

"That's amazing, Dakota!"

"It would be if I wasn't me," she said, her voice heavy.

I guess I understood that. There were times I thought I'd never be good for anyone, but now my life was overflowing with love. "Come on, sis. You've come a long way over the last few years, and Tim loves you so much."

She barked out a sick laugh. "There are some things love can't erase, sis."

I pinched the bridge of my nose. *God, please help.* "What do you mean?"

"It means nothing can change my past. I wish I could escape it, but it's always there lurking in ambush, ready to destroy me."

Her words struck a familiar note with me. Running away from my past was something I had done all too often.

"That's not true. Your past doesn't define you unless you let it," I said firmly, like Joe used to tell me when I didn't believe him.

"The hell it doesn't!" she said with resolution.

I could hear the raw pain in her voice, the resignation that was all too familiar. I sat there for a few minutes in silence, and I shot up another prayer for help. How could I help her see that she was believing a lie? "You're going to be okay, Dakota," I finally said.

"I wish I could believe that, but no matter how hard I try to forget, Ryan is always there, bringing retribution." Her voice trembled as she said his name, and I felt my stomach churn.

"But he's gone, sis. He can't hurt you anymore."

"If only that were true," she said in a whisper, sounding like a scared child.

Sadness shrouded me as I thought of how Dakota had been getting better over the past few years, even ready for Tim's proposal—until this.

A voice from within whispered quietly, *Fear doesn't always lead to the dark side.* Peace settled over me at the soft familiar voice.

"Dakota, I know it may sound strange, but when I was praying just now, I felt like God said..." I hesitated. Was this really God? I truly hoped it was. 'Fear doesn't always lead to the dark side.'"

She sucked in a sharp breath. "What did you just say?"

"Fear doesn't always lead to the dark side. From *Star Wars*," I repeated.

She was quiet for so long that I thought she may have hung up. "Dakota?"

"I gotta go," she murmured, and then the line went blank. I looked at my phone, feeling bewildered, hoping she was okay.

Joe walked into the room. "I think Lillie is out for the count. She didn't even make a peep when I laid her down."

At least that was one less thing I'd have to worry about. "So, what did Tim say? I didn't get much out of Dakota."

Joe sighed and sat back down with me. "He said they were having a great time, but when he proposed, she freaked out and ran out of the room."

Anxiety tightened my stomach again. I clutched the edge of my blanket, my fingers white-knuckled. "That doesn't make sense. I wonder if something happened to her recently."

Joe slid in next to me and put his hand on my back. "What exactly did she say?"

"I don't know. She didn't make a whole lot of sense, but she did say that Ryan was always there, bringing retribution."

Joe's his brow furrowed. "What could that even mean? Ryan's dead. Nothing has happened for two years. What could have possibly changed now?"

The questions hung in the air between us, thick and unanswerable. I wished I knew. "I don't know, but I'm worried about her."

"Do you think you should call her back?" Joe asked with concern.

"No, she needs space." Knowing Dakota, she probably wouldn't answer anyway—not after hanging up on me.

Joe pulled me into a comforting embrace. "How are you holding up, T? There was a lot of drama to process today."

"There definitely was ..." I closed my eyes and leaned into his chest. "But I'm okay, just really tired."

"Let's get you to bed then." He stood and offered his hand to me.

I took hold of it and barely managed to stand up. The six-month baby bump made it extra hard for me. He followed me into the bathroom, where we did our nightly routine. As I finished brushing my teeth, worried thoughts invaded my mind. What did Dakota mean about her past bringing retribution? And why would she take off after Tim proposed?

Joe wrapped his arms around me once more. "I can see the worry on your face, my love."

Leaning into him, I smiled weakly and responded, "You know me so well."

"Your feelings are valid, but I believe that everything is going to be okay."

Nodding slowly, I swallowed the knot forming in my throat. He was right—God had brought us through worse trials than this before. His embrace tightened around me, and he prayed softly, his voice a balm on the fears that gnawed at me. My dad's liver damage and the conversation with Dakota both played in my mind, a relentless torrent of what ifs. But as Joe's words rose and fell, I found myself clinging to them, finding solace in his steadfast faith. A tear crept down my cheek as I remembered that God's faithfulness had unfolded in our lives before, and I had to trust that He would do the same now.

CHAPTER 8

January 21, 9:45 p.m.

DAKOTA

I drove toward the restaurant, heart pounding, trying to make sense of Tamara's words. *Fear doesn't always lead to the dark side?* What did that even mean? How could she have known my thoughts? I hadn't even shared how that line affected me with Tim. Only God knew how that one little line mixed with everything else in my messed-up life had sent me reeling. Fear had always led me down dark paths, but this time it was tearing me apart.

I absolutely could not lose Tim. Once I let him in, he possessed my whole body, mind and soul. To lose Tim would be the death of me, but right now I felt like I was damned either way. If I walked away from Tim, those druggy lowlifes would have nothing on him. But if I walked away, I would lose the one person who had always loved me unconditionally.

He was more than a soul mate, more than a lover—he was my rock, my safe haven in this chaotic world. Tim had always been there for me, even when I was lost in the darkest corners of my addiction. He had seen me at my worst and loved me even more fiercely. His touch could heal the deepest wounds within me, and his presence alone brought me a sense of peace that I had never known before.

I pulled my car back into the parking lot and slammed the door as I stepped out. I dragged my feet up the stairs to Bed and Breakfast, hoping Tim was still there.

Maria greeted me once again, her demeanor cheerful as ever, but her face held a hint of concern. She must have thought I was insane, but I couldn't even bring myself to care. "Is Tim still here?" Could she sense the desperation in my voice? Heat flushed my cheeks. Everyone who worked here probably knew that Tim had intended on proposing tonight.

Maria's expression softened, and she nodded toward the grand room.

Embarrassment shrouded me, but I walked toward the room. What kind of person runs out of a proposal from the love of her life? Each step felt heavier than the last as I made my way through the restaurant. Laughter and chatter echoed around me, a backdrop of normality against the tumult inside my head. I couldn't believe Tim was still here. I had told him to give me a minute, and that minute had stretched into almost an hour. Did he have that much faith in me?

I hesitated at the door, fear gripping my chest, afraid to know what was going to greet me. Gathering courage, I pushed on the hard wood, and the door creaked open. The room was mostly dark except for the candles on the table and the full moon shining through the expansive window.

Tim sat at the table, hunched over, his attention fixated on the glimmering ring resting in his hands.

With cautious steps, I inched closer to him, hoping to break through the walls of his anguish. His eyes finally met mine, and in that moment, I saw the storm brewing in his gaze—a mix of confusion, worry, and something else. My gut twisted with the realization that it was doubt. Doubt I'd put there.

I stepped closer, my heart heavy with regret and sorrow. With every stride, my legs felt weaker, threatening to crumble beneath the weight of my actions.

Kneeling before him, I took his hand in mine. My body

trembled and tears streamed down my face, blurring the contours of his face.

"I'm so sorry, Tim. I'm so sorry," I whispered, my voice barely audible, choked with remorse.

He looked at me, his features filled with a mixture of pain and understanding. His hand reached out, gently cupping my cheek. "Coda," he said, his voice tender but raw. " If you're not ready for marriage, it's okay."

Anger tore through me more intensely than the sadness. If Ryan were still alive, I would hunt him down and kill him myself for this. Because the honest truth was, if Tim would have proposed yesterday, before my past came to threaten to tear us apart, I would have said yes without hesitation. I had worked so hard over the last year and a half to be someone worthy of Tim's love. I'd done everything in my power to let go of my past so I could have a future with Tim. "You don't understand. I do want to marry you. I absolutely want to be with you for the rest of my life."

He tilted his head to the side, hurt overshadowing his features. "You don't have to say that, Dakota. I don't want you to do something if your heart is not fully in it." Tim gently squeezed my hands in his, a look of resignation passing over his face.

Frustration grew inside me as I tried to find the right words to make Tim understand. "Timothy James Moore, you have been my best friend since we were children. You never gave up on me even when I was absolutely horrible to you. You have loved me way more than I will ever deserve. I have been happier with you for the last year and a half than I have been in my entire life! I love you, Tim, and I absolutely want to marry you."

"You do?" The corners of his lips twitched, his countenance lightening with a glimmer of hope.

"With everything in me."

"Dakota," he whispered, his voice filled with a mix of disbelief and overwhelming joy. "Are you absolutely sure about this? After what happened tonight?"

I nodded fervently, my eyes burning with a fierce resolve. "I'm more sure than I've ever been about anything."

A radiant smile blossomed across his face, and he pulled the ring from the box and slid it on my left ring finger. Then he pulled me onto his lap and drew me into a tender, passionate kiss. Our lips met with a desperate urgency, an affirmation of the mutual love and longing we felt. His arms wrapped around me like a warm, protective shield as if he would ward off any danger that dared to come near me. The taste of his lips, the strong beat of his heart against my own, the comforting scent of him—all of it made me feel so safe, so loved, soothing a place inside me that had been rattled all day. Because of Tim, I could actually envision a future that I wanted. Because of Tim, I was living a life worth living. Because of Tim, I had actually had something to lose.

Tim pulled away breathless, a look of intoxication filling his face. He gently caressed my cheek, taking in every inch of me, as if committing my features to memory. "I got us a room for the night," he whispered. "Let's go upstairs."

I nodded in agreement, but kissed him again before climbing off his lap. Grabbing my hand, he pulled me forward, out of the room and up the stairs. He opened the door, pulled me in and then shut it behind. He pushed me gently against the wall and pinned my arms against it. His eyes grew deep with emotion as he looked into my soul. "I love you."

"I love you more," I said, and for the first time in our relationship, I actually believed it. Somewhere along the way, because of Tim my ability to love had been restored.

His lips twitched as he searched my face. "You're going to be my wife, Dakota." His intense gaze bore into me, caressing my soul with an indescribable tenderness.

The heat that flooded through me was immediate and intense.

My emotions soared with desire and fear, happiness and doubt all rolled into one surge through me.

His hand moved to trace the line of my jaw, then down to the hollow of my throat where his fingers lingered, exploring the skin over my rapidly beating pulse.

"Kiss me," I whispered, my words barely audible over the pounding of my own heart.

His lips came close, hovering over mine. The energy that came off of him was electrifying and his smoldering gaze undid me. "You're going to be my wife," he whispered again.

What was he doing to me? Those words were like a declaration eliciting such intense feelings within me, such intense desire. His lips finally touched mine in a soft, lingering kiss that held the promise of a thousand tomorrows. His hands moved tenderly down my arms, leaving a trail of goosebumps in their wake before they found their home on the small of my back, pulling me impossibly closer. I was going to be Tim wife. Those words seared into me in the most intoxicating way. There was nothing about my past or my present that could change our future. I would be Tim's wife. And that was that.

CHAPTER 9

January 22, 8:30 a.m.

DAKOTA

As the morning grey light gently filtered through the curtains, Tim pulled me in closer into his strong, secure embrace. His heartbeat, steady and calm, hummed against my ear. His arms felt like a protective shield, warding off the fears that threatened to invade our little bubble of happiness. Rain pelted against the window in a lulling rhythm, providing a steady drumming soundtrack to the peaceful moment.

I traced the lines of his face with my fingertips, then ran them through his tousled hair, taking in his perfection, letting this moment and the weight of what happened last night sink in. Tim and I were engaged. Never in a million years did I ever think that I, Dakota Jensen, would be able to say that.

But even as the corners of my lips tilted up, a knot of fear tightened in my stomach.

I wanted to tell Tim about what happened yesterday and the real reason I fled the restaurant, but Avery's threat loomed overhead.

Don't you dare tell your boyfriend about this visit or he'll pay.

Avery's voice echoed in my mind, his words reverberating like the ominous tolling of a church bell. I pushed the thoughts away.

Today was a day to celebrate our new life together, a life full of promises and potential.

Maybe I was making a bigger deal in my mind about this than it really was. It was just one package, right? And I didn't know what was in said package. All I had to do was follow simple instructions and it would all be over; then I'd go back to this wonderful life that I was building with Tim, and no one would be the wiser.

But why was there a pit in my stomach saying that it couldn't be that simple? And it literally made no sense at all. Why after all this time would they have me do this?

Fear unfurled within me as my mind went down the dark alleys—the plethora of sick reasons there could be. I snuggled deeper into Tim, willing the terrible thoughts to go away.

Tim stirred, and his eyes flitted open, then a sleepy grin crept up his face. "Good morning, beautiful."

I kissed him softly. "Morning."

Tim leaned away to look at me, then ran his finger along my brow line. "What's going on in that beautiful mind of yours?"

"Well, I don't know how beautiful it is." I laughed lightly, trying to dispel the tension building within me. "More like a bit twisted and sick."

Tim chuckled, his warm breath tickling my ear as he spoke. "It's beautiful to me."

"That's because you're weird," I teased, poking his side lightly. He laughed and swatted my hand away, grinning at me like I was the sun itself.

"True... but I still want to know what you're thinking about."

I leaned in closer and spoke in a whisper. "I was hoping that you made arrangements for us to be in this bed and breakfast for the rest of the week, so we don't have to go anywhere or see anyone."

"I wish," he said as his fingers danced along my back. "But we both have work tomorrow."

"Ugh..." I pulled the covers over my head in revolt. "Sometimes I hate adulting."

Tim chuckled softly, his fingers still tracing delicate patterns on my back. "Right? Adulting can be a real buzzkill."

I peeked out from under the covers, pouting. "Totally. I mean, who even invented this whole 'work' thing, anyway?"

Tim grinned, leaning in to kiss the tip of my nose. "Some long-dead responsible person probably. But hey, we've got today. Let's make it count."

"You're right. So, what should we do with our precious day?"

Tim pretended to ponder the question, rubbing his chin thoughtfully. "Well, first, I think we need a breakfast fit for champions. Pancakes maybe?"

"With whipped cream and strawberries?" I asked, mood brightening at the prospect. "And bacon?"

"That goes without saying," he responded with a playful grin. "What about after breakfast?"

My playful grin mirrored his as I pondered, resting a finger on my chin in an exaggerated display of thought. "Well, after our indulgent breakfast, how about continuing our *Star Wars* marathon in bed?"

"Sounds perfect," Tim agreed, his grin widening at the thought. "And what about a pillow fort?"

"A pillow fort?" I threw him a sideways grin, thinking of our childhood and how we spent most rainy Saturdays. "You're such a dork."

"But the best kind of dork," he retorted, grinning even wider. And with a swift move, he tugged at the covers, nestling us in it.

"And an excellent fort builder," I added with a giggle, nuzzling into his side as he drew the blankets around us.

"Exactly." He chuckled, pulling me closer and pressing a kiss to my forehead. "But probably somewhere in the middle of all of this self-indulgent extravaganza, we should probably call and tell our families the big news."

He was right. I glanced at the clock. It was already almost 9am. Tamara would definitely be awake. After hanging up on her last night, she'd be concerned. I needed to call my mom first, but then I'd call Tamara to let her know that I was okay.

CHAPTER 10
January 22, 2:00 p.m.
TIM

After our pancake breakfast, we snuggled on the couch together. The steady rhythm of raindrops drumming against the windowpane echoed through our dimly lit room. Dakota traced circles on my chest, and I marveled at how such a simple touch could send waves of tranquility through me.

I thought of our night together after she had come back to the restaurant. Being with her after she said yes to my proposal was like being caught in a dream that I was afraid to wake from—surreal and beautiful but tinged with the fear that she might disappear again. It was hard to believe we were actually engaged. It was a moment I'd hoped for since we were kids, but with the path she had gone down, I'd thought it would never be possible.

Beneath the warmth of her touch, I couldn't help but remember the girl she used to be—the girl who laughed freely under the summer sun and had eyes that brimmed with innocence. In moments like now, as I held her close and listened to her steady breathing, I saw glimpses of that girl. But she was also now the beautiful resilient woman who had clawed her way out of the dark abyss of addiction, emerging stronger and more determined. Revitalized, like a phoenix reborn from its ashes, she was more beautiful than ever.

Our gazes met, and her lips curved into that smile that never failed to make me weak.

"So, who should we call first?" I asked, wanting to shout it from the rooftops that we were engaged.

Dakota reached for her phone. "Definitely my mom."

As Dakota found her mom's number, I closed my eyes and took a deep breath, relishing in the moment. The rain outside picked up, pitter-pattering against the windows with renewed vigor, matching my pulse.

Dakota turned on the speaker phone, and a ringing sound filled the room. Finally, the line clicked, and a soft voice echoed through the speakers.

"Dakota? Is that you?"

"Hey, Mom." She glanced at me with a nervous expression. "Umm, I have some news."

"Oh yeah? What's going on?" She sounded cautious, which made sense with Dakota's history.

"Tim asked me to marry him last night, and I said yes."

"Oh, that's wonderful, sweetheart."

Dakota released a breath she'd been holding, and her face lit up with relief. "I'm glad you think so; could you please tell Dad for me?" Dakota and her dad had come a long way over the last few years, but their relationship was still a bit strained.

"Absolutely, honey. I know he will be really happy for you. He thinks Tim is great guy, and so do I."

A soft warmth spread through my chest at her words. I was glad they approved of Dakota's choice, and I couldn't be happier. We were finally moving forward, putting Dakota's tortured past behind us and embracing the future we'd always dreamed of.

"Thanks, Mom. There are so many people to tell, it just makes it easier."

"I understand," she said softly, the tenderness in her voice seeping through the phone lines. "Just remember, honey. This is your moment to relish, and there's no need to worry about anyone else."

"Of course, Mom. I'll remember that." Dakota ended the call and turned towards me, a questioning smile in her expression.

"Let's call Aunt Sage next," I suggested, wanting to keep the momentum going and share our happiness with those who mattered most to us. Dakota nodded and squeezed my hand.

As I found Sage's number, she traced circles on my hand. Sage had been there for me last night when Dakota had run out on my engagement. How would she respond now that Dakota and I had made up and she had said yes? I hoped she wouldn't bring up the subject, but Sage was known for her straightforwardness. Sage had always been a source of comfort and wisdom for me, but at times her words cut deep, revealing truths I'd rather not face. The line connected, and her warm voice filled the room.

"Hey, Tim, I was just thinking about you, wondering how things went after we spoke last night."

Dakota gave me a questioning glance, her hand freezing mid-circle. I probably should have told her that I had called Sage for advice before this phone call.

"That's actually why I'm calling. She's sitting next to me now, and you're on speaker phone. Dakota came back last night, and she said yes."

A soft gasp escaped her lips, followed by a deep chuckle. "Well, congratulations to the both of you. Marriage is not an easy road, but if you truly love each other, it's worth the fight."

"Thank you, Sage," Dakota said softly, her voice bubbling with gratitude and relief. "We'll remember that."

Sage's words lingered in the air, bringing a strange sense of foreboding. Marriage was not an easy road, and with Dakota's and my challenges, it may even be harder. In many ways the deck had been stacked against us from the beginning, but we were still here, more in love than ever. The scars might remain, but they were a testament to our strength, our resilience, and our love.

As we hung up with Sage, I pulled Dakota closer to me, basking in the afterglow of telling those we loved about our big news. The sound of the rain was a soothing background melody, and I felt her body relax against mine.

"I love you," I whispered, pressing a soft kiss to her forehead.

"I love you too," she murmured.

And in that moment, there was nothing else in the world that mattered but us. The rain outside fell harder, but it was drowned out by the steady rhythm of our breathing as we sat there in each other's arms. The future was uncertain, but I knew that as long as we had each other, we could face anything that lay ahead.

Dakota lifted her head off my chest. "We better call Tamara and Joe. Tamara is probably worried after the call from me last night."

My forehead creased. What was said on that phone call? Why would she be that worried?

Before I could ask, Dakota had already hit send on her phone and put in on speaker.

"Dakota?" Tamara answered, her voice heavy with concern.

"Yeah, sis, it's me. Is Joe around? Tim is sitting here with me and would like to tell you both something."

"Yeah, he's right here. Let me put it on speaker." In the background, I could hear Lillie's giggles and playful squeals, the sweet symphony of a happy toddler.

"Hey, guys!" Joe greeted us warmly. "What's up?"

"Well," I said, taking the phone from Dakota, "As you both know, I asked Dakota to marry me last night, and she said yes."

"Congratulations!" Tamara exclaimed, her voice ringing with genuine joy. "Oh, I'm so happy for you both!"

Meanwhile, Joe's laughter rumbled in the background like distant thunder, adding to the joyous atmosphere. "That's wonderful news!" Joe chimed in, his enthusiasm echoing through the room. "But I have to say, I think I deserve some credit here," Joe playfully added, and I could almost see his teasing grin through the phone. "After all, it's happening at our establishment and I oversaw the food and decor, right?"

Tamara and Dakota both laughed, the sound bringing a smile

to my face. A bubble of amusement formed within me, threatening to spill over into laughter as well.

"True, true," Tamara said, her tone dripping with good-natured sarcasm. "But let's not forget whose idea it was in the first place." She paused for dramatic effect, adding, "You can thank your soon-to-be sister-in-law for that stroke of genius."

"I'm forever in your debt." I conceded playfully, chuckling, warmth spreading through me. The laughter, the teasing, the joy —they were such simple, everyday things but felt so precious in that moment. My mind raced with thoughts of gratitude for these people who had become my family.

"I know my little sister well enough to know what would make her happiest," Tamara replied, triumph evident in her voice.

As we continued to chat with Tamara and Joe, the room filled with an aura of calm, a reprieve from the turmoil that had been our lives.

I loved seeing Dakota like this, completely involved in their silly banter. Joe and Tamara had been such a support over the last few years. They were the healthiest part of Dakota's family and a constant reminder that love could win despite the opposition.

As Dakota ended the call, I pulled away from her and reached for the remote. "You ready for Episode Two?"

She tilted her head to the side, a question in her features. "Don't you want to call your parents?"

Her question brought me up short. I knew it wouldn't be an easy phone call, and I didn't want to overshadow our day with my mother's doubts. Truth was, my mom had never approved of Dakota—not even when we were kids. Sometimes I wondered if she blamed herself for our relationship. When I was ten years old, my parents were laid off from their Boeing jobs in Everett Washington, causing our income to be reduced significantly. That financial hardship had forced us into that trailer park in Quilcene Washington, and it was there that my path crossed with Dakota's. We were instant friends—inseparable, even—until she started doing drugs.

I shook off the thoughts. Today was about Dakota and me, and I didn't want anything to dampen the magic of this moment.

"I can call them later. For now, I'd like to just focus on being with you for the rest of the day."

"I'm good with that." And then she leaned in and gave me a sweet kiss.

We settled into the couch, her head resting on my chest and my fingers playing with her hair. I pressed play, and the familiar opening credits began to roll.

As we watched the epic battles unfold on screen, I couldn't help but feel a certain kinship with the characters, their fight for redemption echoing my own struggles to overcome fear and forge a brighter future with Dakota.

In the midst of the movie, I glanced at Dakota's serene face, her eyes reflecting the light from the screen as she leaned into me.

"Tim," she whispered, her voice barely audible above the sound of the rain and the movie. "I love you."

"Love you too, Dakota," I replied, my heart swelling with gratitude for this moment, this woman, this love that had somehow managed to survive against all odds.

CHAPTER 11

January 22, 1:20 p.m.

TAMARA

After leaving church, I drove towards my parents' home with a heavy heart and Lillie sleeping in the backseat. Outside the sky was a typical winter day in Aberdeen Washington, gray and overcast, though the rain had stopped for the moment.

The news of my dad's deteriorating health from yesterday weighed heavily on me as I drove, agitating old wounds. And then came Dakota's phone call, which only made things ten times worse. Even though she and Tim reassured me this morning about their engagement, a lingering fear still clung to me like a second skin.

Everything happening so close together had ripped old wounds open again, wounds I thought had healed. And I needed help to process it all.

Reaching for my phone, I told Siri to dial Hope Chapel. After a few rings, Kathy, the church secretary, answered the phone with a cheerful voice. "Hope Chapel, Kathy speaking; how may I help?"

"Hi, Kathy," I said, glancing at Lillie. She stirred a little, her lips making a sucking motion while she slept. She was one of the biggest reasons I was making this call. I wanted to make sure I was staying in an emotionally healthy place for her. "This is Tamara Phillips. I'd like to make a virtual appointment with David."

"Absolutely, dear. Let me check his availability. Is this an emergency?"

"No, no, nothing like that. Just wanted to catch up." Over the last few years, I'd tried to find a counselor here in town that suited me, but I never found one, so I continued to see David off and on via video calls. It didn't matter if it was over a computer screen, David was the best.

"Okay, well then. It looks like he has an availability next Wednesday at 9 AM. Does that work?"

"Yes, that would be great." Joe could take Lillie on a little play date that morning before he left for work.

"Great, I've penciled you in for next Wednesday. David will look forward to catching up with you," Kathy replied warmly before ending the call.

With a sense of relief, I ended the call and turned onto Highway 101. The familiar sight of the coastal landscape, with its evergreens and rugged cliffs lining the gray sea, offered a sense of comfort. Also knowing that I had the support of David through this battle made me feel safer.

In the back seat, Lillie stirred and made a cooing sound, but her eyes remained closed.

Dark clouds began to gather above, casting an ominous shadow over the ocean as a chill wind rattled the vehicle. I yawned, glancing at the rear-view mirror at Lillie again, wishing she would have let me sleep in more this morning, but she woke around 5:45 am. Needless to say, we could both use a nap, but she was the only one who got one. But that was mom-life for you. I ran my hand along my swollen stomach, feeling the familiar flutter of my second child. This one was a fighter, always kicking and squirming, reminding me of its presence.

Not that I could forget its presence with the size of my baby bump. That was the other reason Joe thought I was having a boy. I was carrying this one so much differently than Lillie and Hope.

It also could have had something to do with having three babies in 4 years' time. My mind lingered on Hope for a moment, and the normal mix of emotions swirled through me. Longing for this child who was being raised by Levi and Sarah—a wonderful couple who adopted her in a moment and time I wasn't ready for a child. Sadness that I didn't have the privilege of raising her myself. And joy knowing that she was in the best place she could possibly be in, being raised by some of the best people I knew.

Lillie made cooing sounds again, but this time she was starting to wake. I glanced at her, and she gave me a sleepy grin, her chubby cheeks scrunching adorably as she stretched her little arms and legs.

I turned into my parents' driveway and parked before climbing out of my SUV. The wind whipped at my coat as I unbuckled Lillie from her seat and hoisted her onto my hip. She nuzzled against me, burying her face in the crook of my neck. Her warm breath made the goosebumps on my skin recede slightly as I headed towards the house. The weight of the situation felt heavy on my shoulders as I walked, and inwardly, I prayed for God to be w in this conversation. With a deep breath, I reached out and rang the doorbell, the sound echoing through the quiet neighborhood.

As I stood on the doorstep, my mind filled with doubts. How would my dad react to this visit? Would he be angry, defensive, or dismissive? I hoped that the love he had for us would be enough to push him to fight through his demons. I prayed that he would find the strength to choose life over the destructive path he had been treading.

Finally, the door creaked open and my dad stood on the threshold. His face was drawn, shadows tucked deep under his eyes, but at the sight of Lillie and me, a soft smile played on his lips. "Tamara?"

"Hi, Dad. Can we come in?" I replied, trying to keep my tone steady and light. The cold air nipped at our faces as we waited for his answer.

Lillie made a silly noise like she was blowing bubbles.

Dad reached for Lillie. "Of course, sweetheart."

She giggled with glee as I handed her off to her grandpa. I smiled at their interaction, but dread weighed down my mood. I was here to beg him to stop drinking to slow the deterioration of his liver, but how does one begin such a conversation?

My father led us into the living room and gently placed Lillie on the floor near a designated play area, thoughtfully created by my parents for their grandchildren. The scent of stale alcohol filled the room, a constant reminder of the battles that had taken place within these walls. I took a moment to admire the new photographs on display of my brother Josiah's family. His wife's lively eyes sparkled with happiness, and their daughter Mia, now almost three years old, was growing up too quickly. It saddened me to know that they were so far away and that my niece was growing up without knowing our family.

"Dad, I need to talk to you about something." I turned from the pictures and met his gaze, which bore a trace of apprehension. He must have sensed the gravity in my tone.

"Of course," he replied, sinking into his worn-out armchair, a cup of black coffee in his hands.

"It's about your drinking."

His features held a mixture of weariness and defiance in them. "Tamara, I don't need another lecture. I get enough of that from your mother."

"Dad, this isn't a lecture," I replied gently, trying to keep the desperation out of my voice. "I'm worried about you." I could see the pain etched on his face, the struggle he had been fighting for far too long. But I couldn't let that deter me. I had to be strong, for him, for Lillie, and for our family.

"Tamara—"

I interrupted him but quickly softened my tone. "Please, just hear me out. I love you, Dad," I continued, my voice filled with a mix of sadness and determination. "You've come so far in so many ways over the last couple of years, but your drinking is literally killing you."

Silence hung in the air as my words settled in, heavy as a funeral shroud. His face went hard, and anger flared in his eyes. For a moment, I thought he would lash out, but he sighed deeply and ran a hand through his graying hair.

I grabbed ahold of his calloused hand with both of mine. "Dad, please hear my heart. I know life hasn't been easy on you... Especially after Gabriel died."

Dad flinched at the mention of my brother's name, the raw pain still visible on his face. Out of all of us, Dad took Gabriel's death the hardest. Nathan a close second. Which did not help that Nathan was his primary drinking buddy. It was as if a part of both of them had died the day they had learned of his death. Dad had always been a drinker, but he drank more after, drowning in the guilt of his own culpability.

"Dad, I understand that you're hurting," I said softly, my voice trembling slightly. "But drinking doesn't help. It won't bring him back. It's only killing you and hurting our family."

Dad looked at Lillie, his face softening with a mixture of love and regret. I could see the internal struggle he was facing, the battle between his addiction and his love for his family. His eyes misted over, his emotions bubbling to the surface. It was clear that my words had struck a chord within him, but would that be enough?

"I want to change," he finally choked out. "But it's harder than you can imagine." He made eye contact with me, and I could see the demons he battled behind his expression. A lifetime of regret, sorrow and the burdens of past generations. "But I will try for you, sweetheart. And for our precious Lillie."

Tears pooled in my eyes. "Thank you, Dad," I said softly, squeezing his hand back. It was a small step, but it was a step nonetheless. A glimmer of hope in the midst of the spiraling turmoil around our family.

Maybe, just maybe, this would be the turning point. Maybe, with love and support, we could help him overcome his demons.

CHAPTER 12

January 22: 6:00 p.m.

DAKOTA

The warmth of Tim's arms enveloped me, anchoring me in the present moment. The faint scent of Tim's cologne, a mix of sandalwood and citrus, lingered in the air around us. I felt safe, cocooned within the sanctuary of our cozy room.

A knock sounded at the door, and Tim untangled himself from me to answer it.

About a half hour ago we had finished the second episode of *Star Wars* and had ordered room service. He opened the door, and a gentleman dressed in black slacks and a white shirt wheeled in a cart with an array of food had been artfully arranged. Tim handed him a twenty and the guy quickly left.

"I hope you're hungry," Tim said with a grin.

I approached the feast laid out, and the sight was almost overwhelming: a culinary masterpiece, complete with vibrant colors and mouthwatering aromas that beckoned my senses.

A bowl brimming with fresh fruit—juicy strawberries, plump blueberries, and succulent slices of mango—provided a visual symphony of color and taste. Beside it, a silver platter featured an assortment of cheeses and cured meats, each piece meticulously arranged to create a tantalizing mosaic. The centerpiece was a steaming dish of pasta, its rich tomato sauce simmering atop a bed

63

of tender noodles, the fragrant garlic and oregano wafting its delicious aroma in the air.

I could feel my hips grow just looking at it. With the amount we were eating, I would have to hit the gym double time next week.

Tim grabbed a blueberry and popped it in his mouth. "This was a bit more than I expected."

I laughed at the understatement. It wasn't just a bit more; it was enough to feed an entire precinct.

"Well, it's not every day we get to indulge like this," I replied, grabbing a slice of cheese and savoring its creamy texture.

He pointed his fork at me with a nod. "Good point. We are celebrating right."

"Anything goes," I said with a wink.

As we ate, the conversation flowed easily between us, punctuated by occasional bursts of laughter. For a moment, it felt like time had slowed down, allowing us to fully appreciate the simple pleasure of good food and even better company.

After we finished our meal, Tim relaxed with a content smile, then he grabbed my hand and pulled me into him. He grabbed the remote as we settled, flicking through the menu until he found Episode Three.

As the movie began, I snuggled closer to Tim, his arms enveloping me in a protective embrace.

The glow of the screen cast a soft, flickering light on our faces as the movie played. The surround sound system immersed us in the world of *Star Wars*, and the iconic opening crawl rolled across the screen.

Revenge of the Sith had always been my favorite, though I somewhat hated to admit it to myself. It was because I understood Anakin's struggle and how he eventually fell into the dark side. This time as I watched it, I couldn't help but draw parallels between his struggle and my own.

It was as if I were watching a distorted reflection of myself, battling my inner demons and fears with every choice I made.

"Do you think Anakin ever really stood a chance?" I whispered, my voice barely audible over the sounds of lightsabers clashing.

Tim turned to look at me, his eyes reflective in the flickering light of the television. He considered my question for a moment before he spoke. "I think everyone has a choice," he said quietly. "Anakin chose his path."

My chest tightened, and I swallowed hard, the edges of my vision blurring as if underwater. I wasn't sure if it was the raw honesty of his words or the hidden layers that they held. He was right. Anakin had made his choice, and so had I, more than once in my life. I, too, had given in to darkness at times, allowing fear and addiction to consume me. But now, in this new chapter of my life, I wanted so desperately to overcome those old shadows. But with this new darkness trying to grip me, I didn't feel like I had a choice. And that terrified me to my core.

Tamara's words from last night replayed in my mind. *Fear doesn't always lead to the dark side.* But how could that be true? I pondered her words, trying to make sense of them in the context of my own life. Fear had been a constant companion, driving me towards addiction and self-destruction. Was it possible that there was a different path, one where fear could help instead of hinder?

Fear, in some ways, led me back to Tim last night. I had been so afraid of losing him, but there was also this greater fear looming over me. That somehow being connected to him would put him in greater danger.

But as I sat there in the warmth of Tim's embrace, watching Anakin's downfall unfold on the screen, I realized something. Fear and love were two sides of the same coin, and it was up to me to choose which one would guide my actions. Would I let fear lead me down the path of destruction, or would I choose love and let it light the way toward redemption? A choice, Tim had said. And maybe that was all it was—a choice.

A choice to accept my past mistakes and move forward. A choice to trust in the strength of my love for Tim and let that guide me—a choice to believe in myself, despite the fears that whispered otherwise.

I turned my attention again to the movie just as Anakin's transformation to Darth Vader was complete. The depth of his fall from grace left a chill running down my spine. But as Episode Three drew to a close, Tim reached over and squeezed my hand reassuringly.

"You know, there's something really beautiful about how these movies show that even when things seem darkest, there's always hope."

"Hope?" I repeated in a question.

"Exactly," Tim said as his fingers traced my cheek softly. "And I want you to remember that no matter what we face, we'll do it together. You don't have to carry the weight of your fears alone."

Tears welled in my eyes at Tim's words, grateful for his unwavering support. As the screen faded to black and the room was bathed in darkness, I realized that perhaps the true power of love lay not in its ability to protect us from harm, but rather in the strength it granted us to face our demons head-on, hand in hand.

"Thank you," I whispered, holding onto Tim tightly as the world outside our little sanctuary continued to spin. "For everything."

"Always." As I looked into Tim's unwavering gaze, I realized that this was more than just a fleeting moment of peace. Yesterday my past had tried to pull me back into its unfathomable darkness, but here in Tim's arms a new determination welled in me. I would find a way out of its deceitful snares and start the life with Tim that both of us deserved.

Tim leaned in for another kiss, his lips tender and sweet against mine. "I love you, Dakota," he said, his voice low and steady as he rested his head against mine.

"I know," I murmured, leaning in to press my lips to his once again. "So, what do you want to do now? We could watch another movie, Episode Four."

Tim checked his phone and sighed. "I would love to, but we

should be getting back. We have a three-hour drive ahead of us, and we both have to work tomorrow."

Nothing in me wanted to leave the sanctuary of this hotel room, but Tim was right. The real world, with all its harsh realities and unavoidable challenges, was waiting for us. We couldn't stay in this fairytale forever.

"Okay," I agreed reluctantly, detangling myself from his warm embrace. He pulled me back, placing a gentle kiss on my forehead before standing to gather his belongings scattered around the room. As I watched him prepare to leave, a pang of fear lodged itself firmly in my chest. The past few days' events had reminded me of how fragile life was. My past wasn't just going to disappear. I would have to find a way to fight it.

Tim grabbed our overnight bags and headed to the door. "After you," he said sweetly, opening my door for me.

I nodded silently and stepped out of the room, wishing we could stay a little longer. We both quickly made our way to our separate cars, and I watched as Tim started his engine.

As the rumble of his car filled the quiet parking lot, I slid into my own vehicle. Looking in the rearview mirror, my eyes met Tim's through the darkness. His comforting gaze held mine for a few precious moments before driving forward, leading us into reality and away from our temporary escape. I swallowed hard, the taste of fear sour on my tongue. Gripping the steering wheel more firmly, I followed Tim's taillights out of the parking lot.

CHAPTER 13

January 23, 5:00 a.m.

TIM

The alarm buzzed its shrill cry at five in the morning, pulling me from a restless sleep. I slapped the snooze button and snuggled into Dakota for a few more minutes of warmth and comfort, her dark hair a gentle cascade against my chest as her steady breaths lured me towards the precipice of sleep once more. The alarm rang again, and I reluctantly rolled out of bed, my feet hitting the cold hardwood floor with a soft thud. The morning chill bit into my skin as I shuffled towards the bathroom.

Yawning, I trudged to the bathroom and splashed cold water on my face. The shock jolted me awake, the icy tendrils of the water piercing through the fog of sleep that still clung to me. I stepped into the shower, letting the hot water wash away the last remnants of the night's restless dreams. It was a dream I'd often had when Dakota was in her addiction. Her sunken eyes devoid of life, her soul trapped within a prison not of her making. In the nightmare, I was always stuck on the outside, powerless to save her, to pull her back from the edge. The fury of helplessness was always raw and visceral, a cruel mockery of my role as a protector.

I shook off the image, focusing on the spray of the showerhead. The stream drummed against my skin, creating a rhythmic lullaby that eased the tension from my muscles and for that moment, I allowed the water to drown the ominous memories. Dakota wasn't there anymore. She had made it through the dark tunnel of addiction and emerged, bruised but resilient, at the other end.

With a sigh, I stepped out of the shower and wrapped a towel around my waist. Dakota was with me now. We were engaged to be married and were building a life together. She was taking one day at a time, and so was I.

After drying off, I put on my police uniform. The dark blue fabric was crisp and neatly pressed, emphasizing the weight of my responsibilities. My badge gleamed against my chest as I looked at my reflection in the mirror. At only twenty-four years old, I had already faced more challenges than some do in a lifetime. But every day, I wore that badge with pride, knowing it represented my dedication to justice, law and order, and above all, protecting others. Especially Dakota.

Once ready for the day, I poured myself a cup of coffee and I settled at the kitchen table with my laptop. I opened the schedule for my final term of my bachelor's degree in criminal justice. Two of the classes seemed like easy A's—courses I could breeze through without much effort. But the third class was the last of my required courses: Restorative Justice. My upbringing had instilled a strong belief in retribution, an eye for an eye, a tooth for a tooth. On the other hand, restorative justice focused on healing the harm caused by an offense, emphasizing restitution and the reintegration of offenders into the community. With the evil I'd seen in my lifetime, I wasn't sure how I felt about it. Not to mention, it had a twelve-page research paper due at the end of the class.

Damn. Good thing my other two classes were a breeze. Otherwise, I'd be screwed with my mounting case work.

Closing the laptop with a sigh, I stood and walked to my room. Dakota was still asleep, her long dark hair fanned out on the pillow, her face a picture of serene beauty. I couldn't help but watch her for a moment, a sense of protectiveness filling me. I wished with everything inside me that I could shield her from all the evil in the world.

I leaned down to press a gentle kiss on her forehead. "I love you."

Her eyes fluttered open for a moment, a hint of a smile playing on her lips. "Love you too. Be safe today."

"Always," I promised before leaving our small bungalow.

On the way to work, I stopped by for donuts. It wasn't a normal thing, but I was still in a celebratory mood because of our engagement. And for my coworkers, the cliché held true—cops really did love donuts.

Stepping out of my car into the crisp morning air, my breath formed small puffs of fog as I stepped toward the donut shop. The familiar jingle of the doorbell greeted me as I entered, the warm scent of freshly baked pastries enveloping me like a comforting hug. Quickly scanning the display case, I selected an assortment of glazed and filled treats, hoping to appease the diverse tastes of my coworkers. Two dozen should be enough. I handed over my cash to the friendly cashier and put the change in the tip jar along with a five-dollar bill.

As I drove to work, I tried to focus on the road ahead, but I kept thinking about asking my boss for a raise. I'd toyed with the idea for over a month, mentally rehearsing how I would ask. I knew I deserved it. I had been working hard, putting in long hours, and even going above and beyond by pursuing my Criminal Justice degree. Yet the nagging fear of rejection gnawed at me, reminding me of the times I had faltered—the cases that remained unsolved.

Pulling into the police station's parking lot, I grabbed the donuts and headed inside. The familiar sights and sounds of the bustling precinct helped to ground me—the sense of camaraderie among my coworkers providing a small sense of comfort.

With the two boxes of donuts in hand, I made my way over to the breakroom, a motley array of mismatched chairs and tables that somehow felt more like home than any other part of the precinct. The scent of fresh coffee and the buzz of conversation filled the air—a comforting reminder that we were all in this together.

I set boxes on the table. "Help yourself, guys."

"Donuts?" Detective Carla Ramirez asked with a wink. "What's the occasion?"

Carla was ten years my senior, but was my confidante, my mentor, and most importantly, my friend. We've worked together since I started at Jefferson County Police Department, a little over four years ago, but earlier this year as I climbed the ranks I became her partner.

"Well... I asked Dakota to marry me," I announced to the room with a large grin. "And she said yes!"

Carla's face lit with a warm smile, and she threw her arms around me in an uncharacteristically emotional display. "That's amazing, Tim. I'm so happy for both of you."

The room filled with a chorus of congratulatory exclamations and hearty pats on the back.

"Thanks, guys," I said as a warm glow spread through me. Their support meant the world to me, especially given how much Dakota and I had been through together.

As the conversation continued, I told them more about the proposal, sharing the intimate details of our candlelit dinner and the quiet moment we shared after she said yes. I left out the part where she ran out of the room and was MIA for over an hour, of course.

"Man, I gotta say, I never pegged you as such a romantic." Officer Martinez laughed, nudging me playfully. "But seriously, congrats, Tim."

"Thanks, man," I shot back with a grin, appreciating the easy banter that always came from him. "But we better get to work before the Sarge comes and puts an end to this party."

"No one's holding you here, my brother." Martinez shoved half of a donut in his mouth at once.

I shook my head, with a chuckle turning towards the captain's office. "How are you not a thousand pounds?" I called over my shoulder with a laugh.

"Don't be jealous, Tim. Just cause you have to eat like a bird to stay fit!" he called back, the words muffled by his mouthful of donut. The precinct echoed with laughter at that, and I found myself joining in.

"Whatever, dude." But the joke abruptly died on my lips as I looked into the captain's office. I gathered myself and rapped softly at the door.

"Come in," came the gruff reply from within.

Captain Simmons sat behind his desk, reviewing paperwork with that intense.

"Do you have a moment, sir? I have something I'd like to discuss with you," I said hesitantly.

"Of course, Officer Moore, come in." He set his paperwork and gestured for me to take a seat. "What can I help you with?"

"Sir, I've been thinking about my performance lately, and I believe that I've been putting in a lot of hard work and dedication on the force," I began, trying to sound confident despite the nerves gnawing at me. "I feel that I've grown as an officer, and I was hoping we could discuss the possibility of a raise."

Captain Simmons took a moment to consider his words before asking me, "How is the Mendez case progressing?"

The Mendez case. The mention of it twisted my gut like a knife. Ever since I was promoted last year it had been a thorn in my side. Even before my promotion, I was determined to uncover the true mastermind behind Ryan Cooke's drug ring. Ryan had been the ruthless dealer who had terrorized Dakota for years, but I believed there was someone else pulling the strings. All signs pointed toward Victor Mendez, and yet I felt like I was chasing my tail with this case, always a step behind. Ramirez and I had found leads connecting Mendez to Ryan, but each one seemed to lead us nowhere.

"Sir, I truly believe we are close to a breakthrough," I

responded with sincerity. "I have confidence that we will catch him soon."

Simmons was silent for a moment, his face betraying no emotion as he steepled his fingers. That always made me nervous. It's like he was playing chess in his head, thinking five moves ahead. "Moore." He leaned back in his creaky chair. "Feelings don't crack cases," Captain Simmons said firmly, his steely gaze boring into me. "You nail this guy, and we'll see about that raise."

"Understood, sir." I nodded respectfully.

As I left the office, the weight of the unspoken words hung heavy like a storm cloud.

I kept my head down as I headed to my cubicle. Capturing Mendez was not just about a pay raise; it was much more. It was about justice for Dakota and all the countless, faceless victims I'd never met, but whose stories had kept me awake at night. The scent of coffee and drying ink filled my nostrils as I pored over documents and photographs, searching for any clue that could lead to Mendez's downfall. There was a house in Brinnon that kept being highlighted, but it didn't make sense. Brinnon was just a tiny town on the Olympic peninsula known for its peaceful living and charming docks, not a place for a drug kingpin. But something in my gut told me not to rule it out entirely. Maybe the simplicity of Brinnon was just another facade, a means to mask the darkness that lurked beneath.

As the day wore on, my nerves frayed, and the pressure mounted. Each piece of evidence seemed to slip through my fingers like water, no closer to a solid lead than when I'd started.

I couldn't shake the idea that Mendez was the key to everything, the puppet master behind Ryan Cooke and the drug epidemic plaguing Jefferson County. As I pored over case files and witness statements, the hours slipped by in a haze of coffee and frustration. My boss's words played through my mind, a constant reminder of what was at stake.

Feelings don't crack cases.

But sometimes they did... the infamous hunch that cops talk about before the breakthrough.

"Hey, Moore, you still focused on the Mendez case?" My partner Ramirez came over with a folder in her hand. "You know we have other cases just as pressing right?"

I nodded. "When I asked the captain about a raise, he specifically mentioned the Mendez case in response."

Ramirez tilted her head, understanding dawning in her eyes. She grabbed a nearby chair and pulled it up to my desk, settling down with a sigh. "Alright, let's see what we've got."

CHAPTER 14

January 24, 5:20 a.m.

TAMARA

Trepidation churned in my stomach as I emerged from the darkness of sleep. All night long, my dreams had been plagued by nightmares—first of Dakota, then my dad—as if my subconscious was trying to warn me of impending danger.

But it was Dakota's nightmare that truly shook me to my core. We were at the old Ninety-Nine Diner, our bodies tied tightly together just like the night Ryan had tried to end us both. As the flames crept closer, licking at our skin, Ryan's maniacal laughter echoed through the air, spewing threats and obscenities at us. Dakota and I struggled frantically against our restraints, but the ropes only dug deeper into our wrists, cutting off circulation and causing excruciating pain.

With a sudden jolt, I woke. Throwing off the covers, I hurried downstairs to check on Lillie.

She was safely snuggled into her bed, her angelic face peaceful and serene. I stood there for about ten minutes, watching her breathe, silently thanking God that she would never have to face the horrors I had experienced. Joe and I would always keep her safe and help guide her through life's challenges.

Climbing the stairs, I thought about the nightmare and

wondered why I dreamt about Ryan. He had been dead for a little over two years. He couldn't hurt me or Dakota anymore.

I shook my head, forcing myself to push the chilling thoughts away. But for all my efforts, I couldn't shake off the nagging feeling that something was terribly wrong. The sinking dread in the pit of my stomach was hard to ignore.

As I lay in bed again, I curled up next to Joe, seeking solace in his warmth. Silently, I thanked God for all that he'd done in the past few years—for our family and for the love Joe and I shared that had only grown stronger since we wed. The tension in my body began to ease as I let sleep take me once more.

But sleep wasn't done with me yet. This time, my dad appeared in my dreams, wasting away before his family as his liver continued to deteriorate. The next scene was even more vivid: I stood by a hospital bed, saying goodbye as he took his last breath.

Tears streamed down my cheeks, and a heavy weight settled on my mind as I woke. My eyes flickered open before dawn, the room bathed in a soft gray light. Shadows danced on the walls, the remnants of my nightmares still lingering in the dimly lit room. My pulse raced as I tried to shake off the images that had tormented me throughout the night. The soft rustle of sheets drew my attention, and I turned my head to find Joe lying beside me, his expression filled with concern.

"You okay, T?" he asked, his deep voice gentle and soothing.

"Rough night," I mumbled, struggling to keep my voice steady, still reeling from the vivid nightmares.

He ran a gentle hand across my brow line and tucked a loose strand of hair behind my ear. "You want to talk about it?"

I hesitated, unsure if I was ready to relive the vivid terror of my dreams, but the weight of the emotions trapped inside me begged for release. "Every time I went to sleep, I saw Dakota trapped, her face twisted in terror, and heard Ryan's cruel laughter echoing in the background." I paused, swallowing hard as the image of my father's gaunt face and lifeless body flashed through my mind. "And then, Dad... His eyes stared into nothingness as he took his last breath. It felt so real, Joe."

His hand froze on my cheek, his featues filled with a mixture of sorrow and empathy. He knew all too well the pain of losing a parent.

He pulled me into an embrace, tucking my head under his chin. His arms held me tightly, as if he could keep the nightmares at bay with sheer force.

"I'm here," he whispered, pressing his lips to my forehead. "I've got you."

The warmth of his body seeped into mine. He kissed my forehead, his lips lingering for a moment as if trying to absorb my pain.

I clung to him, my fingers digging into the fabric of his shirt, drawing comfort from his presence. The tears that I had been holding back spilled down my cheeks, wetting the collar of his shirt.

"It's okay, T," he murmured, his hand gently rubbing circles on my back. His voice was like a soft lullaby, combating the lingering echoes of my nightmares. I clung to it, and to him, letting his presence anchor me in reality.

"I just wish I could protect them."

Joe tightened his hold on me, pressing me flush against him. "It's going to be okay T. We've been through so much together already. We'll face whatever comes our way, and we'll do it as a family."

I tried to focus on his unwavering strength, to let his conviction seep into my bones and chase away the lingering shadows. But as I lay in the darkness, listening to the steady rhythm of Joe's breathing, I couldn't help but feel that something ominous was lurking just beyond our reach, waiting for the perfect moment to strike.

"Joe?" I whispered, my voice wavering with fear.

"Right here, T," he murmured, his breath warm against my hair.

"I'm scared," I admitted.

His hand found mine in the darkness, his fingers threading through mine, offering a solid, much-needed anchor. He gently whispered a prayer, asking God to comfort me and bring me peace. As his words filled the air, I could feel the tension in my body slowly dissipate. In the darkness, his whispers became my lifeline, my beacon of hope. His strength began to fill me as he called on our faith, a shared connection that had always kept us grounded in times of turmoil.

"Thank you," I said, turning to press my face into his chest, basking in the comfort of his arms. "I'm so thankful for you and the life we've built together."

"I'm grateful too, T," he whispered back, his lips pressing a soft kiss to the crown of my head. "We've been through so much, but we always come out stronger."

My heart swelled with gratitude and affection for this man who had become my rock. I basked in the comfort of his arms, the feeling of love washing away the fears. His lips met mine in a deep, slow kiss, each tender caress communicating the depth of our shared love. The kiss deepened, and I ran my hands around his broad shoulders and into his dark hair, letting the strands sift through my fingers. He gave a low, contented hum against my lips, and I melted further into him. Two years of marriage had done nothing to dampen our desire for each other. "I love you," he whispered between kisses, his breath fanning warmly against my cheeks. "I love you so much, Tamara."

"I love you too," I whispered back. My pulse quickened as he pulled me closer, his strong arms encircling me. I allowed myself to get lost in the moment, in the warmth of his embrace, in the slow exploration of our lips.

Lillie's cries rose from downstairs.

Joe groaned as he pulled his lips away, and then rested his forehead against mine. "Please let her go back to sleep," he prayed with a chuckle.

I giggled at his frustration. It seemed like this had been the pattern for the last few months every time we had tried to be intimate. "Oh, the joys of parenting."

"Shhhh." He crushed his lips against mine once more just as Lillie cried again.

"I don't think she's going back to sleep, babe."

Joe gave an exaggerated sigh, pressing a final kiss to my forehead before disentangling from our embrace and then rolled out of bed.

"It's probably for the best," I said as I followed him. "You need to get to work."

"It's definitely not for the best," he said, smirking at me from over his shoulder as we walked into Lillie's room. "I would have gladly been late."

Lillie's tear-streaked face calmed when she saw us, and her tiny fingers reached out to grasp Joe's hand. Joe picked her up and snuggled her close. "It's okay, baby girl. Daddy has you." He rocked her soothingly, his deep voice lulling her into a calm.

Lillie nuzzled deeper into Joe's shoulder, her little hands curling around the collar of his shirt. Joe chuckled, kissing the top of her tiny head as he continued to sway gently. His eyes met mine across the room, a soft smile on his face. It was moments like this that made every struggle worth it.

CHAPTER 15

January 26, 10:32 a.m.

DAKOTA

The sky outside the window was a mass of thick gray clouds, unleashing the usual Washington storm. I stood behind the cash register, hoping that it would stop, mainly because the constant rain meant fewer customers. This meant the day would drag on, and I needed it to pass quickly.

From the moment I got out of bed this morning, a sense of dread had settled in my stomach. It had been days since my encounter with Ricky and his crew, and I was constantly on edge, waiting for them to give me instructions.

Trying to steady my trembling hands, I took a deep breath before starting my usual routine of restocking shelves and cleaning countertops. My phone weighed heavily in my pocket, a constant reminder of the anxiety that consumed me.

"Hey, Dakota," my coworker Sally greeted me, but I barely registered her presence.

"Hi," I mumbled as I tried to focus on the task at hand. But every time I reached for a bottle of beer to stock the empty shelves, my mind drifted to the threats Avery had made to me about Tim.

The addict in me wanted to take a six-pack into the back and drink them all in one go to silence the anxiety.

My phone seemed to constantly pulse with potential danger, taunting me with its silence. Unable to resist, I pulled it out and checked for any missed calls or messages. Nothing. Swallowing hard, I shoved it into my pocket and continued working.

"Are you okay?" Sally asked.

"Fine," I lied, offering another strained smile.

Time seemed to crawl by, each second dragging on like an eternity. I glanced at the clock every few minutes, the ticking sound echoing in my ears, heightening my unease.

Avery's words raced through my mind on repeat. *You don't want to see what we'll do to your cop boyfriend if you don't.*

The storm continued to beat down relentlessly outside, keeping the customers away. I looked at my phone again. Why wouldn't they just call me, so I could get this stupid task over with and be done with it? I desperately wanted to go back to my happy life with Tim and forget any of this ever happened.

I glanced at the ring on my finger and longed to be in Ocean Shores, away from this dreary place. Spending the day with Tim, watching *Star Wars* movies and snuggling in between making out sessions, was like a slice of heaven amidst of this hell called earth.

With the shelves stocked, I forced myself to move on to my next task—cleaning the bathroom. It was a small, dingy space that smelled faintly of bleach and stale urine. Barf. So disgusting. I scoured the toilet, cleaned the mirrors and swept and mopped the floor, but it didn't help the appearance of the room much. Oh well.

I emerged from the bathroom into the store, taking a deep breath to rid myself of the overpowering smell of disinfectant. My gaze immediately landed on the coffee machine, which was almost full but most likely in need of a new pot. No one enjoyed the taste of burnt coffee. I reached for a filter and the canister from the cupboard, my nose now filled with the sharp scent of freshly ground beans as I measured out the perfect amount.

From out of nowhere, a hand touched my waist. I jumped

and let out a scream, my heart raising. Coffee grounds scattered across the floor like tiny, dark pebbles. I flipped around, terrified.

Tim stood in front of me in his wet police uniform, hair drenched with a silly grin on his face. "I so got you back," he said with a chuckle.

I smacked him on the arm and glared at him. "What the hell, Tim? This is my place of employment."

"All's fair in love and war," he replied, mouth curling at the edges.

"Whatever," I snarled, fuming as I walked across the room for the broom and dustpan. "I seriously just cleaned this whole place."

"Babe." He took the broom from me and swept the mess. "Don't be mad."

He swept the scattered coffee grounds, his well-muscled arms flexing as he worked. I watched him, my annoyance melting away as the sight of him working so diligently to clean the mess he'd startled me into making. Why did he have to be so endearing?

I held the dustpan for him to sweep into, refusing to look at him. Then I dumped the grounds in the garbage and grabbed another coffee filter. Once I had added the grounds, I pressed the start button, and the coffee began to brew.

"Dakota," Tim said, turning me toward him, "I'm sorry, okay. Don't be mad."

"What are you even doing here?" I grumbled, trying to keep my stern demeanor but failing miserably as I felt myself being pulled into the warmth of his sincere apology.

Tim scanned the store, and I followed his gaze. Sally was busy restocking cigarettes behind the counter. He brought his pointer finger to his mouth, motioning for me to be quiet. Then he grabbed by the elbow and pulled me into the back room where only employees were supposed to go. He pushed me against the wall, his expression intense as he studied my face.

"What's going on, Tim? Why are you here?"

"I missed you," he said so simply and earnestly that it disarmed me for a moment. His brown eyes were soft pools that locked onto mine and wouldn't let go.

"Seriously?" I grumbled, even as my throat tightened with unshed tears. My hands clenched and unclenched at my sides, part of me itching to reach out and touch him, the other part knowing I should keep my distance. Tim tilted his head slightly, his thumb gently brushing against my cheek.

His lips found mine then, hungry and insistent, and the world around me blurred into insignificance. It was a tender kiss, almost hesitant as though he was afraid I would push him away. But I couldn't. I was anchored in place, held captive by the soft pressure of his lips on mine, the intoxicating scent of him filling my senses. His hands slid down my back, pulling me closer, and our bodies melded together like two puzzle pieces that had finally found their match. "I love you so much, Dakota. I can't wait for you to be my wife."

The weight of my secrets weighed on me, pushing me deep into the cold shadows, even as Tim's words tried to pull me into the warmth of his love. Could I really marry Tim with these lies I was being forced into? Fear suddenly resurfaced along with a stab of self-hatred. I hated lying to Tim.

"Tim, we can't do this here," I gasped, pushing him away. "What if someone sees?"

He nodded, breathless, conceding, his gaze still locked on mine, filled with such adoration that made my stomach twist with guilt. "I just wanted you to know I was thinking about you," he said and pushed a lock of hair away from my face. "That you're always right here." Taking hold of my hand, he placed it over his heart.

A part of me broke at the depth of love in his eyes. Love that I would never be worthy of.

As he left the room, I leaned against the wall and took a few minutes to regroup. I ran my hands over my rumpled shirt, grabbed a box of spearmint gum to stock front and walked out front as if nothing had happened.

Sally gave me a suspicious look as I stepped behind the counter to tend the cash machine. I pretended not to see it. It wasn't like she was Miss Goody-Two-Shoes. I was pretty sure her past was as gnarly as mine. Making out with my fiancé at work was definitely not the worst thing I'd ever done.

But it was guilt, not Sally's judgment, that was the real predator. I wondered if Tim would look at me the same way if he knew the whole truth about Victor's demands. That I had finally escaped from Ryan's grasps only to be sucked in by a new monster. I wasn't sure how it had happened, but I was now caught once more in a web of secrets that threatened to suffocate me. Only now, I had so much more to lose.

CHAPTER 16

January 25, 11:16 a.m.

TIM

As I made my way back to the station, the sun peeked out from behind a cloud, though there was still a light drizzle coming down from the dark gray sky. With hesitant fingers, I pulled out my phone and dialed my mom's number. I had been avoiding this call for days, not ready to face her reaction to the news of my engagement to Dakota. Inhaling deeply, I pressed the call button and waited for the familiar ringing sound to connect us. My parents had relocated to the east coast a few years ago for their jobs, and our distance seemed to only grow with time.

"Tim?" Mom's voice crackled over the line, her normally warm tone laced with a tinge of worry.

"Hi, Mom. I was calling with some big news." Might as well just go for it. Rip the BAND-AID® off.

"News? Is everything okay, Tim?" The worry in her voice heightened, adding a lump in my throat I hadn't anticipated.

"Yeah, everything's fine. More than fine." I forced out a laugh, hoping it sounded more convincing to her than it did to me. "I...um...I proposed to Dakota, and she said yes."

The silence on the other end of the line was deafening. I could hear the cogs grinding in my mother's mind, trying to fit this new piece into a puzzle she'd been trying to solve for years.

I knew this was going to be a difficult conversation, but I had hoped that somehow, she would be happy for me. Tension built in my chest as I waited for her response.

Mom let out a heavy sigh on the other end, one that seemed to stretch on for ages. "Tim, I... I don't know what to say." Her voice was filled with a mix of disappointment and concern. "Are you sure about this? I mean, you're still so young, and marriage is a big commitment."

My heart sank at her words even though I had known this would be her reaction. "Mom, I understand your concerns, but Dakota and I have known each other our whole lives. We love each other, and we both want this."

Her tone grew even more somber. "Tim, you've only been dating for a year. And Dakota is an addict. How do you know she won't relapse?"

Her words hit me like a punch to the gut, stealing the breath from my lungs.

Would she ever give Dakota a chance? "First of all, we've been dating for two years, and in that time, I've seen so much growth in her. She's been working her program faithfully, one day at a time. I'm proud of her, Mom. I just wish you could see her how I do."

More silence ...

Then, finally, Mom spoke again. Her voice was soft, barely above a whisper, but it carried a weight that cleaved the air like a sharpened blade. "I just don't think you fully understand what you're getting into. Marriage is hard work. It requires time and sacrifice. Do you think Dakota is ready for that?"

Frustration grew within me as I pulled into the station. I had always admired my mom's strong-willed nature, but in that moment, it felt like she was using it to cast doubt on my decision to marry Dakota. Turning off the engine, I leaned back in the driver's seat, clutching the phone to my ear tighter than necessary. "I actually do. You don't know her like I do."

"You have to see it from my perspective." Her words were more of a plea now, laced with an undercurrent of worry. "I have dreams for you. I want to see you happy. I want to have grandchildren. Do you think she would be a good mother? Does she even want children?"

I swallowed the emotion rising in my throat. After seeing the way Dakota was with Lillie, I thought she would be a great mother someday—if she wanted children.

"Mom, I love you, but that's between me and Dakota. We will make that decision when we are ready."

The truth was I did want children someday...But I wanted Dakota more.

When she spoke again, it sounded like she was fighting tears. "I've only ever wanted what was best for you. I don't think this is the best decision, but it sounds like you're determined to make it."

The rain picked up, falling steadily on the windshield. I honestly didn't know how to respond. "Mom, I do understand your concerns, but I'm asking you to trust me on this. Dakota is the one for me. It's always been her."

"I know..." she said, her voice softening. "I may not agree with this decision, but you are my son, and I will always love you."

"Love you too, Mom." I said and hung up the phone, stepping out of my car.

With a deep breath, I closed the door behind me and braced myself for the biting cold air that greeted me like shards of ice. Hurrying into the station, I tried to push away the lingering conversation with my mother and the chill in my bones. Her doubts about my relationship with Dakota were not going to get to me. There was a time when I thought I had lost Dakota forever. But now that we were together, nothing would come between us. Not even my own mother's reservations. I had seen the best and worst of Dakota, and I still believed in her, still loved her. I was determined to stand by her side no matter what challenges came our way.

CHAPTER 17

January 27, 5:27 p.m.

DAKOTA

The dusk was settling in, painting the sky with hues of purple and crimson as I toiled outside near the dumpster, breaking boxes into piles. The gritty symphony of crunching cardboard mingled with the distant hum of traffic. I was so ready to be done for the day and get home to Tim—to snuggle into him for a relaxing night in front of the television continuing our *Star Wars* marathon. Tim had been looking forward to Episode Four, though it was probably my least favorite episode.

It would be nice to relax with him and take a break from the whirlwind of emotions that had dominated the day. When I wasn't thinking about Victor and the looming package he wanted me to run for him, I was thinking about my dad and his declining health. I hadn't talked to Tamara about it since Mom had called with the news, and my guess was that she wasn't handling it well.

As I broke down the last box, I reached for my phone and found Tamara's number.

I lit a smoke and hit the call button, holding my breath as it began to ring. Tamara had always been the strong one, the one who held it together when everything else threatened to fall apart. She had been my rock so many times, but now I knew I had to be hers. I just really didn't know how.

ELISHEBA HAXBY & JESSE VINCENT

"Hey," she answered after a few rings, sounding tired. Guilt pinged my insides. I hoped she was okay. She had a lot on her plate with Lillie, being pregnant and now this thing with Dad. I should not have bugged her with my drama the other night.

"How are you holding up, sis?" I asked.

"I'm...doing okay," she said after a pause. "It's been tough though."

I exhaled a plume of smoke into the air, watching it dissipate. "Yeah, I can imagine." I wished that I was better at this, but my knee jerk reaction had always been to get high when things got rough. Being there for people was a new skill. One I wasn't sure I would master in my lifetime.

Tamara hesitated for a moment before answering, her tone cautiously hopeful. "Yeah, I talked to him the other day and he said he'd try to quit drinking. He knows his liver is starting to fail. He wants to get better, Dakota."

Try—the word hung heavy in the air. That did not sound promising. I thought about the *Star Wars* Marathon with Tim. Though we hadn't got to that episode in our rewatch yet, I recalled Yoda's iconic line. "Do or do not. There is no try." I tended to agree with Yoda. 'Trying' at his point was like spinning stuck tires in mud, only to make a bigger mess without breaking free. But I kept that thought to myself, not wanting to upset Tamara further. She deserved not to worry.

I forced optimism into my voice and took another drag. "Perhaps with the support of the family, he really can quit." Oh man, I was so not good at this. Could she hear the lie in my voice?

"Thanks, Dakota," she whispered, gratitude softening her words. "That means a lot to me. I just hope this is the wake-up call he needs."

"Me too, sis," I agreed as my throat tightened.

I stubbed out my cigarette. The bitter taste lingered in my mouth, reflecting the sour worry that clenched at my heart. This wasn't the life I wanted for Tamara or for our father. But it seemed to be the one we were stuck with, a cruel joke from a universe that didn't give two cents about what we wanted.

We spoke for a few more minutes before I had to end the call and get back to work. As I walked inside, my thoughts returned to Tim and the choices I'd made to protect him. Why hadn't I heard from Ricky? Had this all been some sort of cruel way to mess with me? Yeah, right? If Victor was anything like Ryan, this sick game was far from over. They were just winding me real tight before they made their move.

CHAPTER 18

January 27, 5:45 p.m.

TIM

My pulse pounded in my eardrums as I crouched low in the dark alley, my police cruiser hidden behind a row of rundown buildings. The rain was unrelenting, each drop stinging as they battered against my skin and soaked through my uniform, but I hardly noticed. My focus was fixed on the shadowy figure a few streets down who was conducting business which was not exactly legal.

The pulsating red and blue lights casting eerie shadows around the dim alley were turned off. They would've been a dead giveaway. Instead, the glow from a single grimy streetlight provided just enough light for me to make out the exchange happening.

"Suspected narcotics deal happening at West and 5th," I reported quietly into my shoulder radio, a cold knot of dread unfurling in my stomach. Things like this, they never went smoothly.

"Copy that," Ramirez responded immediately, her voice steady and reliable as always. "I'm only two blocks away. Hang tight."

The suspect, a burly silhouette under the scarce streetlight, must've sensed something because he stiffened suddenly and turned to look in my direction. His gaze didn't find me tucked away in the shadows, but he bolted anyway.

"He's on the move!" I relayed into the radio while already pushing out of cover and dashing after him. The rain was a blur as I tore down the alley, every slick step a risk in the downpour. But there wasn't any time for caution. If he got away, that was another night this city was under the thumb of dealers and their poison.

He had a head start, but I was gaining on him. Each desperate stride propelled me forward, closer and closer. The adrenaline coursing through my veins sharpened my senses, made me acutely aware of everything—the driving rain, the thunder rumbling in the distance, the escapee's ragged pants echoing off the alley walls.

"Tim, be careful!" Ramirez's voice came through again, fraught with concern. But her warning came too late. Suddenly, the suspect whipped around and fired a shot at me. The world seemed to slow as I threw myself to the side.

The bullet whistled by me, embedding itself into a brick wall behind me. My heart pounded in my ears as I picked myself up from the wet ground. Ignoring the pain that shot through me from what felt like bruised ribs, I took off after him again.

Just as I rounded the corner, Ramirez's cruiser screeched onto the street ahead of him. The suspect skidded to a halt, his figure momentarily illuminated in the harsh glow of her headlights. He was trapped between us. His head flicked back and forth as he weighed his options—the outstretched arms of the law on one side, a dead-end on the other.

His desperate gaze landed on a rusty fire escape hanging above him. With a frantic surge of energy, he lunged towards it, trying to scramble up. I gritted my teeth and forced my legs to move faster, crashing into him before he could get far. The impact sent us both sprawling onto the wet asphalt.

The rain suddenly seemed louder, pinging off the metal around us as we grappled on the ground. I twisted his arm behind his back and slapped cuffs onto his wrist with practiced efficiency.

"You have the right to remain silent," I recited, my voice steadier than I felt. The rain clung to my eyelashes, blurring the edges of the world. "Anything you say can and will be used against you in a court of law."

His struggles ceased and he went limp beneath me, cursing fiercely under his breath. A wave of relief washed over me. It was over. We had him.

Carla was quickly at my side, her own gun held out and ready. "You okay?" she asked, worry lining her features.

"I'm fine," I assured her with a weak smile, despite the ache in my ribs telling a different story.

"Backup's on the way," she announced, her voice echoing slightly in the narrow alleyway. "Good job, Tim."

I reached into the man's pocket and pulled out a small plastic bag filled with tiny blue pills. Fentanyl. I looked at Ramirez with a grim expression, lifting the bag. This was the drug Victor Mendez was pushing. As I watched the raindrops strike against the translucent bag, I tasted a bitter victory on my tongue. This could be one of Victor's men. If we could just squeeze him for information, maybe we could find a solid lead. Maybe we could bring Victor down once and for all.

Ramirez grimaced at the sight of the bag. "Nasty stuff."

"You can say that again," I muttered, pocketing it as evidence and reaching into his other pocket for his wallet. "Let's get him in the back of the squad car."

With Ramirez's help, we hauled our catch to his feet. He was a big man, solid with muscles I could feel even through the layers of wet clothing. Once in the car, I looked at his I.D. Ethan Jones. A small piece of the larger, more dangerous puzzle that was Victor Mandez.

My mind buzzed with adrenaline and thoughts of Dakota. I glanced at my watch. She'd be waiting, blissfully ignorant of what just happened. I eyed the perp in the rearview mirror and clenched my jaw. If I had anything to do with it, she would stay that way. Safe and removed from all this darkness and danger.

"See you at the station," Ramirez said and then turned toward her cruiser, her coat flicking water droplets as she moved.

"Thanks, Remerez," I responded, starting the car. The metal beast rumbled to life beneath me, adding its own voice to the symphony of the storm outside.

As I drove to the station, my mind kept wandering to Dakota. We were supposed to continue our marathon tonight, but it looked like I would be stuck at the station, interrogating Ethan Jones.

When I arrived at the station, Ramirez was already there, sheltered under the awning as she waited for me. We didn't say anything as we hauled Ethan out of the car and into the precinct, our actions synchronized by years of experience.

Inside, the fluorescent lights lit up Ethan's' face, revealing a myriad of scars that told tales of a hardened criminal. Victor sure knew how to pick them.

As we guided him towards the interrogation room, I could feel my heart pounding, not from fear but anticipation.

I tried to maintain a calm and confident exterior in front of the suspect, but inside, I was a bundle of nerves. Ethan was our best lead to getting some information on Victor, and the gravity of that was not lost on me. Any misstep now, any wrong turn, could foil our chances of bringing Victor down.

I took a step closer to Ethan, my eyes never leaving his face. The dim light of the interrogation room did little to reveal his true intentions, but I could sense the cunning intelligence lurking beneath his façade.

As I shut the door behind us, his gaze met mine, cold and calculating. This was not a man who would break easily.

"We're going to have a nice long chat, Ethan," I told him, my voice steady despite the adrenaline pumping through my veins. His only response was a wry smirk that did nothing to ease my apprehension.

For the next few hours, we danced around each other in a

verbal sparring match. I prodded and pried, pushing for any information he might have on Victor. But Ethan was skilled at dodging questions and offering half-truths. He had clearly been in this sort of situation before. Ramirez relieved me for a spell, her method of interrogation more patient and methodical, but even her gentle approach yielded nothing from the stone-faced Ethan.

Part of me admired his resilience; the other half cursed it. Every passing minute was a minute I wasn't with Dakota.

I studied him from behind the glass, trying to gauge his weaknesses, searching for any cracks in his armor that I could exploit. But Ethan was a master at concealing his vulnerabilities, like a skilled magician who could make even the most astute observer question their own senses.

As she probed for more information, I found myself thinking about Dakota again. The image of her haunted eyes and that vulnerable look she got when she thought I wasn't watching. The thought of her being anywhere near this world, this darkness, made me clench my fists in helpless rage.

Ramirez left the room and entered the area where I was watching behind the glass. "This guy is a waste of time," she muttered, running a hand through her hair. "He's not gonna crack."

"I know..." I whispered, my focus never leaving Ethan who sat smirking in satisfaction at our frustration. "But we need to try, Ramirez. He's all we have for now."

Ramirez sighed again, more resigned this time, and nodded. "Alright, lets call it for now though. We can try again tomorrow."

As I stood and stretched my muscles, the image of Dakota crept into my mind again. This was supposed to be our night, our time. And here I was stuck dancing with a devil.

I stepped out of the small room and shot Dakota a text, apologizing again for missing our marathon and promising to make it up to her as soon as possible.

As we walked out of the building and into the courtyard, I

took a deep breath of the fresh air. The storm had passed, but I couldn't shake off the tense feeling in my chest. I knew we were running out of time to crack this case, and I couldn't bear the thought of letting Victor escape through our grasp.

CHAPTER 19
February 1, 9:30 a.m.
TAMARA

I sat at my desk, opened my laptop and pressed the power button. My body ached with exhaustion, making it difficult to focus on anything but the overwhelming desire to sleep. With a sigh, I waited for the screen to load so I could log in to my Skype call with David. It had been a busy morning, getting Lillie ready to send with Joe on their daddy daughter date. Joe had wanted to make sure I had plenty of space to process things with David.

Honestly, I wasn't quite sure what was going on with me. I'd been on edge ever since I found out about my dad's diagnosis. And though Joe had been stepping up more with Lillie to give me space to spend time with God praying over the situation, I never was able to really come to peace. There was this constant buzzing in the back of my brain—a sick foreboding I couldn't shake. Several times that week, I had the same recurring nightmares. Each time they would leave me reeling emotionally for hours. I hated it because I felt like Lillie deserved better than an exhausted, stressed-out mom.

As I waited for the call to connect, I tried to remember the last time I had a session with David. It may have been over a year. Probably around the time Dakota had relapsed. That had been a really hard couple weeks, but things had mellowed out after that.

Dakota had really dug into her program, and I got busy with motherhood. It had been natural to let this connection with David go. He had led me through so much healing, it was time to learn to stand on my own. Ever since that day last week though, I had felt like I was stumbling down a dark path once again.

David's face finally appeared on the screen, interrupting my thoughts. "Hey, Tamara. It's so good to see you. How have you been?" he asked gently.

A pang of guilt hit my stomach for neglecting our sessions. I let out a deep breath, feeling tears prick at the corners of my eyes. I tried to smile back, but the muscles in my face felt heavy. "To be honest, it's been a rough few weeks." My baby nudged me in the side as if it was saying good morning. I ran my hand over my swollen belly, drawing comfort from the tiny life within me.

David leaned forward and rested his hand on his chin. "I figured something must have happened. It's been a long time since I've seen you on my calendar."

"Yeah, I'm sorry about that." I looked away.

"No need to apologize," David reassured me, his tone soothing. "We're here now. So, what's been happening?

I hesitated for a moment, gathering my thoughts. I was so thankful for David. He'd been there for Joe and me for so much in the beginning, helping me work through the pain of my past and then counseling us through some difficult transitions in the first few months of our marriage.

I blinked back the tears, pushing them away in the corner of my eyes. "It's been a really hard few weeks. First, my dad was diagnosed with cirrhosis of the liver and then I got a really strange call from Dakota the night Tim proposed to her."

David's eyebrows knitted together in a worried frown. "That's a lot to deal with, Tamara. I'm sorry to hear about your father. How is he doing now? And this call from Dakota, can you tell me more about it?"

I rubbed my temples, the beginnings of a headache creeping up on me. "She was really emotional, which isn't like her. And then she said that Ryan was always there, bringing retribution. But Ryan's been dead for two years. He can't hurt her anymore. It didn't make sense, but she seemed scared."

David thoughtfully ran a hand on his chin. "It definitely sounds concerning, especially considering Dakota's past. Sometimes trauma can resurface in strange ways. The fear of Ryan may be something she never fully processed."

I nodded slowly, my palm still pressed against my forehead. "The thing that doesn't make sense is how much fear I have been struggling with since then. I mean, I know God is trustworthy. He's brought me through so much."

David leaned back in his chair, letting out a long breath. "It sounds like you're being pretty hard on yourself. The truth is, you've been through a lot. And you've had your own trauma with Ryan. It makes complete sense that you would be feeling the way you are."

The memories of Ryan's cruelty, his manipulation, still lingered in the darkest corners of my mind. After years of being on the run from him, then he tried to kill Dakota and me. I shivered at the memory, a cold sweat forming on my neck. I could still recall the terror that had gripped me that night, a palpable fear that threatened to consume me whole.

Taking a deep breath, I recentered on the present. "I know, but over the last few years I've made huge strides putting the past behind me and working through that trauma. I just feel like I've come so far, and this seems like going backwards."

"You have come so far, and I'm so proud of you," David said emphatically, his gaze steady and full with the weight of sincerity. "But with the amount of trauma you and your family have endured, it is only natural when dangers arise that you may still experience triggers. When you think of the depths you were in when you first started on this journey to heal, you are miles away from that place now."

David's words seeped into me, softening the hard edges of my self-doubt. "You're right. I just thought I was free of all those emotional flashbacks."

"I understand, Tamara. Emotional healing isn't a linear process. It's okay to have setbacks. It doesn't mean you're back at square one; it means you're human, processing the depth of the experiences you've survived. It's a testimony to your resilience that you can face these moments and still find the strength to move forward."

I bit the inside of my cheek. I hated these kinds of setbacks. "I just wish this cycle of fear would be broken for good. I mean, people deal with stressors like this every day, and I don't see them falling apart."

David's expression held a gentle concern as he considered my words.

"Tamara, I know it can feel like you are falling apart, but from my perspective, you are courageously overcoming and facing your fears without running. Think about how much more emotional capacity you have now than you did when we first met."

That was true. When David first met me, I had been so closed off, so guarded, an emotional fortress built from the rubble of my traumatic past. "Yeah, I guess you are right ..."

"It's not about guessing, Tamara. It's about acknowledging the vast strides you've made over time. Some people just stay stuck in their cycles all their life, refusing to do the hard work of overcoming, you are doing it, and you are doing it well."

Tears welled in my eyes at the fatherly encouragement. "Thank you, David. It is good to remember how far I have come. I guess sometimes I am just tired of looking at how much more I have to overcome."

"Do you still have your list of promises?"

"I do, and I continue to add to it."

"Great, I encourage you to read over that list when you have fears. God has brought you through so much already; he will get you through this too. Life does not always get easier, we just get stronger. And with God, you have what it takes. Just remember to go super easy on yourself right now. With your pregnancy, everything is already more heightened, and that's super normal, but I do think there are some added layers here."

I nodded again, a mix of gratitude and apprehension flooding through me. We prayed and ended the call. Sitting alone in the stillness that followed, I ran my hands over my growing belly, the tangible evidence of new life within me. A flutter beneath my fingertips made me smile, a little nudge that seemed to say, 'I'm here, Mom.'

Tears streamed down my cheeks as I whispered a fervent prayer, one of love, of fear, of hope. "Stay strong, little one," I murmured, my hands still cradling my belly. "We've got this."

One thing I had learned through my past trials was that breakthroughs often come after the darkest nights. The nights were certainly dark now and the fear a heavy shroud that seemed to mute the world around me. But as I sat there, feeling the signs of life from within, I also felt a tiny flicker of something else. Perhaps it was strength, perhaps it was resilience, maybe even a touch of faith.

CHAPTER 20
February 3, 7:34 p.m.
DAKOTA

I sat in the dimly lit room, surrounded by the familiar faces of my fellow NA members. The topic of discussion tonight was the dreaded fifth step, and as each person shared their fears, regrets, and hopes about this crucial phase, frustration built inside me.

"Step Five," Richard, the group leader began, his voice low and resonant, "is about admitting to God, to ourselves, and to another human being the exact nature of our wrongs."

I had already thoroughly worked this step, exposing my deepest, darkest secrets to God and my sponsor. It was a painful process, but I had done it. I had faced my demons head-on, and I thought I had left them behind. But the truth was that demons have a way of reappearing, especially when you least expect them.

As I sat listening to others share their experiences, anger began to boil beneath my skin, like a tempest in a teapot. It wasn't fair. Should I have to work this step again? Was it fair to ask me to delve into my past once more when I had been forced into a situation I never wanted to be a part of? It felt like a cruel twist of fate, a punishment for my past mistakes.

"Drugs controlled my life for so long," a woman across from me said quietly, voice quavering, clutching a tissue. "I stole from my family, lied to people who cared about me... I've hurt so many."

I shifted uncomfortably in my seat, the weight of my present secret pressing on my chest. Didn't intention matter? There wasn't a thing inside me that wanted to do Victor's bidding. I had actually thought I had escaped that life.

I started to zone out, focusing on an old water stain on the ceiling as others continued to share their multitude of sins. My mind was spinning, a whirlwind of thoughts and fears. This room once felt like a sanctuary, a place of healing. But now it felt more like a court where I was judged without mercy.

The familiar smell of stale coffee and old books did little to soothe my nerves now. A somber tone hung in the air, thick and unyielding, as more confessions spilled forth, each one a reminder of the battles we were all fighting.

The raw honesty of those around me only amplified my guilt and self-pity. This totally sucked. The last week or so, I'd been full of fear, looking over my shoulders, wondering when the moment would come, when I would be forced to do this thing I didn't want to do.

"Sometimes," a woman next to me whispered, her voice cracking, "I feel like a monster for what I've done." Her words struck a painful chord within me as I fought against the memories clawing their way to the surface. My chest constricted as if a vice grip held my heart in place.

"Thank you for sharing," Richard said, his voice gentle but firm. "It's important to remember that Step Five is about acknowledging our past and making amends. We can't change what we've done, but we can learn and grow from it."

If only that were true. For the last year and a half, I had given myself fully to the program, working every step with diligence, but now that didn't seem to matter.

"Does anyone else want to share?" the leader asked, his question hanging heavy in the air.

I remained silent, teeth grinding together as I tried to fight the torrent of emotions threatening to drown me. A part of me wanted to unload this secret—to spill my guts to this room of fellow screw-ups, but I stayed silent, keeping it all in.

An older man spoke about his relapse with a monotonous drone, much like the others before him.

"Sometimes, it feels like we're stuck in a loop," a woman across the circle said, her voice soft and tremulous. "But it's important to remember that we're moving forward, even when it doesn't seem like it."

"Progress, not perfection," someone else chimed in, and several people nodded in agreement.

"Exactly," someone else said. "We can't change our past, but we can take control of our future."

Her words echoed in my mind, taunting me. Control? What control did I have over the horrible things I was being forced into? Why did I have to admit to wrongs that weren't mine to begin with?

"Would anyone else like to share?" Richard asked, scanning the faces of those gathered.

To my relief, the room remained silent. I swallowed hard, the lump in my throat growing with every second that ticked by.

"Alright," the leader finally said. "Let's close with the Serenity Prayer."

I bowed my head, mouthing the words along with the others.

"God, grant me the serenity to accept the things I cannot change, courage to change the things I can, and wisdom to know the difference."

As the last syllable left my lips, my phone buzzed in my pocket. I snuck a quick glance at it and froze. Avery's name lit the screen.

"Excuse me," I whispered, slipping out of my chair and making my way toward the back of the room, my heart racing. My fingers were trembling as I unlocked the screen and read the message.

"Someone's watching you. Be ready."

My breath caught in my throat, a strangled gasp escaping my lips as the walls of reality crashed around me. The words on my phone seemed to pulse with menace, each letter a promise of the danger that lurked in the shadows.

I pressed my hands against the cool wall to steady myself. This was a good thing. Soon I would deliver the package and then it would all be over. I would never have to think about Justin, Avery or Victor ever again. I'd be free to live a happy life with Tim.

"Copy that." I typed out, my fingers hovering over the 'send' button, hesitating, my mind revolting. I didn't want to do this... but I didn't have a choice. I hit send and the familiar sense of dread washed over me, leaving me feeling cold and hollow.

"Details soon. Be ready. Or else." He sent the words with a gun and skull and crossbones emoji.

The message was clear, the ultimatum laid bare—complete the assignment, or suffer the consequences. The darkness beckoned, and I could do nothing but follow, praying that one day I might find a way to escape its grasp for good.

"Alright," I whispered to myself, wiping away the tears that had spill down my cheeks. "I'll be ready."

And with those words, I headed outside, head hung low, the weight of my past actions settling heavily upon my shoulders as I prepared to face whatever lay in wait in the darkness of the night.

CHAPTER 21

February 3, 8:16 p.m.

TIM

The bluish glare of the laptop screen cast a ghostly hue across my face as I sat hunched at my desk. My fingers hovered above the keyboard, itching to type out my anger and confusion; instead, they only managed a nervous drumming on the worn wooden surface of my desk. Restorative Justice. That's what I was supposed to be learning about, but it felt like I was trying to learn a foreign language.

According to the text on the screen, restorative justice focused on the rehabilitation of offenders through reconciliation with victims and the community at large. It sought to repair the harm caused by crime while offering a chance for redemption. A chance for redemption? The thought pissed me off. I didn't want redemption for people like Ryan or Victor. Not after the hell they reeked on society.

For a full minute, I tried to imagine a man like Victor Mendez sitting in a room with those he'd hurt, trying to make amends. The image just wouldn't form. It clashed with everything I believed about justice. Surely, the principles in this class did not apply to the truly evil people like him.

Then there were people like Dakota. She had done bad things, perhaps even terrible things, but she'd been driven by pain, desperately seeking a way out of the dark labyrinth her childhood had locked her in. But she was more the exception than the rule.

I refocused on the screen and continued to read. *If the perpetrator is willing to make amends, there is hope for reintegration.* Bingo! There it was. There had to be a willingness to make amends to the victims. But what if someone like Victor played this restorative justice game? What if he went through the process and said everything that he was supposed to say, but once he was released, he'd be on the street again, back to his old ways? Using the system to slip back among unsuspecting prey. The thought made my skin crawl. That was the danger of this model. Narcissistic psychopaths could play the system, and no one would be the wiser until it was too late. Nope, it was better to stick with the current system with all of its flaws than take the chance of letting the wrong people go free.

The screen continued to glare relentlessly at me, unfazed by my internal turmoil. The word "reconciliation" seemed to pulsate with each beat of my heart, mocking my convictions. A part of me wanted to take justice into my own hands with Victor. With everything I'd discovered over the last few months, it was completely clear that he had been Ryan's boss. The one he answered to.

That meant that he was just as responsible for the torment Dakota had endured. He was probably the one supplying the drugs at Quilcene High School when Dakota started doing meth. And now far worse than meth was flowing through those halls. Over the last six months there had been three deaths by overdose at Quilcene High School alone. I knew in my guts Victor was the source of it all. The cold hard truth was there were monsters in this world who were beyond redemption.

I brought my attention to the class once more. I stared at the screen, trying to focus the words blurred together. I felt like I stood on the edge of a precipice, staring into an abyss of questions to which I had no answers. All the while, time was ticking away, and people were dying while psychopaths were running free, glorying in their reign of terror. I had to decide for myself what justice really meant.

Frustrated, I slammed my laptop shut, unable to think about this another second.

Man, I wanted a beer, but ever since Dakota had moved in, I didn't keep alcohol in the house. Instead, I went to my garage, which I had converted into an at home gym, and hopped on the treadmill. I couldn't think about Victor Mendez or Restorative Justice any more tonight.

I went through the warm-up and then began pushing myself, running as fast as I could on a level ten incline. Try as I might, I could not repress the images that my mind conjured up. Victor's victims played on repeat like a bad movie. The innocent people who had gotten caught in the crossfire of his drug empire, the families torn apart by his merciless pursuit of power. Their faces were twisted in agony as they cried out for help that never came. Each one struck a chord deep within me, fueling my determination to stop him at any cost. But more than anything, it was the thought of Dakota potentially caught in the crossfire that terrified me the most.

My chest tightened with anger, and I fought to keep it from consuming me completely. I pushed faster, my pulse in the 190s. Victor was a black hole of evil that sucked out everything good and light around him. It was like staring into the abyss of human cruelty, a place where no hope or redemption could be found.

I slowed my pace to catch my breath, sweat dripping from my forehead.

"Tim!" Dakota called out. "I got us pizza on the way home."

The sound of her voice momentarily pulled me out of the hellish darkness I had been spiraling into. I slowed the treadmill to a stop and stepped off. "Be right out!" I called out and grabbed a towel and patted the sweat of my brow. Closing my eyes, I took a few more deep breaths to collect myself. I didn't want Dakota to know how stressed out I was about work. That was part of our lives that we didn't really talk about. The less she knew, the safer she would be, especially now that I was working on the Mendez case.

I walked out of the garage and back into the house. "How was your meeting?"

"Oh, ya know. Same old, same old. People moaning about their crappy lives, trying to grapple with surrendering to a Higher Power. Blah, blah, blah."

I chuckled at her sarcasm. "Well, alright." I walked to the cupboard, grabbed two plates and handed her one. "Thanks for dinner."

"You know this is about as good as it gets for my culinary expertise," she said with a wry grin, reaching for a piece of meat lovers pizza.

"I probably should have thought of that before I asked you to marry me."

"Right?" She nodded in agreement, a playful expression lighting her face. But there was something off in her tone. "No take backs."

What was that? Did she really think I would ever want to take myself back from her? "Coda, I never want to take this back." I set down my plate and reached for her, pulling her into me, her body tucking perfectly into mine.

Her arms wrapped around my waist, her head resting on my chest. "I know... It's just sometimes." She fell silent for a long moment, her fingers tracing idle patterns over my shirt.

I pulled away and searched her face. "Sometimes what?"

A battle seemed to rage behind her eyes as if there was something she wanted to tell me but didn't know how.

"Talk to me," I said with a bit of desperation in my tone.

She sighed and looked away. "Just sometimes the demons of my past really haunt me."

With a gentle finger, I pulled her face toward me. A tear slid down her face. My heart ached for her. "Did something happen at the meeting?"

"Yeah." She shook away the emotion. "I, ah, there was just an old friend I used to run with there. Remember Lisa?"

I nodded. Images of the night I had followed Dakota home from the casino to protect her from Ryan; but I had disrupted a fight with her and Lisa instead. That in many ways was where our journey restarted.

Dakota glanced away from me again. I hated it. I wanted so badly for her to know that she could be vulnerable with me. "Well, tonight she was there, and she kept glaring at me from across the room. It made me feel judged and somewhat angry. She was the one who betrayed me to Ryan. I don't know, I hate it when my past feels this close."

A burning sensation overtook me at the mention of Ryan's name, and I made a mental note to do some investigating on Lisa. In moments like these, I wondered if keeping Dakota in this town was the best idea. There were too many shadows lurking in every corner. Her meetings should be a safe place to heal, not a place to bring up the past.

But instead of voicing my concerns, I simply pulled her into a tight embrace. "I'm so sorry, Dakota. I hate that you have to deal with this. But know that I'm here for you, always." My words felt inadequate, but it was all I could offer her right now.

Dakota leaned into me, and she cried into my chest. I held her tightly, hating to see her in pain like this. But maybe it was a sign of deeper healing. That she he was finally letting some of her deeper emotions out. She was finally letting some of her vulnerability show.

Whispering soothing words, I gently stroked her hair, my touch a tender caress against her tear-stained cheeks. I wanted her to know that she was not alone, that I was here for her, unwavering in my support. With each passing moment, I hoped to convey the depth of my love, the unwavering devotion that resided within my heart.

Dakota slowly lifted her head, her eyes red and swollen. She looked at me, searching for reassurance.

ELISHEBA HAXBY & JESSE VINCENT

I wiped away the remnants of her tears, my touch gentle yet firm. "You're stronger than you know, Dakota," I whispered, my voice filled with conviction. "You've come so far, and I believe in you."

Her cheeks grew flush and there was a pain behind her eyes. Whatever happened at that NA meeting had affected her in places I didn't understand. Perhaps there was no way that I could. "This pizza is getting cold," she whispered as if trying to take the attention off of herself.

A part of me wanted to press her. To ask her why this encounter with Lisa had affected her so deeply. But I let it go for now. I knew her. If I pushed after she had let me in this far, the walls could easily go back up. "Cold pizza is better."

"Yeah, right." She pushed my shoulder playfully as she reached for her plate.

And just like that, the emotional scene was over. We grabbed our plates, loaded them with pizza and settled into the couch for *Star Wars* Episode Five.

CHAPTER 22

February 5, 5:46 p.m.

TAMARA

The sun was dipping below the horizon, casting a warm golden glow over Aberdeen as we drove home from our family day out. Lillie sat quietly in her car seat, her curly dark hair framing her innocent eyes as they drooped with exhaustion. The baby kicked inside me, and Joe's hand found mine. Our fingers intertwined and he smiled warmly. My heart expanded at the love I felt for our growing family. It made me miss the rest of my family.

"Hey, babe," I said. "Would you be okay with us stopping by my parents' house on the way home? It's been a while since I've seen my mom, and I'm pretty sure she's off today."

"Absolutely." He turned on his blinker to head on East Wishkah Blvd. A few minutes later we pulled in front of my parents house. Mom's car was in the driveway and so was my brother Nathan's. Nice. Two for the price of one.

Joe parked the car and we got out, Lillie now awake and excited to see her grandparents. Joe helped her out of the car seat, scooping her into his strong arms.

Joe led us to the front door, his presence always providing a sense of security and comfort. The door creaked open, revealing my mother's familiar face, her warm smile instantly putting my mind at ease.

"Tamara, Joe, Lillie! What a surprise!" Mom exclaimed, enveloping us in a hug. "Come in, come in!"

As we stepped inside love and gratitude swelled with in me for this place, for these people. For a moment, it felt as though we were a normal family again, without the shadows of fear looming over us.

"Mom," I said softly, my voice thick with emotion. "It's so good to see you."

"Likewise, sweetheart," she replied.

As I rounded the corner into the kitchen, the sight that met me was like a punch to the gut. There sat Nathan and Dad, sitting across from each other, both with a half finished beer in front of them and empty shot glasses beside them. A bottle of Jameson Whiskey sat in the middle of the table. Disappointment and then anger rose within me. Dad had promised that he would try to stop drinking, but now he was here with Nathan betraying his word.

My steps faltered, a bitter taste creeping into my throat. Joe, sensing my discomfort, put his hand on the small of my back and offered a comforting squeeze.

I was a idiot to think Dad would ever change—that my heartfelt pleading with him would be enough. Did it not matter that he had beginning stage liver failure? Didn't Nathan care that drinking with Dad was only encouraging his behavior?

I took a deep breath, trying to calm myself as Lillie ran towards Nathan, her giggles filling the room. Joe followed close behind me as we entered the kitchen. His strong hand was warm on my back, a steady anchor amidst the storm brewing inside me.

"Hey, Lills." Nathan scooped Lillie up with a jovial laugh, her childish delight sparking a flicker of affection in his features. But the sight did little to abate my rising storm of emotions.

"Dad," I said, struggling to keep my voice steady. "I thought you were done with this."

He looked at me, his eyes bloodshot and his words slurred. "Tammy, I'm not hurting anyone. Just having a drink with my son. Let me be."

"You're hurting yourself, Dad," I replied, my throat tight. "And you're hurting us by not taking care of yourself."

Nathan set Lillie on the floor and spoke. "We're just having a good time, sis. No need to ruin it."

"Take Lillie into the living room," I whispered to Joe, forcing a smile for his sake. "I'll be right there."

He nodded, expression flickering with concern before leading our daughter away. I took a deep breath, and fought the tears that threatened to come. "I'm not trying to ruin your fun, Nathan. I'm trying to save our father's life. Don't you care about his health?"

"Of course, I care, but he's a grown man. He can make his own decisions."

"He can't make his own decisions if he's not in the right state of mind," I argued, my voice growing louder. "He's going to die if he keeps this up. Don't you see that?"

Dad raised his hand in a placating gesture. "I know you're worried, Tammy, but I can handle my own life."

"But you're not handling it." I tried to quiet my tone, but it wasn't working. "You're slowly killing yourself, and you don't even care about the people who love you. Is this really what you want? To die alone, with nobody by your side?"

Tears streamed down my face as I spoke, my insides aching with the pain of watching my family fall apart. Nathan stood, his tall frame towering over me. "Let's talk outside."

Joe appeared in the doorway then, face lined with concern. Lillie was behind him in the living room playing with Mom completely oblivious. I gave Joe a reassuring nod and then followed Nathan out to the front porch.

Once outside, Nathan turned toward me, an apology lining his features. "I'm sorry, Tamara. I didn't mean to upset you like that. We just wanted to spend some time together, you know? There are things going on with me that you don't know about."

I took a deep breath, reigning in my anger as a new concern threaded through me. "Nathan, what is it?" I asked, my voice shaky. "What's going on?"

"Tamara, I..." Nathan trailed off, searching for words that couldn't be found. And in that moment, I realized that no matter how angry I was, my love for my brother would never waver.

I stepped closer to him, placing a comforting hand on his arm. "Tell me, Nathan," I pleaded. "Whatever it is, we can handle it together."

His gaze penetrated mine, and I saw an unfamiliar vulnerability in his features. He took a shaky breath, running a hand through his hair. He shifted uncomfortably on his feet.

"Please, Nathan," I implored softly, fighting back tears. "Tell me what's going on. Let me help you."

Finally, he looked at me, his expression brimming with vulnerability and fear. "Something's wrong, Tamara," he admitted, hoarsely. "Amanda and I...we're not okay. And I don't know how to fix it."

My chest tightened at his confession. He had always been the strong one, the one who laughed in the face of adversity. To see him like this, so lost and afraid, filled me with an overwhelming sense of sadness and empathy.

"Tell me everything," I said softly, squeezing his arm gently. "I'm here for you, Nathan."

"She's been... he began, his voice cracking. "Distant lately. Cold. We barely talk anymore, and when we do, it feels like she's a million miles away." Hurt and confusion etched across his face as he spoke. It made me want to shield him from the storm.

"I've been trying to fix us. To make it better, but sometimes I feel like it may be too late."

As I absorbed his words, a surge of sorrow washed over me. Amanda had always been so sweet and supportive of me. But I couldn't help the surge of protective instinct rise within me. Why would she be treating Nathan like this?

"I don't know what to do, Tam," he whispered, his voice trembling. "I'm scared. I'm scared that I'm losing her, and I don't know how to fix it. I don't want to lose my family."

His vulnerability tore at my heartstrings, and I couldn't

supress my own tears any longer. They streamed down my face, mingling with the salty air as I pulled him into a tight hug.

"Listen to me, Nathan," I murmured into his ear, my voice thick. "You are not alone in this. Whatever happens, I'm here."

We stood there for a moment, embracing each other beneath the vast expanse of the night sky. I felt his body tremble against mine, and I knew that the road ahead would be difficult.

We made our way back inside, where my mom and Joe were engaged in quiet conversation, their voices soft and soothing. Lillie was curled up on the couch, dozing off with a book in her lap, oblivious to the storms brewing around her. Dad sat in front of the television, a stoic expression on his face. I went and knelt before him and gently touched his knee, drawing his attention away from the old western he was half-watching on the screen.

"Dad." I searched his face. "I want you to know that I love you no matter what, but for the sake of your family, I'm begging you to stop drinking."

A sadness crept into his face, an acknowledgement of the truth I had spoken. He looked at me for a moment, then to his half-empty whiskey glass on the coffee table.

"I know, Tammy," he said softly. "I promise to try. That's all I can do right now."

I wished so badly that he could give me more of a guarantee, but I knew that such promises were not made easily, nor kept lightly. I squeezed his hand tightly before standing and turning. Joe had already gathered Lillie into his arms as if he knew it was time to go. I gave my mom a hug and whispered solemn words of encouragement into her ear. She nodded, a single tear escaping.

As Joe and I walked to the car, each movement felt ponderous and heavy. Joe buckled Lillie into her car seat and got in the driver's seat, his hands tightly gripping at the steering wheel. I slid into the passenger seat, staring blankly out of the window at the house we were leaving behind.

On the way home, I racked my brain about who I could reach out for support regarding Dad. Mom was already enabling, and now with Nathan going through his own issues, I couldn't count on him to help. I did trust Dakota, but even though she had come a long way, her tactics still were a bit too fiery and judgmental. So that just left Josiah, the brother who lived over a thousand miles away and kept himself aloof from the family chaos.

I found his number and hit send before I could talk myself out of it. After a couple of rings, he picked up.

"Tammy?" His voice came through clearly on the speaker, sounding surprised.

"Hi, Josiah," I mustered, trying to keep my voice steady.

"It's so good to hear from you," Josiah said. "I've been meaning to reach out to you too. Is everything okay?" His voice held a note of concern, a slight crack in his otherwise stoic visage.

I took a deep breath, trying to find the right words. "It's about Dad," I said, my voice cracking. "I'm really worried about him."

Josiah was silent for a moment, and I could practically see him on the other end of the line, brow furrowing, wheels turning. "Mom told me about his liver condition," he said finally, his tone heavy with regret. "But she didn't give me the details. Is it bad?"

I nodded, forgetting for a moment that he couldn't see me. "It definitely can be if he doesn't quit drinking."

Josiah exhaled sharply, a sound of frustration and worry. "Does he...does he know that? Does he understand how serious this is?"

Next to me, Joe reached over and gently squeezed my hand. The city lights outside the window flickered and danced, casting ethereal shadows in the car.

"Yes, the other day, I practically begged him to stop drinking, and he said he would, but when I went over there tonight, he and Nathan were hitting the bottle pretty hard."

"I'm so sorry," he said with a sigh. "It's moments like this that I wished I lived closer—"

"I wish you did too," I confessed. "But I thought maybe...maybe if he heard it from you..."

There was a brief pause on the other end of the line before

Josiah replied with a soft, "Of course. I'll call him first thing in the morning."

"Thank you," I managed to say, my voice quivering.

"No need to thank me. He's our father." His voice was soft, like a comforting blanket wrapping around me from miles away. "We can't just watch him walk this path without intervening."

As I ended the call, my gaze drifted out of the car window. The city night was a blur of neon lights and shadowed buildings, the streets slick with the remnants of rain. I felt Joe's hand on mine, his grip warm and firm, grounding me to reality as I swam in my thoughts. It seemed there was a storm brewing around our family and somehow I stood in the eye of it. The calm center of a whirlwind of fear and uncertainty, carrying the burdens of their lives on my shoulders.

CHAPTER 23

February 8, 11:00 p.m.

DAKOTA

The fluorescent lights of the gas station flickered above me as I swiped my timecard, signaling the end of another grueling shift. My phone buzzed in my pocket, and I pulled it out to find a text from Avery.

Meet me behind the station after your shift.

Uneasiness curled in my belly, a shadowy serpent of dread as I stared at the text message. Now? At eleven o'clock at night? I texted a thumbs up emoji and shoved my phone in my pocket.

I grabbed my jacket and made my way to the back of the gas station. The air was damp and cool, the scent of gasoline lingering in the night air. In the distance, the rumble of an engine resonated through the quiet darkness.

As I rounded the corner, an older Oldsmobile, its headlights dimmed, waited ominously in the shadows. With the dull light of the streetlight overhead, I could see Justin and Avery through the windshield. My pulse thudded in my ears as I approached the car.

Justin rolled down the window and spoke, his voice low and tense. "Get in."

My heart jackhammered against my rib cage as I hesitated by the open window. This wasn't part of the deal. With shaky hands,

I reached for the door handle. Protesting would only make this worse.

Swallowing hard, I glanced around and then slid into the musty seat, the foul scent of stale beer and cigarettes washing over me. The worn-out upholstery felt cold and rough against my skin as I pulled the door shut. My chest tightened, and I struggled to draw in a full breath. I was a caged animal awaiting its fate.

"I need you to listen very carefully, Dakota. Your life depends on it." Avery spoke in a cool yet menacing tone. "You will do exactly what we say. Nothing more. Nothing less. Do you understand me?"

So many sarcastic lines ran through my head. What do I look like? An idiot? Moron is my second language. Naw, I'm deaf in both ears. Instead, I kept my mouth shut and nodded.

Justin grunted in the front seat, his knuckles turning white as he clenched his grip on the steering wheel.

"First of all, I want you to shut off anything on your phone that would let anyone track you," Avery continued in that same calm, cold tone. "Do it now so I can see you."

I pulled out my phone and showed him what I was doing as I turned off the tracking capabilities, trying to keep my hands steady. They were like dogs—if they sensed fear, the attack would be swift and merciless.

"Once we're done here, I want you to go straight to your car and follow us to the next location. From there, you will get the package and the rest of the instructions. Comprende?"

I nodded again.

"You're awfully quiet tonight, Dakota," Justin said, looking at me in the rearview mirror, his eyes hard and scrutinizing. "What's the matter? Cat got your tongue?"

I gave him a hard glare, my blood boiling at his taunt. "That's cause there's nothing to say."

"That's right." Avery spoke this time. "We own you, Dakota. Never forget that."

I swallowed, pushing down the sensation of revulsion. How

many times had Ryan told me that? How was Ryan still my puppet master even beyond the grave?

"How could I forget?" I asked, my voice cold, my body aching for some sort of relief from this hell that I'd stepped into.

Justin cackled a sick, menacing laugh that made my skin crawl. The addict in me flared with angry lustful thoughts, begging me to ask these guys for a line. Anything to take away the torture of this moment. I reached for the door handle. I had to get out of here before I threw away a year and a half of sobriety. "Let's just get this over with," I said and then stumbled out of the door. On the way to my car, I said Tim's name over and over again like a mantra. He was the reason I was doing this. I had to do this to keep him safe.

The night air was chilly, but I only felt the oppressive heat of terror coursing through me. I climbed into my car and followed them out of the parking lot. They stopped at the four corners stop sign, and then turned on Center Road toward Quilcene. My mind stayed on Tim as I drove. Was he asleep by now? Would he be worried if he woke and found I hadn't made it home? What would I tell him when I arrived hours late from work? I wanted to call him, to tell him about this evil that had appeared at my doorstep, but I couldn't risk putting him in danger.

The night air was thick with tension as we made our way through the winding roads, the beam of my headlights slicing through the darkness. As the familiar sights of Quilcene came into view, I gripped the steering wheel tighter. We took a left on Linger Longer Road, over the bridge and another left on Muncie Ave. Panic threatened to swallow me whole as we pulled into the old drug house where Ryan used to live. I parked behind the Oldsmobile and watched Avery and Justin exit the vehicle. I stayed frozen, praying they wouldn't force me to go in there. The house looked exactly as I remembered, the chipping paint and broken windows a painful reminder of the dark path I'd once walked.

Justin motioned for me to follow them into the house, his

cruel smirk making my blood run colder. Bracing myself, I slowly unbuckled my seatbelt and stepped out of the car.

Everything in me screamed at me to turn back, but I knew there was no other option. To my surprise, they didn't come with me inside. They stopped at the doorway and stood guard as I went forward.

The door creaked open, and Ricky stood there, his expression wary but not unkind. He handed me a small package wrapped in brown paper. "I'm sorry about this, Dakota," Ricky's voice was low and fraught with regret.

He handed me a separate piece of paper, and I took it, my trembling hands, all too aware what it likely contained. "If it were up to me, you would have been kept out of this. But Victor—" Ricky paused as if to catch himself before saying too much.

Strange thing was, I actually believed him. My fingers fumbled with the package, my mind spinning with dread.

"The address is on the paper. Make sure you do everything as they said."

I nodded and clutched the package tightly, turning toward my car. With one last glance around the place that had once haunted my nightmares, I walked down the driveway.

"You on your own now, Dakota. Don't screw this up," Avery said with malice in his voice. I typed the address into the gps and pulled out of the driveway. What would Tim think if he knew what I was doing? How could I ever face him again after tonight?

As I wound my way over Mt. Walker toward Brinnon, the shadows cast by the full moon seemed to twist and stretch, forming sinister shapes that mirrored my inner turmoil.

What was Victor's end game? Would this be the only thing he asked of me or would there be more tasks to come? And could I ever hope to escape the tangled web I'd allowed myself to become ensnared in?

"Maybe I should just tell Tim," I whispered to myself as I gripped the steering wheel tighter. "Together, we might stand a chance against Victor." But even as the words left my lips, I knew it wasn't possible. The threat to Tim had been clear. Who knew what kind of suffering they would inflict on him if I didn't do this thing?

As I drove through the darkness, I found my mind circling back to that moment when Tim had gently slipped the engagement ring on my finger. His features were filled with so much love and faith—faith in me, faith in us. How could I betray that? "Tim," I whispered his name like a prayer into the chilling night air. The love that I felt for him, consuming and all-encompassing, was now my greatest weapon and my deepest weakness.

I continued on to the address on the screen, gripping the steering wheel so tightly that my knuckles turned white. From the outside, the house I pulled in front of looked normal. Harmless. Nothing like the trap house in Quilcene. I parked the car and took a deep, shaky breath. With the package in hand, I steeled myself and stepped out into the chilled night air. As I slowly walked to the house, the gravel crunched under my shoes, breaking the silence of nighttime. I rapped on the door and waited.

"Who's there?" a gruff voice called through the cracked door as I knocked hesitantly.

"It's Dakota... I've got something for you."

The door opened just enough for a scarred, unshaven face to peer out at me. "Well, come on in then," he said gruffly, pulling the door open wider.

I stepped inside, the stench of stale smoke and sweat hitting me like a punch to the gut. Memories of my past life threatened to overwhelm me, but I fought against them as I handed over the package.

"For your troubles; enjoy." He tossed a small bag of meth in exchange for the parcel. "Now get out of here."

I clutched the bag tightly, the familiar texture of the plastic awakening the addict inside me like a slumbering beast. As I left the house, the door slammed shut behind me with a resounding thud, sealing away the darkness that had once held me captive.

In the car, I stared at the bag of meth in my shaking hands. The plastic crinkled under my touch and the tiny crystals gleamed under the glow of the streetlight. The addict inside me roared for it as the weight of the lies and the danger I'd been forced back into clung to me. *We own you, Dakota.* Avery's words slithered through my brain like a venomous serpent, hissing and coiling around my resolve.

I threw the bag onto the passenger seat and tore my gaze away from it. I had to get out of here. I started the car, my hands trembling on the keys as I slipped it into the ignition. The engine growled to life, breaking the silence that had descended. I pushed my foot flat on the gas pedal and the tires screeched beneath me, tearing me away from the house. I drove recklessly through the dim-lit streets, the glow of streetlights flashing past in a blur.

The small bag of meth sat ominously on the passenger seat, its contents glinting malevolently in the faint glow of the dashboard lights. The addict whispered my name, promising relief, escape—a lie I knew too well.

I would *not* do this to myself. I would not do this to Tim.

Tears welled in my eyes, blurring my vision as I thought about Tim sleeping peacefully at home, unaware of the danger he was in and the lies I was telling to protect him. Could I really do this alone? Was I strong enough to resist the pull of my old life? I glanced over at the bag of meth. This was all so cruel. Why would they even give me meth? They were toying with me, trying to show me how weak I really was.

The bag seemed to pulse with a dark energy as I navigated the winding roads toward home. Each whispered temptation was a siren's song, each glinting crystal a tempting promise of oblivion. It was my own Pandora's box, a haunting reminder of the person I used to be—the person I swore I'd never become again. I knew I should just throw it out of the window, but I couldn't. The magnetic pull it had on me was too strong, like some twisted kind of gravitational force.

My knuckles clentced tighter as I fought the urge to reach for the bag, to taste that familiar high just one more time.

Tim. The strength in his eyes, the warmth of his smile—how could I possibly betray him like this?

As I pulled into our driveway, the weight of my actions threatened to crush me. I steeled myself, grabbing the bag and stepping out of the car.

With each step toward the house, the bag grew heavier in my hand, a symbol of the lies and danger I'd brought to our doorstep. I paused for a moment, taking in the quiet stillness of our home. The darkness was almost comforting, providing a brief respite from the reality of what I'd done.

I tiptoed to our bedroom, the floorboards creaking softly beneath my feet. As I stood in the doorway, my eyes were drawn to Tim's sleeping form. His chest rose and fell steadily, the rhythm of his breaths a soothing melody.

I stood there for an eternal moment, watching him sleep. The weight of the bag in my hand became unbearable. I couldn't let it destroy us.

With a sudden burst of resolve, I raced to the bathroom and flung the meth into the toilet. The tiny crystals seemed to scream as they swirled down the drain, but I refused to listen.

I stood there, staring at the empty toilet bowl, my hands trembling. The meth was gone, and I had made their stupid drop. It was over now. For a long time, I stood there, calming myself from the night's events. It was over. Finally, I made my way into our bedroom and slid into bed next to Tim. In spite of everything that had happened tonight, I knew one thing. I loved Tim more than anything or anyone on the planet. What I had done was wrong to the core, but I did it because I loved this man that I held in my arms more than life itself. His life was a hundred times more valuable than mine. And I would do whatever it took to keep him safe.

CHAPTER 24

February 9, 7:45 a.m.

DAKOTA

I jolted awake, the weight of last night's events pressing on my chest, making it hard to breathe. I reached out for Tim, but he wasn't there. The sheets were cool and empty, the faint scent of his aftershave still lingering in the air. Thoughts of last night engulfed me. Delivering the package, the man handing me the drugs, the addict within me struggling to be unleashed. With a groan, I pushed myself off the bed. My head throbbed with a pulsating pain, matching the rhythm of my heartbeat. My hands trembled as I ran them through my tangled hair, each strand seeming to whisper accusations and reminders of my weaknesses. I tried to block out the memories that continued to assail my mind—the feel of the small plastic bag in my hand, the promise of oblivion, the guilt that gnawed at my insides like a ravenous beast.

Stumbling towards the bathroom, I squinted into the light of the sun beaming through the window. My reflection in the mirror was a hollow echo of myself. There were dark shadows under my eyes, contrasting with my pale face, devoid of color except for the redness around my dry, bloodshot eyes.

I turned on the cold tap. The chill ran over my fingers, grounding me in reality even as my head screamed to retreat from what was real. Cupping water in my hands, I splashed it against my face, letting the cold droplets shock my system awake. The cold didn't erase the guilt, but it did provide a temporary reprieve before the storm of my shame came thundering back.

"Get it together, Dakota," I muttered to myself, slapping some water onto my cheeks. Truth was, it had been a battle, but I had overcome. I didn't do the drugs. That had to mean something, right? As I brushed my teeth, the shame I'd been struggling with flared into an anger—the truth dawning on me, like fire pouring through my veins. Victor was well acquainted with my past. Giving me those drugs was a cold, calculated move on his part. He was trying to drag me deeper into his clutches. Rage and fear twisted together inside me, a lethal cocktail that threatened to consume me from within. How dare they try to manipulate me like this? How dare they use the very thing that had nearly destroyed me as a weapon against me?

Damn it! I had been so close—just one decision away from throwing away everything I'd fought so hard to rebuild.

My fists clenched in impotent rage. The desire to punch something, anything, burst within me like a hot spring. But what good would it do? Victor was out there, untouchable in his fortress, while I was here—trapped within the four walls of my own personal hell.

I couldn't stay in this room any longer—I needed Tim, the one person who wasn't tainted by the darkness. With that desperate thought driving me forward, I stumbled out of the bedroom and into the small hallway, my legs still weak beneath me but growing stronger with each step.

The smell of cooking bacon wafted toward me as I approached the kitchen. Tim stood at the stove, his back to me as he flipped over a strip with practiced ease. The sight of him— dependable, protective Tim—was like the first sunbeam piercing through a clouded morning. For a moment, I allowed myself to simply breathe in the comforting normalcy of the scene.

"Hey," Tim said softly, turning to look at me.

"Morning," I replied, forcing a smile. I didn't want him to see the storm raging within me, not when he was trying so hard to help me build a better future. "Breakfast smells amazing. You didn't have to do all this," I added, trying to inject some lightness into my voice as I gestured towards the stove.

"I know," he said softly, "but I wanted to. You deserve a good start to the day."

I nodded, not trusting myself to speak. I didn't deserve his kindness, but I was grateful for it nonetheless. Feeling a sudden need to occupy my hands, I walked across the room to the coffee pot.

"Are you okay, Dakota?" Tim's voice reached me as I was pouring myself a cup. I didn't turn around as I tried to steady my trembling hands.

"Yeah, just... couldn't sleep, you know?" I felt his stare burning into my back, the concern palpable in the air between us. Silently, I pleaded he wouldn't push further. I was a glass teetering on the edge, ready to shatter at the slightest touch.

"Bad dreams?" he asked, moving closer, leaving the bacon sizzling on the stove.

"Something like that." The lie tasted bitter on my tongue, and I swallowed hard, almost choking on it. Tim's hand came to rest lightly on my shoulder, but I didn't turn around. I couldn't face him, not with the demons of my past still clawing at me, not when I was still teetering on the edge of this precipice.

"You got home really late last night..." His words trailed off as he hovered behind me, a tense silence hanging in the air like a thick cloud of fog. His touch was light, gentle, but even so, I could feel his anxiety pulsating through his skin and into mine.

"Uh, yeah." I finally turned to face him, putting down my coffee. As I took in his worried gaze, so full of love and tender concern, I wanted to tell him everything—about Victor, about the temptation I'd faced last night, about my fear that I'd never truly escape my past. But there were so many reasons I couldn't. "I just... ran into a friend from group, and we ended up talking for hours. You know how it is."

Tim frowned, the creases in his forehead deepening. "A friend?" he asked, his voice carefully neutral. "Anyone I know?"

"Um..." My mind raced, searching for a name that wouldn't arouse suspicion, but all I could think of were the ghosts from my past—people I desperately wanted to leave behind. "Not really. Just someone from NA. They needed a friend."

"Right," Tim said, clearly unconvinced. He turned back to the stove, and took the pan off the burner, but I could feel the weight of his unspoken questions pressing on me, threatening to crush me beneath their burden.

I stared at the floor, my fingers gripping the edge of the counter. I hated lying to Tim, hated the way it made me feel like I was betraying both him and myself. But the alternative—telling him the truth—was unthinkable. I had to protect him.

"Listen, Dakota," Tim said, his voice low and serious as he faced me once more. "I can't help but worry about you. We've been through so much together, and I just... I need to know that you're okay."

My throat tightened, and for a moment, I couldn't speak. The love and concern in his expression broke my heart, even as it filled me with determination to prove that I could be the person he believed I could be.

"Tim, I promise you, I'm okay." The words felt like shards of glass in my throat, but I forced myself to continue. "It's just... sometimes things are harder than I thought they would be. But I'm trying, I really am."

I reached across the counter, my fingers brushing against his in a silent plea for understanding.

For a long moment, he just stood there, looking at me. "Where were you last night, Dakota?" Tim probed. "I want the truth."

"I already told you. I was out with friends."

"And you didn't think to text me?" His voice was more hurt than angry, a wounded sound that tugged at my heart. "Did you not think I'd be worried?"

"I..." My voice faltered. "I just got caught in the moment and lost track of time."

"Lost track of time?'" I could see the gears turning in his head, the doubt creeping in. His shoulders tensed as he crossed his arms over his chest. "Come on, Dakota. Who were you with?"

"Does it really matter?" I snapped, my fear bubbling over into irritation. "I just... needed a break, okay?"

"Of course, it matters!" he said, his voice escalating with frustration. "Who were you with?"

Fear and shame mingled within me. *Don't you dare tell your cop boyfriend or he'll pay.* Avery's threat echoed through my mind, a chilling reminder of the reason I couldn't tell him.

"Tim," I began hesitantly, the words catching in my throat. "You have to understand that some things... they're just too hard to talk about. But trust me when I say that I'm doing everything I can to stay on the right path."

His jaw clenched as he studied me. The silence between us grew heavy, charged with unspoken fears and doubts. And then, finally, he asked the question that cut to my core.

"Are you using again, Dakota?"

"What? No!" I snapped, my hands balling into fists at my sides. "You know how hard I've worked to stay sober, to prove to you—and to myself—that I'm not that person anymore!"

His expression didn't change, eyes still hard on mine, but I saw something flicker in them. Doubt? Fear? Both probably. "Then what is? I'm not an idiot, Dakota. I know something is going on."

I hesitated, my heart pounding in my chest. As I stood there, locked in my own private hell, I realized just how much I had to lose. And I swore to myself that no matter what it took, I wouldn't let the darkness win. Not this time. Tears rolled down my cheeks as the lies formed in my mind. More like half-truths that would keep him safe but could potentially ruin us. I let out a sigh and began to speak. "Last night, right around the end of my shift, Justin and Avery came into the gas station to get some beer and smokes."

Tim stiffened. "You were with Justin and Avery?"

"No! But they came in and were messing with me. Talking about Ryan and some of the messed-up things he'd done to me. They were drunk and being jerks throwing out ever insult they could at me, calling me a pig lover and telling me how disgusting I was."

Tim's cheeks grew red, and a vein pulsed on his forehead.

"By the time they left, I felt so humiliated and triggered, like I would never be free from that life I have been trying to escape. I would always be a prisoner to it." Though the story was a lie, I was speaking from a truthful place inside me. That was how I had felt last night. "When I got to my car, I found a gram of meth sitting on my seat. It's like they had planted it there, hoping that I would fall, so they would have that same power that Ryan had on me."

Tim's gaze smoldered with fury, now. "I was tempted." I confessed. "I drove around for hours, fighting the demons they had unleashed on me. A huge part of me wanted to get high and forget, but there was this other part of me that finally brought me home. It was my love for you that kept me sober in the face of such an onslaught."

Anger twisted Tim's features for a moment, before it settled into a grim determination. He clenched his fists at his sides, hard enough that I could see the whites of his knuckles in the dim light. "I will kill them," he growled under his breath, the fury flashing in his eyes.

I tried to protest, but he was already stalking toward the door. It slammed behind him with enough force to rattle the window panes. I flinched and stumbled against the wall, a strangled plea dying on my lips.

CHAPTER 25

February 9, 8:20 a.m.

TIM

I stormed away from the house. Dakota's tearful confession reverberated in my mind, the image of driving around last night tormented by those sick criminals. My chest tightened with anger, not toward her, but at the thought of someone trying to sabotage her recovery.

I got into my car and drove through the quiet suburban neighborhood, the once comforting familiarity now tainted by fear and suspicion. As I made my way to the police station, my thoughts raced back to Dakota. She had come so far, and those low lives tried to take that from her. My jaw clenched so tight it ached. I would find them and make them pay for this. By the end of this day, they would know if they ever messed with Dakota again, the consequence would hurt them for the rest of their lives.

My fingers locked onto the steering wheel in a death grip, my knuckles turning pale from the pressure. I knew I had to do something, anything, to protect her. It wasn't enough to be supportive and caring. I had to be her shield against those who sought to harm her.

I entered the station and headed straight to my desk. No one needed to know what I was doing or that I was using my resources to track down a personal vendetta. As I settled into my office and sifted through the information, a cold determination settled over me. For better or worse, Dakota was the love of my life, and I'd be damned if I let anyone or anything hurt her. My resolve to gather as much information as possible on Justin and Avery only intensified as I dug deeper into their backgrounds.

The dim glow of the computer screen cast eerie shadows on the walls of my office as I sat hunched over the keyboard, searching for any scrap of information that might help me protect Dakota. My fingers trembled with a mix of rage and fear, but I forced them to remain steady as I typed in Justin's and Avery's names.

"Tim, what are you doing here on your day off?" asked a concerned voice from the doorway. I glanced to see Jenna, her brow furrowed with worry. Her attention shifted to the screen, trying to make sense of the data before her.

"I just had a hunch, and I needed to look into it." I clicked off the screen, hoping she hadn't seen the names.

"You couldn't have waited until your next shift for that?" she asked with a hint of suspicion. Or was I being paranoid?

I shrugged. "It was really bugging me, and I had nothing else going on."

"Alright. Well, I hope it pans out. Let me know if you need help with anything."

"Thanks, Jenna. I will."

I watched her walk away and then turned to my computer and scanned the files on Justin and Avery. They had been arrested on minor drug charges more than once, but that was it. They were small fry, but their repeated brushes with the law hinted at something more sinister lurking beneath the surface. What could have been their possible motivation to mess with Dakota? After looking at their criminal record, I searched the database to see if either of them had a car registered in their name. Justin had an older gray Oldsmobile; the license plate was CD9 463. Avery had nothing. What a loser. I wrote the information on a notepad and logged out of my computer. As I stood from my desk, my heart pounded like a jackhammer in my chest. No time to waste. Dakota needed me. I grabbed my jacket and made my way through the dimly lit station, careful not to draw attention to myself.

I slipped out into the cool air, the weight of my decision settling heavily on my shoulders. The police officer inside me screamed at me to turn back and do this the right way; I ignored the cop part of my mind and climbed into my car.

Driving through shadier parts of town, I clutched the steering wheel tight. Fear gnawed at the edges of my consciousness, but I pushed it aside, focusing on the task at hand.

CHAPTER 26

February 9, 9:50 a.m.

DAKOTA

Panic choked my senses as I stared at the clock. Nearly two hours had gone by since Tim left, and terror had been my constant companion since he stormed out. *I will kill them.* His angry words tormented me. Why hadn't I lied better? Why had I mentioned Justin and Avery's names? I had been so flustered by our growing fight, I hadn't considered the potential consequences. If he found Justin and Avery and roughed them up, telling them to stay away from me, they would assume the worst. They would believe that I had told Tim the truth. Or worse, Tim could find them, agitate a hornet's nest and get himself killed.

A few minutes after he left, I'd tried calling him to talk some sense into him only to hear his phone vibrating on the counter. In his blind rage, he had left it behind and now I had no way to get ahold of him. No way to know he was okay.

Every horrible scenario imaginable played though my head as I paced our home, my hands wringing out the hem of my shirt. Each tick of the clock felt like a death knell, reverberating the possible outcomes of Tim's wrath. A tight knot formed in my stomach as the thoughts assailed me like a swarm of bees stinging relentlessly. My mind was a cesspool of fear and guilt. Guilt that I had violated the trust we had built. Fear for what my past could do to harm Tim. The cold, prickling sensation of tears threatened to spill, but I blinked them away stubbornly. This was no time for tears.

"Higher Power, let him be safe," I whispered into the empty house, fidgeting with the engagement ring on my finger, a symbol of our hopeful future now caught in the crosshairs of my past. The wind howled outside, and I pulled the sweater tighter around me as if it could shield me from this fear.

What if somehow he found out the truth about last night? What if he found out I've been lying to him? Would that be the final straw for us? Would he ever be able to forgive me? Damn it! I hadn't wanted to lie. I hadn't wanted this. Didn't that count for something?

Tears fell down my cheeks, and the weight of uncertainty settled on my shoulders. The minutes ticked away relentlessly, each second stretching out like an eternity. I couldn't lose him—not when I was just beginning to truly find him, to let myself truly love him.

"Tim." His name left my lips in a choked whisper. The silence of the house echoed back at me, mocking the desperation in my voice.

The more time passed, the more I felt like a marionette whose strings were being pulled by an invisible puppeteer, a cruel one who delighted in my torment. My head throbbed with each frantic heartbeat, and the coldness of the winter air cutting through the cracks and crevices of our home felt like a physical assault.

I desperately tried to focus on something—anything—to keep my spiraling thoughts at bay. I turned on the television and scrolled through my phone. Yet it was no use. The room spun around me like a carousel out of control, and all I could see were images of Tim hurt or worse.

Tears blurred my vision, each one a bearing witness to the fear gnawing at my soul. The thought of him being surrounded by those leeches who had once been part of my life ... it was unbearable.

Eventually, I found myself in our bedroom, hunkered down in our bed wrapped in our blankets as tears poured like waterfalls off my cheeks. This wasn't me. I didn't cry like this. I wasn't weak like this.

But there I was, sobbing, my body wracked with uncontrollable quivers. The room was filled with a hollow silence that pressed in from all sides like an unending void, amplifying the sound of my heartbreak.

I clung to Tim's pillow, inhaling the lingering scent of him. The smell was reassuringly familiar—a mix of his musky cologne and the spicy undertone of his skin. In that moment, I was deeply aware of how much I loved Timothy Moore. More than I ever thought possible.

CHAPTER 27

February 9, 11:55 a.m.

TIM

"Come on, where are you?" I muttered, frustration mounting as I searched for any sign of Justin's Oldsmobile. Gray clouds loomed in the sky, casting an ominous shadow over the rundown neighborhood. Disquiet gnawed at my insides, a pit viper coiling itself tighter and tighter. The houses were riddled with decay, windows boarded up, paint peeling off in patches.

As I rounded a corner, my pulse jumped at the sight of the old gray Oldsmobile parked in front of an older home that I was all too familiar with. Rameriz and I had scouted out the place several times over the last few months in connection with the Mendez case. I cursed under my breath. Justin and Avery were in league with Mendez? Had they acted alone just to mess with Dakota? Or was there something even more sinister going on here?

As I watched the house, tension coiled in my gut like a spring, ready to snap. Anger simmered beneath the surface, fueled by images of Dakota's haunted eyes as she told me of the planted drugs in her car and her struggle against old demons. Was this all a twisted game to Victor? Luring her back into the drug ring like some kind of sick puppeteer?

I grabbed my gun, slipped it into the back of my jeans and opened my car door. As I climbed out, I could feel the blood pulsing in my veins. I took a step toward the house. A flicker of movement from the upstairs window caught my attention. I hesitated, torn between the desire to confront Justin and Avery and the knowledge that taking down Victor would have a greater impact. I couldn't risk blowing this, but I had to fight the urge to barge in and demand answers. What if they knew where Dakota was? What if they planned to hurt her?

My hands tightened into fists and my jaw clenched in frustration as I weighed my options against one another. I forced myself to turn away, making my way back to my car. I couldn't risk ruining this, not when I was so close.

I took a deep breath, trying to calm my nerves as I slid into the driver's seat. I glanced at the dashboard clock: 12:17 pm. My thoughts turned to Dakota, and my heart twisted with guilt. It had been four hours since I left her at the house after confronting her about her behavior. I'd been so blinded by rage and the need to protect her from these lowlifes that I hadn't thought about what it may have looked like to her.

I started my car, the engine rumbling to life as a wave of regret washed over me. I should have been more patient, more understanding. Dakota was fighting her demons, and I had only added to her burden. Before I put the car into drive, a man wearing a hoodie approached my car and knocked on the window. I opened the window a crack, my hand instinctively reaching for the gun at my back.

"Can I help you?" he asked.

I looked up and saw his face, shadowed by his hood. "Ricky?" Ryan Cooke's cousin? Last time I'd seen him was about two and a half years ago. I had arrested him on a petty drug charge, which he pleaded guilty to and chose to go to treatment instead of going to jail.

"It's Dakota," I said, going on gut instinct. "Someone planted drugs in her car last night. You wouldn't know anything about that, would you?"

A shadow crossed his face and his jaw tightened as he looked down, avoiding my gaze. What was that in his expression? Anger? Guilt? Or was it something else entirely—like fear? The tension in the air became a palpable, living thing.

"Naw, man, but I will keep an eye out."

He looked at me, and there was a sincerity in his expression that couldn't be feigned. He seemed to know something, and whatever that was, he wasn't happy about it.

I handed him my card. "Please let me know if you have any information."

"Will do," he said, sliding the card into his pocket before walking away and heading into the house. Even though his family was awful, Ricky had always seemed like a good person to me. Kinda like Dakota—born into the wrong family and consumed by circumstances beyond their control. It was like he had no chance.

I took one last look at the house, committing every detail to memory—the peeling paint, the dark windows, the overgrown yard—before driving away. This would have to be dealt with later. For now, I needed to get home to Dakota. She'd been through so much in the last twenty-four hours. She didn't need to be sitting at home by herself worrying about me.

As I stomped on the accelerator, I wished I had remembered my phone so I could call her, but I had been so enraged I hadn't even thought. I just stormed out of there with murder flashing before my eyes. I saw then she didn't need me to go all vigilantly on her behalf. She needed me to be there for her, for us. What she needed was someone to stand by her side, someone to reassure her that she wasn't alone in this fight.

The house seemed too quiet as I pulled into the driveway. Her car was there, but the living room lights were off and the curtains drawn. I eased my car into its usual spot, cut the engine and made my way to our house.

My nerves on edge, I slowly entered the house. The house was dark and the silence was suffocating, broken only by the faint ticking of the living room clock. Apprehension crept along my spine, chilling me to the bone as I gently called out, "Dakota?" The echo of my own voice was the only response.

Fear curled its icy fingers around my guts as I moved hesitantly through the living room and down the hall. I approached our bedroom door and pushed the door open. The lights were off, and the blinds were shut, making it hard to see Dakota curled into a ball on the bed. My pulse pounded in my ears as trepidation twisted my stomach into knots.

"Dakota?" I flicked on the light and her red-rimmed eyes squinted shut. I'd never seen her look so broken. I hurried to her, sliding into bed next to her and pulling her into my arms. She buried her head into my chest, and her body convulsed as she held back sobs. "I'm so sorry, Tim. I'm so sorry. Please forgive me."

My heart broke for her, and I held her tightly to me as if that could somehow shield her from the darkness that threatened to consume us both.

I stroked her hair gently, trying to soothe her sobs. "Shh, it's okay. You have nothing to be sorry for, Dakota. None of this is your fault," I whispered, my voice rough with emotion.

Her body shook as she cried, her tears dampening my shirt. I held her tighter, trying to comfort her in any way I could. "I promise, we'll figure this out together."

Her sobs subsided a bit, and she looked at me with those haunted eyes that held too much pain for someone so young. I hugged her closer, whispering words of comfort, assuring her we'd get through this. I brushed her hair out of her face and cupped her cheek gently. "I love you so much. I'm sorry I took off like that."

"I was so scared," she whispered into my chest. "That you would get hurt. That I'd lose you."

"Dakota." I said her name softly. "You're never going to lose me."

She looked at me, searching my face. I leaned in and kissed her gently, pouring all of my love and reassurance into the gesture. As our lips touched, I felt her relax in my arms, her body melting into mine. Our kiss deepened, our worries momentarily forgotten as we lost ourselves in each other. Her fingers found their way to my hair, her soft touch a contrast to the harsh world that awaited outside the safety of our embrace. The taste of her tears melded with mine as we clung to each other in the dim light. It was a moment of bittersweet surrender, of promising each other that no matter what tomorrow brought, we'd stand together, fight together.

CHAPTER 28

February 10, 3:36 p.m.

TAMARA

The cold, sterile smell of disinfectant hung in the air as I sat in the doctor's office, waiting for the nurse to come take my vitals. I ran my hand over my swollen belly as I took in my reflection from the polished surface of the metallic office cabinet across from me. The worry lines on my forehead seemed more pronounced, and a haunted look dimmed my usually vibrant eyes. Honestly, I felt awful. Ever since the confrontation with Nathan and Dad, my anxiety had been off the charts, and my continued nightmares were a constant reminder of the trials that swirled around my family.

The door creaked open, interrupting my thoughts. A nurse in blue scrubs entered, her white shoes squeaking against the tile floor. She asked me to step on the scale as she did every month, then she took my pulse, which was a little high. After that, she brought out the blood pressure cuff and placed it around my arm. It tightened and squeezed really hard. The nurse's eyebrows creased as she listened through the stethoscope.

"Is something wrong?" I asked, biting the inside of my cheek.

"Your blood pressure is a tad high." She took the cuff off my arm and wrote the numbers on a clipboard. "The doctor will be right with you."

The nurse exited the room, and the door closed behind her with a soft click. High blood pressure... That didn't sound good. I had been under a lot of stress lately, but I hadn't realized just how much it had been affecting me physically. My hand instinctively returned to my belly, rubbing it in soothing circles. Inwardly, I whispered a prayer, attempting to release the knots of worry in my chest.

After a few moments, Dr. Nelson walked in with a friendly smile that helped ease my nerves.

She had me lie back so she could measure my stomach. "You're measuring at 31 centimeters, which is just about perfect for 32 weeks," she said and then looked at my chart. "I see here that your blood pressure is elevated a bit. How has your diet been over the last week?"

As I sat up, I thought of Joe. He always made sure Lillie and I ate well, with lots of fresh fruits and vegetables. "Nothing has changed in my diet. Lots of whole organic foods."

She nodded, jotting down some notes on her chart. "That's good. But stress can also have a big impact on blood pressure. Have there been any changes or challenges in your life lately that may have contributed to your levels?"

I hesitated for a moment before nodding. "There have been some hard things with my family lately."

The doctor nodded sympathetically. "I understand. It's important to realize when you're pregnant, your body is already under a ton of stress, so added stressors can create a bigger impact on your health."

A lump formed in my throat as she spoke. It seemed like every day lately brought a new challenge, and I was struggling to keep up. "What can I do to reduce my stress levels?"

She put the chart down and looked at me. "I recommend that you take some time for yourself, and make sure you're getting enough rest. Stress can also have an impact on your baby's health, so it's important to take care of yourself for both of you."

Nodding, I blinked against the oncoming tears. "I'll try my best."

Dr. Nelson gave a comforting smile, reaching over to give my hand a gentle squeeze. "That's all we can ask." As she walked towards the door, she paused. "Getting some regular exercise can help reduce stress levels as well. It doesn't have to be anything strenuous—a walk on the beach or a leisurely swim could do wonders. Meditation or prenatal yoga might help you too. They'll not only maintain your physical health but can also foster mental peace," she suggested, her words carrying a soothing assurance that somehow, things would eventually align.

As the door clicked shut behind her, I was left alone to process her advice. Slowly, I pulled myself off the examination table and put on my coat. My fingers worked mechanically to button it up, my mind lost in contemplation.

As I stepped out of the doctor's office, the cool breeze caressed my flushed cheeks as if it were trying to soothe my frayed nerves. With each step toward my car, I resolved to implement the stress management techniques Dr. Nelson had shared, but that would only be a temporary solution until I could face the root causes of my turmoil.

My phone suddenly buzzed in my hand, jarring me from my thoughts. The screen displayed Tim's name. "Hello?"

"Tamara, it's Tim. You got a minute?"

What was that in his voice? I took a deep breath, trying to suppress the fear that tried to rise. "Yeah, I got time. What's up?" I unlocked my car with the key fob, opened the door and slid into the driver's seat.

"I'm not sure how much I should tell you, but honestly I'm really worried about Dakota."

I rested my hand on my stomach and closed my eyes, trying to calm my racing heart. After this doctor's visit, I wasn't sure if I could handle anymore drama with my family. "Sure, Tim. What's going on?"

Tim paused for a moment, his breath audible through the

phone. "Well, the other night she got in really late after work. She didn't return any of my calls or texts, and then she came in about three in the morning."

Not good. Was she using again? I waited in silence, not knowing what to say.

"Again, I'm not sure I should tell you much more. It's Dakota's story to tell."

But the silence lingered, heavy and ominous, punctuated only with the sound of Tim's shallow breaths. Finally, I broke it. "Tim"—my voice was steadier than I felt—"I appreciate you respecting her privacy, but if Dakota is in danger or if she's fallen off the wagon again, I need to know. We need to help her."

Tim's sigh was heavy on the other end. "It wasn't like that exactly. When she was at work the other night, some guys from her past came in. From what I know, they were connected to Ryan."

Ryan? I gripped the phone tighter, my guts wrenching at his name as a torrent of awful memories cascading through my mind.

"They said some really messed-up stuff to her, Tamara." Tim paused and took in a long breath.

My skin crawled, thinking of how cruel Ryan could be. Were these guys just as bad?

"When she left work, she found a bag of meth planted in her car." Anger spilled out in Tim's words.

My heart pounded in my ears. What kind of twisted animal would do that to someone? The fact that Ryan and his associates were still causing trouble for my family was infuriating. Dakota had been through enough at their hands. She didn't deserve this.

"Is she okay?" I managed to choke out, struggling to draw in a deep breath.

"She's shaken up but physically okay. I've been staying with her as much as possible to make sure she's safe," Tim replied. "But I'm only one person. I can't be with her for twenty-four-seven."

God, please help me. This was too much. "Is there any way that you could get extra time off and bring her to Ocean Shores?

Getting her out of there and being surrounded by people who love you both might help."

Tim was quiet for a moment, and I could hear the weight of his thoughts in the silence. "I think that might be a good idea, Tamara. We could all use some time away from everything. Give us a chance to regroup and collect ourselves. I'll talk to Dakota and see how she feels about it."

"Please do, Tim," I said, feeling a thin thread of relief. "She needs to know that she's not alone. We're a family, and we stick together, no matter what."

"Please, keep me updated," I pleaded.

"Of course," Tim replied, sounding drained. "We'll figure this out, Tamara. Dakota's strong. And we're stronger together."

His words were soothing, but the chill of fear clung to my bones long after ending the call.

I sat in the car for a few minutes, taking deep breaths to calm my nerves and ease the tension in my body. Once I felt a little more collected, I started the car and drove home.

CHAPTER 29

February 11, 2:20 p.m.

DAKOTA

The door creaked open, the sound grating on my frayed nerves as I stepped into our house. The weight of another day at the gas station and uneventful group meeting hung heavy on my shoulders. To make matters worse, I'd been scheduled for the early morning shift all weekend.

"Tim?" I called out, tossing my keys onto the kitchen counter. No response. A sense of unease crept over me as I walked down the hall to our room. I pushed open the door and there he was. His strong, broad back was facing me as he hunched over our open suitcases, folding shirts and jeans in neat piles. I leaned against the wall and watched him for a minute, my eyes tracing the familiar lines of his body, etched out by the dim light seeping in through our half-drawn curtains. His movements were methodical, almost meditative, even in this mundane task.

"Whatcha doing?" I finally asked.

His movements paused, and he looked over his shoulder, releasing a soft sigh. "Packing." Setting aside a neatly folded pile of clothes, he came around the bed and wrapped his arms around me. The warmth of his embrace enveloped me, chasing away some of the chill that had settled deep in my bones. He planted a gentle kiss on my forehead. "You look tired, babe."

The last few days had been rough as I worked hard at keeping the secret that burned into my soul. I just hoped it was over now. I'd done their dirty work, delivered their package ... it had been silent since then, except for the demon on my shoulder constantly calling me a liar. "I am." I admitted, leaning into him.

"Good thing we have a surprise weekend trip planned," Tim said with a small grin, pulling back slightly to gauge my reaction.

A surprise trip? The sudden break from this monotonous life sounded like a breath of fresh air, but the demon on my shoulder just laughed ominously, picking at the loose threads of my peace. "What are you talking about?"

"Ocean Shores," he announced. "We're going to spend the weekend with Tamara and Joe. It's time to take a breather, don't you think?"

Ocean Shores? I thought of the day after Tim proposed to me. Lounging in the room all day as the storm outside pounded against the building. Ordering room service and watching *Star Wars*. Losing ourselves in each other's embrace. It sounded wonderful, but I was scheduled to work all weekend. "I can't, babe. I work."

"Actually, you don't," he replied, his eyes twinkling with mischief and determination. "I called in a few favors. Mike owes me."

With a raised eyebrow, I pulled away from him. "You called my boss?"

"Sure did." He walked back to the suitcase and continued to organize it. "And he managed to get your shifts covered."

He had just done something so wonderful for me, and yet all I could do was worry about how my actions would haunt us. I swallowed hard, my throat tight. "You shouldn't have done that."

He paused, turning around, looking at me with soft concern.

"Why, love?" he asked gently. "You've been burning the candle at both ends. You need rest."

The affection in his voice hit me hard. I looked away, unable to meet his gaze. I thought about this lie I was carrying around, the unspoken truth that was big enough to tear us apart. "I just feel bad that someone else is stuck with morning shift this weekend."

Tim crossed the room and took my hands, his touch warm and comforting against my skin. "Hey," he said, his voice gentle. "It's time to stop worrying about everyone else for once. This is about you, about us."

"But—"

He silenced me with a finger to my lips. "No buts." He spoke softly yet firmly. "Don't you see? We need this. We need to be together, away from everything else."

I shifted uncomfortably under the weight of his words. Tim was right—we needed to be away. Getting out of Hadlock and spending time with my family did sound nice, but what if being around those I loved only amplified the demons screaming at me?

I sighed, a deep and heavy breath that felt like it was carrying the weight of all my secrets. Tim's face softened, his thumb tracing my hand gently.

"We've both been working so hard, and with everything that's happened in the last few days..."

Guilt twisted my stomach even harder. I knew he was referring to my almost relapse—the one that almost sent both of us off the edge. But he didn't know the full truth behind that night...nor the demons I had been wrestling with since. My eyes clouded with unshed tears, the lump in my throat threatening to choke me.

"Dakota, please," he implored, his grip on my hands tightening ever so slightly "We need this." His words, so full of tenderness and empathy, slowly chipped away at my wall of resistance. Images of the ocean and the soothing sound of crashing waves filled my thoughts, replacing the darkness with a glimmer of hope. It would be good to see Tamara and Joe too. It had been too long.

"Okay," I finally relented. There was relief in his smile, his handsome features brightening in a way that made my heart ache. "Let's do this."

For the next fifteen minutes I went through the motions of helping Tim pack our bags, but inwardly I felt like a zombie—the night of the living dead. I hope this trip would help me break through this funk I'd been in since being forced to lie to Tim.

As we packed our things into suitcases, I watched Tim move around our room: grabbing clothes and toiletries, filling our bags with the things we would need. I loved him so much, but each loving gesture of his—every concerned glance, every touch—felt as though it was a needle piercing through my heart. I knew that if he learned the truth, the real reasons behind my near relapse and my brooding demeanor, our world could possibly break apart.

Watching him from the corner of my eyes, my heart bound with guilt and unease, I made a choice. A choice to fight, for him and for us. I couldn't let these demons destroy what we had built together. If this trip was a lifeline being thrown at me, then I would grab it and cling onto it with everything I had.

CHAPTER 30

February 11, 6:02 p.m.

TAMARA

The aroma of freshly chopped rosemary and thyme wafted in the air as I sat with Lillie on the area rug in the middle of the living room floor, helping her with a wooden puzzle. Joe stood at the stove, stirring a pot of bubbling lemon Parmesan sauce while he chatted with me about my day as we waited for my family to arrive.

Lillie giggled as she placed a wooden puzzle piece into its designated spot, her chubby fingers working diligently. "Great job, Lillie," I praised, clapping my hands together.

"I'm pretty sure we have a genius on our hands." Joe beamed with pride as he turned from the stove to sneak a glance at our daughter.

"Oh, for sure," I tickled Lillie under her chin, causing her to break into a fit of laughter.

This little routine repeated several times with Lillie thoroughly enthralled with the game. I tried to focus on her joy, but my mind kept drifting to yesterday's phone call with Tim. I ached for Dakota and her recent struggle with sobriety. Tim had asked me to not tell Dakota that he had spoken to me about it, but I hoped that time with her this weekend would allow her to confide in me.

A faint knock sounded on the door, and I groaned as I tried to stand. My swollen belly made it a struggle to move easily. Yet Joe was beside me in an instant, his strong arms hoisting me up to a wobble. "I'll get it," he said, pressing a quick kiss against my forehead before striding over to the door.

Through the window, Dakota and Tim stood on the porch, their cheeks rosy from the biting cold. Tim held a brown paper bag and Dakota, carried a couple bottles of sparkling apple cider.

Joe opened the door and invited them inside. "Dakota, Tim! It's so good to see you." He took their coats and hung them up. Lillie eagerly ran to Dakota and wrapped her small arms around her leg. Dakota smiled down at her, and for a moment, I could see the shadows that haunted her eyes lift some. "Hey there, Lillie Bug," Dakota said, ruffling Lillie's hair.

I reached out and pulled Dakota into a hug, holding her tightly to communicate how much I had missed her. To my surprise, she returned the hugged with the same intensity.

"It smells amazing in here, Joe. It's making me even more hungry than I already am," Tim said, laughing as he patted his stomach. Tim put the paper bag on the counter that separated the kitchen from the living room then moved forward to greet Lillie, who extended her arms towards him. He scooped her up and tossed her in the air playfully, catching her in his strong arms. Lillie erupted into giggles, kicking her feet in delight.

Joe chuckled and walked into the kitchen to stir the sauce.

The smell of garlic and butter filled the air, the sauce's aroma adding a homely feel to everything. "Should be ready in twenty-minutes!" Joe called out, his voice floating over the soft hum of the oven.

"Great! I actually brought some snacks to tide us over." Tim stepped toward the kitchen and reached for the paper bag. He pulled out a jar of green olives, a tray of prosciutto, several types of sliced cheese and some crackers. "You got a plate?" he asked Joe.

Just then, there was another knock at the door. I easily answered it this time, opening it to reveal my brother Nathan's familiar grin framed by his short, dark hair. Amanda stood beside him, holding a pie, her auburn hair pulled into a tight ponytail, her slim figure rigid. Colton and Ivy ran forward with sounds of delight, throwing their arms around my legs. "Auntie Tammy."

Nathan's booming laughter filled the air as he took off his coat. "They both really love their Aunt Tammy!" Nathan exclaimed, stepping forward and enveloping me in a bear hug.

Colton then made his round, starting with Joe, but Ivy stayed next to me. I lifted her and gave her a tight squeeze. My heart swelled from the adoration I felt from my beautiful six-year-old niece.

Amanda smiled too, but there was a vacancy behind her expression that hadn't escaped my notice. A flicker of sadness or fatigue maybe, a silent plea for help perhaps. I thought of my conversation with Nathan the other day and the concern of her growing distance.

She lifted a pie pan in the air. "I brought dessert," she said in a low voice, looking at the floor. What was going on with her? This was not the outgoing, bubbly, sister-in-law that I was used to.

Joe walked across the room and took the pie pan from Amanda's hands. "Thank you, Amanda. It looks amazing."

I set Ivy down and hugged Amanda tightly. "So glad you guys could make it."

She pulled away quickly and joined Nathan and the kids in the living room. Colton and Ivy had grabbed a few toys out of Lillie's toybox and sat with her on the floor. Dakota and Tim had already settled in, munching on the snacks that Tim had brought, while Joe finished the sauce.

As we waited for dinner to be ready, we all chatted, making small talk, but I kept glancing at Amanda, noticing the coldness in her. Nathan said the other night that he felt like he was losing her, and he didn't know how to stop it. I watched as Nathan tried his best to act normal with Amanda close by, laughing too loudly at Tim's jokes and slinging his arm around her with an air of forced cheerfulness. Yet she barely reacted to his obvious attempts and continued to gaze out the window, consumed with her own thoughts. I made a note to try to speak with her privately later and tuned into the funny banter between Tim and Nathan.

A few minutes later, Joe announced that dinner was ready. Everyone gathered around the table while I grabbed Lillie and fastened her into her highchair. My heart swelled with thankfulness as I took a seat and looked around at my beautiful family. The warm glow of candles flickered across their faces, casting dancing shadows along the walls. We held hands, and Joe prayed a quick prayer.

"Alright, everyone," Joe said, clapping his hands together. "Let's dig in!"

"Finally!" Tim exclaimed, reaching for the angel hair pasta. "I've been fantasizing about this meal since I walked through the door."

Nathan gave him a playful shove. "Get in line, buddy," he joked, reaching for the platter of roasted chicken. Laughter bubbled from within me, as if it had been trapped inside for far too long, just waiting for permission to escape.

"Careful, Nathan," Joe warned with a grin. "You know how protective Tim can be over his food."

"Hey, I'm not that bad," Tim protested, feigning offense as he scooped a generous helping of steamed vegetables onto his plate.

Meanwhile, Amanda continued to sit quietly, pushing around the food on her plate. Her silence was deafening amidst the joviality at the table. I watched as she twirled her fork aimlessly through her pasta, a pensive expression etched on her face. It was as if she existed in a separate sphere, detached from the laughter and merriment around her. I noticed Nathan glance at her out of the corner of his eye, worry lining his face. He tried to engage her in conversation, but she just responded with one-word answers.

The meal continued in this manner, laughter mixing with the clatter of cutlery while Amanda's silence hung over us like a dark cloud. Occasionally, Lillie would let out a gurgle of glee, momentarily distracting me from my concern for Amanda.

As we chatted, I stole glances at Dakota too. Her shoulders seemed to relax with each passing moment, her laughter mingling with the rest of ours. I silently prayed that this lighthearted atmosphere would continue to ease her pain.

As we ate, we shared stories and jokes, passing dishes around the table and savoring every bite. Colton and Ivy entertained us with their silly antics, and Lillie cheerfully ate her food.

I felt a sense of warmth and contentment, grateful for this moment of togetherness. These were the moments that I lived for —the ones where joy and love outweighed everything else. My gaze swept across the table, taking in Dakota's flushed cheeks and Tim's laughter. Amanda even seemed to thaw a bit, a faint smile playing at the corners of her lips. Nathan's gaze met mine across the table, relief mirrored in his features.

After we finished our meal and cleared the table, Amanda offered to help with the dishes.

Joe took Lillie into the bathroom to clean her up and put her in some fresh clothes and the rest of the gang settled into the living room.

"Is everything okay, Amanda? You don't seem like yourself."

She glanced over her shoulder into the living room, eyeing her family. "Yeah, everything is fine," she said, but her voice was off.

"Okay, well, just know that I'm here if you want to talk."

"Thanks, Tamara. I appreciate that."

I made a mental note to reach out to her sometime during the coming week, hoping to gain some insight into her thoughts and offer my support if needed. She might be reluctant to open up now in front of Nathan and the kids, but maybe if we were in a more private place, she would.

We finished cleaning and joined everyone in the living room. Joe pulled out the game Balderdash, and we spent the next hour laughing and making fun of the silly words and definitions.

As the night unfurled, the glow of family and camaraderie that filled our home was a beacon amidst any lingering shadows of worry. Balderdash brought out the competitive side in all of us, especially Nathan, who had a knack for thinking of the most outrageous and comedic definitions. His antics had us all in stitches, and his energy seemed infectious, drawing out even the most reserved among us. Colton and Ivy were a riot trying to guess the often complicated and ridiculous words, their answers filled with imaginative nonsense that only children could conjure.

Around eight-thirty, Lillie began to fuss, her tiny fists rubbing at tired eyes as she nestled her head into my shoulder. I excused myself and took her to her room. It took about twenty minutes for her nightly routine of putting her pajamas on, brushing her teeth, singing a few songs and reading her favorite bedtime story, "Goodnight Moon". Then Joe came in and said a prayer with her, and within a few more minutes, she was asleep. When we walked back into the living room, Nathan and Amanda were getting the kids ready to leave.

Nathan shook Tim's hand and clapped him on the shoulder, an easy grin on his face. "It was great hanging out with you guys tonight. Tamara said you two are down for the weekend. What do you think about doing a guy's night at Midways tomorrow night?"

Tim nodded and glanced at Joe. "Sounds fun to me. You in, Joe?"

I turned to him to take note of his response. It was somewhat insensitive of Nathan to invite a recovering alcoholic to a bar, but I knew Joe. Drinking wasn't much of a temptation to him anymore. He told me once, after his last relapse, he knew the stakes and it wasn't worth the risk.

"I think I can get the night off," Joe said with a grin, giving me a nod of assurance, his eyes meeting mine in a quiet conversation only we could understand.

"That would be great!" I encouraged, taking Joe's hand in mine and giving it a squeeze. "Then Dakota, Amanda and I could have some girls time here."

"I don't know..." Amanda said, looking a bit irritated at Nathan.

"Oh, come on, Amanda," I said, smiling in assurance and trying to smooth over any discomfort. "It's been a while since we had some good time together. I miss you. And we can see if Mom and Dad can take the kids."

Amanda glanced between Dakota and me. "Okay, if Mom and Dad can take the kids, I'll come."

"I don't know, Dakota said sarcastically. "What would we possibly do without kids or our men taking up our attention?"

The comment was met with a round of laughter. Tim leaned in to kiss her cheek. "I think you'll find something to do."

"Alright, it's settled then," Joe said, clapping his hands together once more, this time with a satisfied grin. "Men to Midways, ladies here."

CHAPTER 31

February 12, 9:32 a.m.

DAKOTA

The room was dank, with the smell of cigarettes, burnt ammonia and cat piss swirling together in the air. I shivered as I stepped forward in the dim light. "Here ya go, Dakota." Avery handed me a glass pipe filled with meth, a menacing grin on his grisly face. "Have as much as you want."

I shook my head, my body buzzing with the war it fought. "No!"

"Come on, Dakota, you know you want to." Justin grabbed the pipe and lit the flame outside of the glass before offering it to me again.

"No!" I stepped backwards, but the addict in me was fixated on the smoke leaking from the pipe.

"Fine!" Justin said and took a long pull from the pipe. Then he lunged forward, placed his mouth over mine and exhaled the smoke. I wrestled and fought against him, but he was too strong.

I woke with a start, sweat beading on my forehead. Taking a deep breath, I glanced around the room to calm my racing pulse. Sunlight beamed through the window of the cozy guest room in Joe and Tamara's home, casting a golden glow on the wooden floor and the soft pastel colors of the room. Tim lay next to me in a peaceful sleep, his features relaxed and serene. The fear dissipated as thoughts of last night seeped into my mind. Sitting around the table with my family, enjoying delicious food, and easy laughs with the people I cared about the most. It was so lighthearted and fun. And now it was a new day, a beautiful one at that. It would be wrong to let hopeless nightmares and fear of the future rob these moments from me.

As Tim stirred, his eyes fluttered open and immediately landed on me. His warm fingers found mine, and they intertwined together.

"Good morning, beautiful," he murmured in his deep, husky voice.

"Morning," I replied softly, leaning into place a gentle kiss on his lips. The warmth of his touch and the taste of his lips pushed away the memory of the nightmare that still lingered in the back of my mind.

The sound of Lillie's happy coos and giggles from downstairs interrupted our peaceful moment together. Tim pulled away with a fond smile on his face. "I think we should probably go join them."

Reluctantly, I agreed and untangled myself from his embrace. After quickly getting dressed, I ran my fingers through my hair in an attempt to tame it. Tim chuckled at my messy hair as he pulled on a shirt. "I personally like your bedhead look."

I smirked and reached for my purse, rummaging through it until I found a rubber band to tie my hair into a ponytail. Tim grabbed hold of my hand and led me out of the room. We made our way to the kitchen where Joe was already busy cooking breakfast. The savory smell of bacon and eggs filled the air, making my stomach growl with hunger. Tamara sat on the couch with Lillie on her lap, reading her a book.

Joe looked up with a cheerful grin as we entered the kitchen. "Good morning, you two. Breakfast will be ready soon. And the coffee has just finished brewing."

Tim gave Joe a nod of thanks before guiding me over to one of the kitchen chairs. I slipped out of his hold and moved towards the coffee machine, pouring myself a cup. The aroma of the freshly brewed concoction hit my nose, and my entire body seemed to sigh with contentment.

I sat on the chair and watched Tamara read to Lillie as they snuggled on the plush couch. The adorable toddler was completely engrossed in the storybook in her mother's hands, her bright blue eyes wide with wonder. A smile tugged at my lips as I took in the peaceful scene before me, grateful for this moment of calm amidst the chaos of daily life.

Soon breakfast was ready, and Joe began dishing out plates of scrambled eggs and strips of crisp bacon, alongside fluffy pancakes topped with a generous dollop of butter.

As we ate our meal, conversation flowed easily around the table. I relaxed into my seat, content to just be here with my family, away from the worries and stresses of the outside world. But as the meal drew to a close, a sense of restlessness crept over me, and thoughts of the nightmare that had plagued me last night resurfaced.

Tamara's voice cut through my troubled thoughts. "It's such a beautiful day outside."

"Yeah," Joe chimed in, pulling out his phone to check the weather app. "It says it's already 43 degrees out, with a high of 59 for the day."

"Perfect weather for our visit," Tim added, lifting his coffee mug to take a sip. "Looks like we lucked out with the timing."

Lillie babbled from her highchair before flinging a fistful of eggs towards Tim, some bits landing in his lap.

"Nice aim, Lills," I chuckled, lifting my hand for a high-five from the precocious toddler. She giggled and threw some food towards me.

"Don't encourage her," Tamara said with a chuckle as she rose from her seat. "Sorry about that, Tim. She gets a bit rowdy when she's finished eating."

Tim laughed and brushed off his lap, waving away the apology. "No harm done, really," he replied warmly, turning towards Lillie, who was now snuggled in Tamara's arms, still giggling. "It's impossible to stay mad at that adorable face anyway."

Lillie squirmed and kicked her feet obviously wanting down. Tamara set her down, and she ran into the living room and began circling the couch.

"She's got more energy than a pack of puppies." Joe chuckled as he watched Lillie play.

Tamara gestured towards me and Tim with a playful grin. "I have a feeling it's because of the company."

Lillie burst into the kitchen again, carrying her little shoes and pointing excitedly towards the front door. We all laughed, enjoying her enthusiasm and eagerness to venture out.

"Do you guys want to go for a walk?" Joe asked, smiling at me and Tim.

"Count me in," I said standing, beginning to clear the dishes from the table. Tim nodded, mirroring my actions on the other side of the table.

Within minutes, we were bundled up and ready to head out to the beach. The winter air was crisp but not too cold, and as we stepped onto the sand, the sun cast a warm glow over the water, its surface shimmering and dancing with the light. Seagulls squawked overhead, and the sound of crashing waves filled our ears, beckoning us towards the shoreline.

"Isn't it beautiful?" Tamara exclaimed, her hair whipping around in the cool wind as she wrapped her jacket tightly around herself.

"Definitely," I agreed, my feet sinking into the sand as they walked. Tim nodded and took hold of my hand as we walked forward.

Joe lifted Lillie onto his shoulders, her delighted squeals and babbling adding to the idyllic scene. He eventually set her down, and she ran ahead of us for a while, releasing some of her boundless energy.

"Sometimes I wish I had her endless supply of energy."

Tamara sighed wistfully, a small hand resting on her growing belly. It was then that I noticed the weariness in her features, stealing some of the usual brightness from her gaze.

My stomach tightened with guilt. Why hadn't I noticed before? Probably because I was consumed with my own selfish drama, too occupied with my worries to observe my sister's fatigue.

Lillie squealed in delight again, pulling me out of my thoughts. She was pointing towards the shoreline where the waves reached their foamy fingers towards her tiny feet. She began making funny faces and pointing out interesting shells and rocks along the shore to Joe and Tamara as they delighted in each one of her finds. A pang of envy mixed with admiration for their little family. Then another wave of guilt for feeling that way.

"Sometimes I wish I could be like them," I whispered to Tim, nodding toward Tamara and Joe. "They just seem so..." I trailed off, unable to find the right words.

"Whole?" Tim suggested, his voice gentle.

"Exactly." I sighed.

Tim stopped and pulled me close, whispering in my ear. "We'll get there, Coda."

I nodded and tried to smile, but fear still lingered in my chest, a tight knot I couldn't quite unravel. I couldn't imagine it. Especially now.

The brilliance of Lillie's laughter pulled our attention toward her. I laughed at her infectious joy, as she darted from one spot to another, her little feet kicking the sand as she went. Even if Tim and I never had a family, I would enjoy the moments with the family I did have. Tim caught up with them quickly, while lingered behind observing the scene unfold. Lillie bent over and rose smiling, lifting the shell in the air. The sun caught the iridescent hues of the shell, making it shimmer like a tiny, captured rainbow.

"Wow! That's beautiful, Lillie," Tim said, crouching down to admire her treasure. Her expression sparkled with pride, and she grabbed hold of his hand, pulling him forward to show him more gems in the sand.

Tim and Tamara followed close behind Lillie, leaving Joe and me alone near the water's edge. As the waves lapped at the shore, my thoughts churned like the foam that fizzled around my feet.

"What's on your mind, sis?" Joe asked, his handsome features sincere and kind. That was the thing with Joe—he was always so observant, but never judgmental. If I was going to tell anyone, it would be him. He'd had his own struggle with addiction and yet he overcame and built this wonderful life with my sister. No wonder my sister loved him so much.

I watched as Lillie darted toward Tim and Tamara, her laughter ringing like wind chimes in the distance.

I turned to Joe. "It's about... my addiction."

His gaze met mine, steady and understanding. "What is it, Dakota?"

"Recently, there was temptation," I admitted, my stomach turning. "It was a real struggle. I almost gave in, and it terrified me. I don't want to go back to that life, but sometimes the darkness feels so strong, like it's closing in on me." As the words spilled out, a weight lifted from my chest, yet simultaneously, a heavy silence fell between us. Joe's features soften with understanding. The ocean's symphony continued unabated, the only sound in our shared silence. The salt from the sea air stung my eyes, or perhaps it was just the tears threatening to fall.

"Hey, it's okay," he said, voice full of empathy. "I know how hard it can be to resist those urges. I've been there too, remember?"

Nodding, I looked at the sand. "But you overcame it," I said, my voice small. "You have a beautiful family now, a successful business. You've made something of yourself. How did you do it?"

Joe sighed. "It wasn't easy. It took a lot of work, and it took time. Every day, I made a choice,—a choice to fight, even when it felt impossible."

"I'm just not sure if I'm as strong as you." And I was sure my demons were ten times gnarlier than his.

"You're stronger than you give yourself credit for," Joe said firmly. "Look at the battles you've already overcome. You've come so far, and Tamara and I are so proud of you."

Joe's words played in my ears, ringing like a mantra, a truth I had somehow let go of. Sometimes it was easy to forget how far I'd come, when all I could see was how much farther I had left to go. I couldn't let my addiction define me. For now, I'd cling to Joe's words like a beacon in the darkness when the shadows became too much.

"Thank you, Joe," I said, grateful for his understanding and support. "It means a lot."

We stood there for a moment, the waves crashing against the shore behind us. A sense of hope flickered to life within me. The wind blew gently against my face, a cool reminder of my vulnerability as I stood there, exposed. The sun shimmered off the ocean, its brilliance contrasting with the darkness that had been lurking within me.

Joe broke the silence, his voice calm and reassuring. "And just so you know, it's normal to have moments of temptation. That's just part of the struggle. But what matters is how you handle it. You just have to remember what's at stake," he said, tilting his head toward Tamara and Tim.

A swell of love washed through me as I watched Tim lift Lillie and swing her around. Joe was right. The stakes were higher than they had ever been. Now that I knew what it was like to be loved like this, I could never lose it.

"Let's catch up with them," Joe suggested and gestured towards the group.

Together, we made our way across the cold sand, but as I walked, I felt a little lighter. The briny scent of the ocean filled my nostrils as the waves crashed against the shore, punctuated by Lillie's infectious giggles.

Lillie noticed us coming close, and she ran toward us, her tiny hands cupped protectively around something precious.

Joe and Tamara exchanged proud smiles, their love for their daughter written plainly on their faces.

"Lillie found something really special," Tim explained, the fondness evident in his voice.

"Can I see?" I ventured, crouching down to Lillie's eye level.

Lillie hesitated momentarily before opening her hands, revealing her treasure. The sight that greeted me was both unexpected and beautiful—a perfect sand dollar, its delicate pattern unbroken by the harshness of the sea.

"Wow, Lills, that's amazing!" I praised, my voice filled with genuine awe. The significance of this fragile token wasn't lost on me—like the sand dollar, I had survived the storms of my past and emerged stronger for it.

Lillie beamed, her cheeks flushed with pride. Her innocence and joy served as a beacon of hope in my otherwise tumultuous world.

As the waves continued to crash around us and the wind whispered through the air, I felt a renewed sense of determination take root within me. Joe's words still echoed in my mind, a reminder that I had the strength to resist temptation and forge a better life for myself. In the face of fear and doubt, I would hold onto this moment—this fragile, beautiful sand dollar—and remember that I, too, could weather the storm.

$\mathcal{F}ebruary$ 12, 7:00 p.m.

TIM

As Joe, Nathan, and I walked into Midways, the familiar smell of beer hit us along with a strange combination of pheromones. I scanned the bar, taking in the unfamiliar scene. The faint hum of chatter, clinking glasses, and the smooth rhythm of blues flowing from the jukebox filled the air. Both pool tables were occupied for the moment, but the dart boards were free. I followed Nathan and Joe to the bar where Charlie, the bar's owner and a good friend of ours, was manning the taps.

"Hey, guys! Great to see you," he greeted us with a broad smile. "What can I get you?"

Joe ordered a Coke, and Nathan ordered a dark beer. "I'll take a Mic Ultra," I said, my gaze drifting towards the pool tables.

"Mic Ultra," Nathan teased, with a grimace. "That's a girl beer, bro."

I shrugged, grinning at his jest. "Guess I'm in touch with my feminine side."

Charlie chuckled, grabbed a chilled glass and set it under the tap. "Nathan's right; you order too many of these and your voice pitch will rise and you'll start wearing pink underwear."

Joe laughed and leaned against the bar, taking a sip of his Coke. "Ahh, he could pull it off though."

"Only if it was a thong," Charlie jabbed as he placed the beer in front of me.

I smirked and took a sip of my beer, enjoying the light and refreshing taste. "You guys are too much."

Nathan smacked me on the shoulder with a grin. "Oh, we're just getting started. We always treated you with kid gloves before, but now that you are marrying my sister, all bets are off."

"He can be relentless," Joe said, chuckling. "You just gotta dish it back harder."

"I think I can hold my own."

"Oh, we'll see about that, Timmy boy." Nathan taunted.

As we bantered, my attention kept drifting to a dark figure in the corner, hidden beneath a hood. His presence was like a blip on my radar, something that didn't seem to fit in with the rest of the crowd. I tried shaking it off, attributing it to cop instincts and years of training.

"Ya'll ready to get your butts kicked?" Nathan nodded toward the pool table which had just opened up. "Because I'm about to show you how it's done."

"Bring it on," Joe challenged, grinning at Nathan as we moved to the pool table.

Charlie waved us off with a laugh, already serving another customer. The bar's atmosphere enveloped us—the smell of alcohol and greasy food, the soft murmur of conversations, and the occasional cheer from a winning dart throw. As much as I tried to immerse myself in the banter and the friendly competition, I couldn't shake off the unnerving presence of the man in my peripheral vision. Without drawing attention, I was able to assess that he wasn't much of a threat, for now. Just a creepy guy sipping his drink.

Nathan chalked his cue and made a flashy break, sending balls scattering around the table with a satisfying clatter. "I'm so about to school you both."

"Sure, you are," I retorted with a laugh, casually watching as

Nathan potted two balls in quick succession. He shot me a cocky grin as he prepared his next shot. "Don't choke now."

"Last time you said that, you choked on the eight ball," Joe quipped.

"Past is past," Nathan retorted, lining up his shot with the flair of a showman. "Watch and learn, boys."

I laughed and took a seat on a tall chair as I watched Nathan's theatrics. He made a show of closing one eye and sticking out his tongue just a little before taking the shot. The cue ball danced under Nathan's guidance, clicking against the others in a rhythm that was nearly hypnotic.

"Man, you're on fire tonight." Joe chuckled, taking a swig from his Coke.

"Nothing like a little pressure to bring out my A-game," Nathan boasted, chalking his cue stick again while I tried to focus on anything but the hooded figure tucked away in the corner.

"Tim, your turn." Joe nudged me, pulling me back to the table where I was supposed to be living in the moment.

"Right," I mumbled, aligning the cue ball, trying to pretend like everything was normal.

Nathan's turn came once more, and he strutted around the table, surveying his domain. He leaned over, aiming for a corner pocket shot. The cue slipped, the white ball danced a cruel tango across the felt, and kissed the eight-ball with a betrayal that ended in a scratch.

"Sssscccratttccccchhh!" Joe roared with laughter, clapping Nathan on the back as he let out a groan of defeat. "The pool gods have spoken!"

"Or you've angered them," I added, unable to help myself from joining in.

Nathan rolled his eyes, passing me his cue stick as he moved away from the table. "Ah, hell," Nathan sighed, shaking his head in mock disappointment. "I'm gonna grab a shot. You want one, Tim?"

"Sure, make it a double," I responded.

When Nathan returned with the shots, we all took a seat around a table and chatted for a bit. Nathan, ever the joker, turned a bit serious as he spoke about Amanda and how his troubled marriage was taking a toll on him. His words were laced with regret and confusion as he confessed, "I just can't seem to reach her." He downed his shot as if trying to drown his sorrows in the burning liquid. "I feel like I'm grasping at straws, trying to figure out what went wrong or more importantly how to fix it."

"Sometimes it takes time, Nate," Joe suggested softly. "Maybe you both just need a little space to figure things out."

"Space." Nathan's face turned sour at the word. "That's what she said the night I started sleeping on the couch."

A knot tightened in my chest at seeing him looking so lost. Pausing for a moment to gather my thoughts, I said, "Nate, sometimes space isn't a bad thing, as long as it doesn't become permanent. Use this time to show her you're still the man she fell in love with."

Nathan waved down a cocktail waitress. "I need another shot for this conversation."

The waitress nodded, disappearing into the crowd, reappearing moments later with a shot glass balanced on a tray. Nathan downed it immediately, wincing. "I'm sorry, guys. We're supposed to be having a fun guys night and I'm bringing everyone down."

"You're not bringing anyone down," Joe reassured him, his voice steady and calm. "We're your family. We want to be there for you."

"Yeah, man. We're all going through things," I reached forward to gently nudge his arm. "I'm dealing with some stuff too." I grimaced, thinking about Dakota's close brush with relapse, the drugs planted in her car—a nightmare scenario that could have ended so differently. Not to mention her tormentors, Justin and Avery. My hand clenched involuntarily at the thought of them.

"You alright there, Tim?" Nathan asked.

I sighed, shaking my head. There was no point in keeping it a secret, not from the two men who had become like brothers to me. And both loved Dakota nearly as much as I did.

"The other night, Dakota didn't get home until about three in the morning." I began, my heart rate increasing as the memory resurfaced. "The next morning, I confronted her about it. She tried to play it off, but the conversation escalated into a fight. I knew in my guts she was lying to my face."

"That's messed up," Nathan interjected.

"Right? But the actual truth of the matter was worse." I paused, a surge of anger swelling in me.

"What happened?" Nathan was on the edge of his seat.

I looked at Joe. I could tell by the hard expression on his face, he already knew. Tamara must have told him. "Some guys she used to party with had come into the gas station she works at and started taunting her, saying some real nasty things about her past."

Nathan's jaw tightened with anger, his hands curling into fists. "Justin and Avery?" The names were spat out like venom, dark and bitter. Joe shifted uncomfortably beside me.

"And it gets worse. When she left work, she found a bag of dope sitting in the driver's seat."

"What the hell, man?" Nathan slammed his fist on the table. The shot glasses rattled against the wooden surface, splashing a little liquor out onto the table. "Did she use?"

I shook my head. "No. She resisted, but she fought that battle until she came home that night."

Joe sighed. "That's tough, man. It's tough for anyone, but especially for her. She's been through hell."

Silence fell over us, only broken by the ambient noise of the bar.

The faint sounds of laughter and clinking glasses mixed with the steady thump of bass from the jukebox in the corner, but it wasn't enough to drown out the tension between us.

"You know what, Tim?" Nathan said suddenly. "Maybe we should teach those pricks a lesson." His eyes flashed with an intensity I hadn't seen before, and for a moment, I was taken aback.

"I almost did. But there is more at stake than them right now."

My response silenced Nathan, his anger simmering beneath the surface as he processed it. Joe gave me a knowing look, aware of the delicate balance I was fighting to maintain.

"Well, if it ever is the right time, count me in as your backup."

Nathan's offer brought a grim smile to my face. "You got it."

Out of the corner of my eye, I noticed the creepy guy again, inching closer to a group of unsuspecting patrons near the dartboard.

"Hey, guys," I interrupted, nodding towards the man. "Do you see that guy over there? He's been giving me a bad feeling all night."

"Which one?" Joe asked, squinting in the dim lighting.

"The one by the dartboard."

As we watched, the man's hand subtly slipped into his jacket pocket and emerged with something shiny—a knife. Without thinking, I sprang into action.

"Stay here," I instructed them as I pushed away from the pool table, my instincts kicking in.

"Hey!" I called out, trying to draw his attention away from the group he was approaching. He turned to face me, glowering as he took me in.

"Put that away," I said forcefully, making sure to project confidence, despite my racing pulse. "This isn't the place for violence."

The man sneered at me, clearly not impressed with my attempt at diplomacy. "Who are you?" he spat and took a step closer. "Some kind of wannabe hero?"

I swallowed hard, knowing I had to be careful about escalating the situation further. The last thing I wanted was for anyone to get hurt.

"Look, you don't want to do this," I said, raising my hands

slightly to show I wasn't a threat. "It's not worth it. Assault with a deadly weapon could mean five to ten."

For a moment, it seemed like the man was considering it, his grip on the weapon wavering ever so slightly. "You don't want to flush 10 years of your life away because the dude is sleeping with your ex."

His expression hardened. That may have been a bit too close to home. The psycho lunged at me with a snarl, knife pointed in my direction.

"Tim!" Nathan shouted from behind me. I easily sidestepped the man's clumsy attack and grabbed his arm, twisting it behind his back. The knife clattered to the floor as he cried out in pain, and I kicked it away before it could be used again.

"Everybody stay calm!" I called out to the bar patrons, who were watching the scene unfold with wide eyes. "I've got this under control."

As I held the struggling man, waiting for the police to arrive, I couldn't help but feel a strange sense of relief. Despite the fear and adrenaline coursing through me, I knew I'd done the right thing.

CHAPTER 33

February 12, 7:45 p.m.

TAMARA

The mouthwatering smells of Chinese takeout and freshly baked chocolate brownies intertwined with the music, creating a sensory experience that made me feel warm and content. The air was filled with the nostalgic mix of 80s and 90s music, transporting me to simpler times. Madonna's "Like a Prayer" had just faded out, replaced by the opening notes of Nirvana's "Smells Like Teen Spirit." The familiar tunes were like old friends, bringing back memories both good and bad. Dakota, Amanda, and I were gathered around the kitchen table, playing Rummy.

"Your turn, Tamara," Dakota said with a smile, but her eyes held a hint of sadness that spoke of inner turmoil. It was a darkness I recognized too well, a constant battle against the ghosts of past mistakes.

"Alright, let's see what I've got." I carefully laid down a set of cards.

"Nice move," Amanda complimented before snatching a card from the deck, but her words seemed forced.

After a few minutes the song changed again, this time to the upbeat rhythm of MC Hammer's "U Can't Touch This."

I chuckled as we recalled our attempts at doing the Hammer dance, feeling a sense of ease and comfort at the shared memory.

Dakota joined in with a snicker, while Amanda's seemingly distant demeanor softened as she laughed along with us.

"We thought we were so cool," Dakota said.

"Oh, I was cool," Amanda chimed in with a playful wink, trying to match our lightheartedness despite her seemingly distant demeanor.

"Of course, you were." I flashed her a silly grin. Suddenly, a sharp kick from my unborn child caught me by surprise and I gasped in pain. Both Dakota and Amanda looked at me with concern.

"Are you okay?" Dakota asked quickly, reaching out to touch my arm.

"Yeah, just a powerful little kicker in here," I said, placing my hand on my swollen belly and massaging the spot that still throbbed.

"Definitely a future soccer player," Amanda joked playfully.

"Or an MMA fighter," Dakota interjected with a mischievous glint in her eye.

"I hope not," I responded with a small groan as I discarded a card.

Shaking her head, Amanda drew a card and added it to her hand. "I swear, Colton is already there. The other day, during a playdate, he body slammed another kid for taking his toy away from him."

"That's freaking awesome," Dakota said with a sarcastic grin. "I love that kid."

Amanda's lips pursed in protest as she laid down a set of three cards and then discarded another with a sigh. "My four-year-old does not need to be exposed to that kind of violence." She fell silent for a moment before conceding with a smirk, "I blame his father." The way she said "father" carried a weight that felt bitter.

Another few beats of silence passed before my mind latched onto a lighter story. "Did I tell you guys what Lillie did the other day while I was in the shower? She covered herself in peanut butter," I interjected, trying to lighten the mood. "She had nodded off in the middle of the floor while watching a cartoon, so I thought I was safe, but when I came downstairs, she had peanut butter everywhere. And I mean everywhere."

Dakota burst out laughing. "I swear, both your kids are hilarious. You need to have your video camera for those moments to record them for Aunt Dakota."

Amanda chuckled softly. "I'd be blowing up your phone on a regular basis with all of Coltan and Ivy's antics."

"I wouldn't mind," Dakota mused.

"Yeah?" I asked, suddenly curious. I paused for a moment, not sure if I should go here, but in the end, I really wanted to know. "Do you think you and Tim will want kids someday?"

Dakota hesitated, her expression shifting from playful to contemplative. "Honestly? I don't know. Until Tim and I got together, I never even considered it. Not with the childhood we had and my addiction issues..." Her voice trailed off.

With a gentle tone, I reassured her. "Whatever you decide, I know you'll make the best choice for both of you." I wished so badly that I could shield her from the ghosts of our past. I reached for her hand. "We've come a long way since then, haven't we?"

She wrapped her hand around mine and gave it a gentle squeeze. "More than I ever thought possible."

Amanda set her cards on the table and looked back and forth between us. "I know this is a difficult topic, but can you tell me about your childhood? Nathan seems to remember it differently, and I want to understand your perspective."

Dakota and I exchanged a glance, as if silently deciding who would speak first. My throat tightened as I recalled our tumultuous upbringing.

"Where do I even begin?" I murmured, struggling to find the words to describe our childhood. "We were born into a family that was broken long before we were part of it. Our dad was raised by an abusive alcoholic, and though he wrestled to keep his demons suppressed, they often won the battle. His anger was volatile, and our mother was too scared to stand up to him. We lived in constant fear, never knowing when the next violent outburst would occur."

"Every day was a battle, and every night a war," Dakota added, her voice hollow and distant. "We became experts at walking on eggshells, sensing the undercurrents in Dad's moods, learning to disappear when we felt a storm brewing."

"Why do you think Nathan talks so differently about your childhood? He never talks bad about your dad."

My lips twitched into a fond smile, thinking of Nathan and his humor and the way he saw life. "That's Nathan's way of coping. He's always been that way."

"It's his superpower," Dakota mused.

"Creating a fantasy world, where the demons we lived with are embellished into heroes," I added. "Nathan protected himself by painting our father as a flawed hero, a decorated soldier battling inner enemies while struggling to raise us right. He molded our past into a palatable narrative."

"Maybe Nathan is just trying to forget and move on," Dakota suggested. "But it's hard to truly heal when there's so much left unspoken."

"That's very true..." I murmured, nodding. The somber atmosphere seemed to thicken around us, the weight of our shared pain pressing against the walls, between the furniture, whispering through the drapes.

"I've been feeling so lonely in my marriage lately," Amanda admitted, pain flowing out in my shaky voice.

Amanda's confession hovered in the air, a raw and vulnerable truth that twisted my heart. Her pale face turned to me, her hazel eyes filled with longing and a sorrow that felt heavy in the room.

"Loneliness can be a cruel companion," I murmured sympathetically. "Especially when you're supposed to be surrounded by love and affection."

Amanda nodded and swallowed hard. "I love Nathan, but there's so many things left unspoken between us."

"Unsaid words can be as dangerous as a wildfire," Dakota said thoughtfully. "They can grow and spread until they consume everything." Her features were filled with understanding, her voice carrying the weight of experiences beyond her years.

"And there's a danger in pretending everything is fine," I added softly. "Because then, you forget that it's not. You keep living in this façade of a perfect marriage until one day it cracks, and the reality floods in." My words hung in the air for a few minutes as we gave Amanda space.

Amanda sighed. "It's just so hard with Nathan sometimes. He avoids things with humor and old memories."

"That's Nathan though. Like a lot of men, he hides behind humor and nostalgia when he can't handle deep emotional conversations," Dakota said, reclining in her chair. "It's one of his his defense mechanisms."

I nodded in agreement, my hand resting on my stomach. "And it's not as if he's consciously doing this to hurt you. It's probably more of an unconscious habit formed over many years."

Amanda sighed heavily and let out a sad laugh. "It's funny, because his humor and lightness was what made me fall in love with him. He was so charismatic and funny in high school. He would make me laugh so hard I'd almost pee my pants. But now, so much coldness has crept between us, and it's like I'm living with a stranger. A stranger who would rather wallow in nostalgia than face our problems head-on."

"Then you need to be honest with him, Amanda. No one can fix something they don't know is broken," I advised, my voice steady and reassuring. "Communication is key. It's not easy to talk about our emotions. But I think it's important for both of you to share your vulnerabilities and work together to heal."

"The thing of it is..." She hesitated. "It's not just about the lack of connection. It's about his drinking. It's gotten pretty bad over the past few years."

Dakota and I exchanged a glance. We both remembered all too well what it was like to live with an alcoholic father. The fear, the uncertainty, the constant tug-of-war between love and resentment.

A heavy silence settled over the room like a suffocating blanket as Amanda's trembling voice faded away. She looked so small, her slim figure slumped in the overstuffed chair, dark hair framing her pale face. It was the first time she'd spoken to us about Nathan's drinking—our shared pain laid bare in the dimly lit living room.

"Addiction runs deep in our family," I whispered, my gaze drifting to Dakota, and my heart swelled with pride at how far she had come. "But Dakota is living proof that the cycle of addiction can be broken."

Amanda's eyes filled with tears, shimmering like fallen stars against the darkness of her despair. "Thank you, Tamara."

I reached out to touch her arm. "We'll get through this, Amanda. Just like Dakota did."

Dakota shifted uncomfortably in her seat, looking anxious. She had come so far, and yet the shadows of her past still clung to her.

"Tamara's right," she spoke hesitantly. "I made so many terrible choices with my life. Many times, I thought I'd die in my addiction, but here I am, fighting through, building a life with Tim. And if I can do it, so can Nathan."

"That means more than you can possibly know." she whispered, her voice thick with gratitude and hope. "Thank you both so much. I don't know what I'd do without you guys."

"You'll never have to find out," Dakota said firmly, her voice filled with conviction. "We got you, girl. We're family."

We sat in a wordless moment, the air around us still and charged with unspoken emotions. The soft melody of "Hold On" by Wilson Phillips filled the air, adding to the already peaceful atmosphere. Amanda let out a small laugh, breaking the silence. "It's like the station was listening in on our conversation."

Dakota smirked and jokingly added, "They call them smart phones for a reason."

The sound of Joe's Jeep pulled into the driveway. I heard three car doors shut and then the sound of Nathan's booming laughter. I glanced at Amanda and hoped for her sake that he wasn't too drunk.

As if reading my thoughts, Amanda's expression shifted to one of anxiety and dread. "He better not be drunk," she whispered, her eyes flickering towards the door.

I squeezed her hand in reassurance. "We're here for you, no matter what."

Footsteps sounded on the porch, and I could hear Nathan teasing Tim, full of laughter and mirth. Joe opened the door and his gaze landed on me, giving me a warm smile. Tim and Nathan came in after him, both obviously buzzed but not too bad.

"Babe," Nathan said cheerfully, walking across the room and putting an arm around her. He smelled like Midways—a mixture of beer, fried food, and stale cologne. "You should have seen Tim." His words slurred a bit. "He's like freaking Dirty Harry or something, taking down the bad guys."

Amanda pushed him away, confusion and irritation lining her expression.

"Don't listen to him," Tim said, taking his place next to Dakota. "He's completely exaggerating.

Joe chuckled and shook his head. "This is what I've been dealing with all night."

"Seriously though," Nathan continued. "There was a guy with a knife."

"What?" Dakota asked, clearly taken back.

"Don't worry, sis. Tim took him down like a scarecrow. The guy was like this." Nathan grabbed a butter knife from the table and crouched like he was going to attack somebody. "And then Tim moved so fast I didn't know what happened. It was crazy."

Tim waved him off with a dramatic eye roll. "He exaggerates."

"Let me get this straight," Dakota said, eyebrows pinched together. "You go have a guys night with my brother, and you get into a knife fight? Unbelievable."

"Babe, it wasn't like that," Tim said quickly, reaching out to lightly grasp Dakota's hand. "I just noticed a guy that seemed off... He pulled a knife and I took him down. End of story."

"Wow." Dakota huffed.

"It was freaking awesome," Nathan said again.

"It was pretty awesome," Joe agreed.

"That's it!" Amanda snapped, standing to her feet, her hands clenched into tight fists, and for a moment, I thought she might launch herself at Nathan in anger. "Enough of this ridiculous bravado. This isn't some action film!" Her voice sounded sharply in the room, making everyone freeze mid-motion. She pointed a finger in Nathan and Tim's direction. "This isn't a joke. A knife fight is not a joke! You could have gotten seriously hurt."

"Come on, Amanda," Nathan said, his smile fading. "Don't be mad. We were just having some fun, right, Tim?"

"Right," Tim agreed.

"Enough!" Her gaze locked onto mine, seeking reassurance and strength. I nodded, conveying my support. "Nathan, we need to go home."

Nathan let out a groan, obviously not thrilled with the idea of leaving the party so early. "Come on, babe. Let's stay a little longer."

But Amanda was already grabbing her coat and purse. "No, Nathan, I mean it. We're leaving now."

Nathan grumbled something to himself as he followed after her as she headed towards the door.

CHAPTER 34

February 13, 8:57 a.m.

TIM

My eyes drooped as I drove to work after dropping Dakota off at our house, but as tired as I was, I felt a sense of renewal after spending the weekend with Dakota's family. Their warmth and acceptance washed away some of the darkness that had tried to consume Dakota and me lately. Thoughts of Dakota walking on the beach, the wind blowing in her hair, interacting with Lillie's excitement as she found various treasures filled my heart. Being there this weekend gave me a glimpse of a simpler life that I craved for us.

As I navigated the familiar streets toward the precinct, my phone buzzed in the cupholder beside me. Glancing at the screen, I saw the words 'unknown number' glaring at me. This was the third time, twice over the weekend and now again. A spike of irritation flared up within me, but I quickly dismissed it. Just another telemarketer trying to sell me something I didn't need.

I pulled into the police station, my mind now back in Ocean Shores and the laughs I shared with the guys last night at Midways. Today was going to be rough with staying out as late as I did, but it was worth it.

The moment I stepped out of my car in the precinct parking lot, my phone alerted me that a voicemail had come through.

Strange. Most telemarketers didn't leave voicemails. A sudden gust of wind whipped around me as I walked toward the entry, ruffling my hair and sending a chill through me.

"Morning, Tim!" Officer Jenkins called out from across the lot, his hand raised in greeting.

"Morning," I replied, throwing an easy smile with a wave, but my mind was now on the voicemail.

"Hey, Moore! Got any hot leads?" Officer Ramirez teased.

"Not yet, but the day is young," I answered, giving her a wink. The camaraderie among us was one of the things I enjoyed about the job, but today my attention was diverted, pulled towards the unknown caller and their message. I settled at my desk and pulled out my phone. Tapping on the screen, I put the phone to my ear and waited for the message to play. The voice that came through was distorted, as though the caller had used something to mask their identity. "Officer Moore." The unnaturally deep tone setting my nerves on edge. "Quit ignoring my calls. I have important information regarding Victor Mendez."

My pulse jackhammered at his name, and I gripped the phone tighter. Was this some kind of sick joke? Or could it be the break we'd been waiting for in the Mendez case?

Scanning the office, I turned on my computer and listened to the message again. Was one of my fellow officers messing with me? The office was buzzing with activity as officers moved about, papers in hand, engrossed in their own cases. No one seemed to pay me any mind. I listened to the voicemail again as I waited for my computer to load. The voice echoed in my ear, its monotone delivery chilling me to the bone. I pulled up the Mendez file and began to scour through it again and again, berating myself for not answering the phone earlier. Would the guy call again, or had I missed my chance?

After a good hour of waiting, I leaned back, frustrated, and took in a breath. The scent of coffee lingered in the air, mixed with the sharp aroma of ink from the printers and papers strewn across desks.

I stood and grabbed my phone, about ready to go to the bathroom. The cell buzzed. I looked at the caller ID. The number. For a moment, all I could hear was the blood pounding in my ears as I swiped the screen to answer the call.

"Officer Moore?" A voice that sounded like Darth Vader filled the line.

"Speaking," I replied, keeping my tone steady despite the adrenaline coursing through my veins.

"There is a house in Brinnon, Washington that holds the key to take down Mendez," the distorted voice continued.

I quickly jotted down the address as he spoke, just in case this guy was legit.

"Who is this?" I asked.

"That's not important," the caller replied with a hint of arrogance. "All you need to know is that I have evidence that can bring him down."

My heart pounded with anticipation as I grappled with the implications his words carried. This could be the breakthrough we desperately needed to dismantle Mendez's operation once and for all. But something about the situation felt off—too convenient, too easy. "How do I know this isn't a trap?"

"You don't." The line went dead, leaving me reeling with uncertainty.

I stood there for a moment, the cold device pressed against my damp palm. Unease twisted in my gut and I frowned, studying the address on my notepad. Was this call a lifeline or a noose? Brinnon? This house had been in question before, but I never able to fully make the connection.

I looked at the computer screen, trying to figure my next move. The Mendez file loomed over me like a dark cloud, its contents filled with horrors that haunted my every waking moment. It was a constant reminder of the man who stalked our city, leaving a trail of blood and misery in his wake. And yet, despite our best efforts, he always seemed to be one step ahead of us.

"Tim?" Ramirez's voice cut through my thoughts. "What's going on? You look like you just saw a zombie or something."

I leaned in close to her and told her everything that just happened, then pointed to the address I had jotted down.

"Caller didn't identify himself, but he claims to know something that could bring Mendez down," I explained.

Ramirez's thick brows furrowed in confusion. "Do you think the call was legit?"

"I don't know," I admitted, studying the address. "But I'm going to find out. You in?"

"Hell, yeah, I'm in."

I loved that about her—she was always all in, fearlessness wrapped in a petite frame.

Ramirez glanced around the bustling office and leaned in closer, lowering her voice. "Let's keep this between us for now. We don't know who we can trust."

I nodded, appreciating her caution. The last thing we needed was a leak in the department. Mendez had already proven his influence ran deep—who knew how far it extended?

As we made our way towards the exit, my mind swam with possibilities and risks.

My car roared to life, its engine purring as it carried us towards our destination. We drove in silence, the weight of our thoughts pressing down on us like an invisible hand. I couldn't help but let my mind wander to Dakota, her bright blue-green eyes that were still a bit haunted even after all her hard work of recovery. It was men like Victor that had left her bruised and scared, but they could never take her beauty and resilience.

As we approached the address, a fierce longing for justice overwhelmed me. I hoped so deeply that this lead would finally give us what we need.

The small town was nestled along the Hood Canal, surrounded by dense forests and rugged mountains. It was the perfect backdrop for hidden secrets and a place where Mendez could have easily established his operations. The house was modest, with a fresh coat of paint in light blue and white trim. The lawn was well-manicured, and the windows were clean and sparkling. It blended in easily with the other houses on the street, unassuming and ordinary.

"I don't know, Tim," Ramirez said as we drove by. "This place is so squeaky clean, you would think Ozzy and Harriet lived here."

I nodded, but something in me wouldn't let this go. Even if I had to break the rules a little, I would find out what was in that house.

CHAPTER 35

February 13, 8:27 p.m.

TAMARA

Joe stood by my side, his hand resting on my shoulder as we gazed at our sweet daughter, finally asleep in her crib. Her dark curls sprawled across the pillow like a halo as her breathing changed. He carefully planted a tender kiss to Lillie's forehead and whispered a soft goodnight. I gently tucked the soft blanket around Lillie's tiny form. "Mommy and Daddy love you so much," I added softly.

We tiptoed out of the nursery, closing the door behind us to ensure that Lillie's slumber remained undisturbed, and then walked down the hall to the living room.

"Whew." Joe sighed, stretching his arms above his head and cracking his back. "Finally got her down."

"Tell me about it," I murmured in agreement. "You ready for our show?"

"Absolutely," Joe said and reached for the remote before relaxing onto the couch. I settled beside him and took out my phone to check the emails and messages that had accumulated throughout the day, while he found our show. My thumb hovered over the screen, hesitating for just a moment as I weighed the necessity of dealing with the outside world against the comfort of snuggling up to Joe and shutting out everything else. But then I saw a text from Nathan, asking for prayer. He said he and Amanda had gotten in a really big fight after leaving our house the other night and she was barely talking to him.

My heart ached for him, and I thought of how Amanda had opened up to Dakota and I the other night. For a moment I paused and said a prayer for both of them, and their children too. For Ivy and Colton's sake, I hoped they could work through their issues. And that Nathan would find a way to quit drinking before it was too late.

Releasing the burden for the moment, I clicked on my email app and caught sight of an email from Sarah Taylor. The subject line read "Levi's Birthday Surprise."

"Ready when you are," Joe said with a wink

"Umm, yeah." I nodded, but my attention stayed on the glowing screen of my phone. "I just got an email from Sarah."

"Sarah?" Joe's brows furrowed as he glanced over, his attention instantly diverted from them television. "It's been a while. Is everything okay?"

"I think so," I said and then began to read.

"Hey, Tamara! I hope all is good with you. Joe and Lillie. Everything is great here in Portland. Hope is growing like a weed and hitting all her physical milestones with ease. Levi and I are convinced she's a genius." Below these words there was a picture of Hope attached. I stared at the picture. Her radiant blue-green eyes sparkled with joy, and a contagious smile lit her round, rosy cheeks. She looked so much like Lillie it made my heart ache for what could have been. A phantom limb—the child that should have been mine but wasn't.

"Isn't she beautiful?" I asked, turning the phone to Joe.

He took hold of my hand, and his eyes misted over with tenderness. "Stunning." His thumb brushed over the back of my hand, soothing me in a way only he could.

A wave of emotion crashed over me as I thought about how our lives would be if things were different. The pitter-patter of tiny feet on hardwood floors that weren't just Lillie's. The heart-melting sound of coordinated laughter.

Joe swiped away a stray tear, his touch as gentle as a feather. His soft expression was filled with a depth of understanding that needed no words. I leaned into his comforting strength, allowing myself a moment to just breathe before finishing the email.

"Levi is turning 40 in June, and I wanted to do something really special for his birthday. The other day, I thought of how much he loved our time in Ocean Shores when we were there for your wedding to Joe. Do you know of any good venues around you that may be available?" A wave of nostalgia washed over me with the image of our wedding day, a memory so vivid that it felt like just yesterday. The sun was setting over the Pacific Ocean, painting the sky with hues of pink and gold as we said our vows in the grand room at our Bed and Breakfast. It had been a wonderful celebration, surrounded by the people who loved us the most.

I looked at Joe, who was deep in thought, probably caught up in the same memories. A slow smile stretched across his face as he nodded, already brainstorming.

"What do you think about throwing Levi's birthday at the B&B?"

"Absolutely." Joe stood and walked across the room to retrieve his laptop. "Let me look at our availability. What's the date?"

"June 16th," I said, watching as he quickly keyed in the information.

"I'd love to gift it to them if it's available." His face was set in concentration as he scrolled through the bookings.

"Absolutely," I agreed with a nod, feeling a warmth spread through me at the thought of being able to provide such a gift for Levi.

Joe's features brightened as he found the date, and a triumphant grin spread across his face. "It's wide open. Nothing's been booked for that weekend yet."

"Perfect," I exhaled, reaching out to squeeze his hand. "Let's do it."

He nodded, fingers already flying across the keys as he blocked out the dates. "Let her know it's theirs if they want it."

"Thank you, Joe," I said as I picked up my phone again, eager to tell Sarah the good news. "Sarah, so great to hear from you. Joe and I just checked the big room we were married in and it is available. If you want it, it's yours." I typed quickly, the words flowing from my fingers. Sarah and Levi had always been such a light to me. It would be wonderful spending some quality time with them. Even though it was still a few months away, I could already picture the decorations, the laughter, the love that would fill every corner of the room. The thought of such tangible joy was a welcome distraction from the worry that had been gnawing at my heart.

CHAPTER 36

February 14, 2:15 p.m.

DAKOTA

I pulled into our driveway, completely exhausted from work. The gravel under the tires crunched like dry bones as the car came to a stop. I sat there for a moment, the engine humming softly in the quiet afternoon. My eyes drifted shut briefly, and I let out a sigh that seemed to drain the last of my energy.

My mind drifted to the weekend and spending time with my family in Ocean Shores. It had been exactly what I needed. It calmed my heart and gave me a sense of hope for the future, even after all of the forced secrets and the almost relapse.

Perhaps now that I had done what those demons wanted, I would be able to push away the guilt and give myself fully to my future with Tim. Because I had realized something the other day when he left for hours after our fight. In those dark moments, where every second felt like an eternity, I understood I loved him too much. If something happened to him, if something broke us, I wouldn't survive it.

Shaking off the heavy thoughts, I opened the car door and stepped out into the crisp fall air. The leaves rustled softly as a breeze kicked up, stirring the sweet smell of damp earth and pine. I walked into our home—the only loving home I ever really known and breathed in, relishing in the smells of hardwood and vanilla scented candles.

I stepped into the kitchen and glanced around, contemplating what I would order for dinner. Then I noticed the small yet elegant bouquet of flowers. It was Valentine's Day, a fact I had tried to ignore all day in the midst of hurried customers and convenient store errands. Tim knew how much I detested the ridiculous commercialized day. Yet there they were, a small rebellion against my usual cynicism. A blush of roses, their petals as pink as morning light, and white lilies nestled between. A small card sat propped against the vase, Tim's familiar scrawl gracing the front. I traced a finger over the soft edges of the petals, a tender smile forming on my lips. I lifted the card and unfolded it carefully.

I know you despise the superficiality of Valentine's Day, but I couldn't resist the urge to express my adoration for you. The world may be consumed by commercialism, but my love for you is pure and unwavering. It always has been. The longer I'm with you, the more I fall in love with you. I can't wait for the day when you become my wife.

I held the note against my chest, overwhelmed with the emotion it stirred in me. So much lately, this man had eclipsed every part of who I was. It was terrifying yet amazing at the same time. I hated stupid days like Valentine's Day because it seemed cheap and superficial. There was nothing about my feelings for Tim that were superficial. Suddenly, I wanted to find a way to express that to him. I wanted to make up for the years I'd pushed him away because of my own selfishness and pain. I just wasn't sure how. I racked my brain, thinking of ways that I could express my love to him that would be meaningful, even sacrificial.

I carefully set the note down, determination growing within me to find a way to reciprocate Tim's love in my own way. I'd do something that he'd never expect. I'd make him a home cooked meal, something I'd never done before. I wasn't even sure I had the ability, but I would try for him.

For the next hour, I scoured the internet, looking for videos on recipes until I found a meal that looked delicious yet simple enough to recreate. Then I took a quick trip to the store to grab the ingredients. When I returned home, I watched the video again as I began to chop, dice and sauté with determination. The kitchen became a battlefield, but I pressed on, envisioning Tim's surprised smile.

As I cooked, I thought about the last couple years of our lives together, about the demons I had faced, the battles within myself, and how Tim had been a constant source of support. His love was an unwavering light that guided me through the shadows.

My eyes stung as I cut the onions, but it wasn't just from their natural effects. Tears welled as my heart overflowed with a mix of gratitude and guilt. Tim didn't deserve the endless sorrow I brought his way, yet he still stood by me. His love never faltered or faded, just like those stubborn ocean waves that never tire of kissing the shore.

This meal that I was preparing was nothing in comparison to the unending reciprocation he deserved. But perhaps it would be one way to show how much I appreciated him.

I glanced at the clock. Tim would be walking through those doors any minute. After dimming the lights, I grabbed the tapered candle I'd purchased at the store, placed it in the holder and lit it.

I set the table and gently placed the flowers Tim gave me in the middle. The timer dinged on the oven, and I crossed the room quickly to take the Baked Chicken Alfredo Pasta and garlic bread from the oven. I placed it in the center of the table and grabbed the salad from the fridge.

I glanced at the table, heat tinging my cheeks. What if Tim thought it was stupid? I shook my head, forcing out the self-doubt. Tonight, it wasn't about me, it was about Tim.

The rumble of a car engine sounded from outside, and my pulse quickened. I ran a hand through my hair, took a deep breath, then rushed across the room to put on our playlist. The door creaked open, and my heart thrummed as I heard his footsteps.

"Dakota?" he called out.

"I'm in here!"

He rounded the corner, and his mouth dropped open as he took in the romantic scene set out before him.

Slowly, he set his phone on the counter and stood rooted on the spot, his gaze flitting from the candles to the perfectly set table and finally, resting on me. "What is all this?"

I smiled nervously, my hands fidgeting as I tried to find the right words. "I wanted to do something special for you, for Valentine's Day."

"Valentine's Day?" He lifted a playful eyebrow as a grin spread across his face. "Okay, where have you put my fiancée?"

"I'm serious, Tim. I wanted to do this for you," I said, feeling vulnerable, which caused fear to rise, but I pushed it down. I wouldn't play the coward and shy away from these emotions that transcended every part of who I was. After everything that we'd been through together. After everything that had happened over the last few weeks, I wanted, no I needed him to know. I stepped forward with fresh courage.

He studied me, with curiosity yet something else. What was it?

I took a breath. "For most of my life, I've run from any true emotion, because inside I was so broken. I've used quick wit and sarcasm to keep people out. To keep you out. But you were so relentlessly loyal. You never once gave up on me, though I pushed you away so many times."

He stepped forward, his expression tender as he looked at me, the candlelight casting a luminous glow on his face. "It's okay, Dakota, we're through all of that."

"I know, but sometimes I wonder if you really understand how much I love you." The energy between us began to intensify as he inched toward me.

"I think I do." He brushed a lock of hair off my face, his warm touch sending tendrils of hope seeping through my veins as the exposure of my sheer honesty left me vulnerable.

I shook my head slowly, looking at him, trying to convey the depth of what I felt. "No, Tim. I've shown you glimpses of it. But today, when I read that note, I wanted you to know that every single day, my love grows for you. Or maybe it's just my capacity to love." I paused, trying to get the words out through the swell of emotions. "Your love has softened me, Tim. It's changed me so deeply, some days, I don't even recognize myself. If something ever happened to you, or to us, I'm pretty sure it would be the end of me."

His arms came around me then, enveloping me in a warmth that soothed my shaking soul. He tilted my chin up and his gaze held mine, solid and unwavering. "Nothing is going to happen to me, Dakota."

Tears spilled over as I thought of the possibility with his line of work. "But it could. The other night, when you came home from the bar, it made me realize that something could happen to you any moment at any time."

"I promise you it won't."

I sniffed, trying to blink away the threatening tears. "I wouldn't survive it if you did."

"Dakota." He said my name with such tenderness it melted every defense. His lips brushed against mine, softly, yet so deep. "I love you so much."

I leaned into the kiss, desperate to be closer to him, to feel the certainty of his presence.

"You're everything to me," he whispered, and it seemed to reverberate through every cell of my body, marking me even more deeply as his. He lifted me into his arms and carried me to our bedroom, leaving the diner untouched and the candle burning in the middle of the table. But it didn't even phase me. The only thing that mattered in that moment was him and the way he completely consumed me.

CHAPTER 37
February 15, 10:24 a.m.

TIM

I sat at my desk in the bustling precinct, surrounded by the low hum of voices and ringing phones. My focus was on the Mendez file, determined to find any connection between Victor and the Brinnon house. My mind flashed to Dakota last night and her honest vulnerability with me. I didn't think it was possible, but I fell deeper in love with her in that moment as she confessed how much she loved me. How much she feared that she would lose me. I understood that fear all too well. For years, while she had been consumed by her addiction, fear had been my constant companion.

Her confession only strengthened my resolve to take down Mendez. To make our world more safe. Sweat beaded on my forehead as I poured over every detail for the tenth time that day, my mind tirelessly circling around the anonymous tip from the distorted voice on the phone. The puzzle taunted me, a maddening enigma that refused to be solved.

But it wasn't just the tip that bothered me. It was the house itself—a quaint little cottage in a small town like Brinnon seemed like an unlikely base for Victor's criminal activities. And why had this mystery informant chosen to reveal it to me? Was it all just some elaborate ploy to throw me off track?

Determined to get answers, I had Ramirez interrogate the only lead we had—Ethan Jones—this time alone. From behind a one-way mirror, I watched as Ramirez slid a photograph of the house across the table towards him. As soon as Ethan saw it, a flicker of surprise and fear crossed his eyes before he quickly masked it with a steely expression. It was as if a curtain had been drawn over him, hiding whatever secret knowledge he possessed.

"I've never seen that place before," Ethan replied coolly, leaning back in his chair and crossing his arms over his chest in defiance. "You're barking up the wrong tree, Detective."

My jaw clenched in frustration as Ramirez continued to grill him for another twenty minutes, but it was no use. Ethan remained as tight-lipped as ever. However, his initial reaction was enough to keep me pursuing this lead.

As I delved deeper into Victor's file again, something clicked in my mind, and I couldn't believe I hadn't thought of it sooner. My fingers moved quickly as I typed "Jefferson County assessor's records" into the search engine, eager to uncover any new information.

The website loaded and I navigated to the page for the property in question. The first few pages displayed basic details, but it was the last page that truly caught my attention. There, in black and white, was the name of the legal owner—Miguel Rodriguez.

"Miguel Rodriguez," I repeated his name, a sense of familiarity stirring inside me. But where had I heard that name before? My mind raced, sifting through past cases and memories in an attempt to make a connection.

Finally, I turned to my computer and typed his name into the database. My fingers tapped against the desk with impatience as I waited for the search results to load.

"Come on, come on," I muttered under my breath, urging the screen to reveal its secrets faster. Finally, the results appeared, and I leaned in closer to scan them. And there it was—an arrest record from eight years ago. Rodriguez had been caught with over two ounces of meth and charged with intent to sell. Despite this, he only served five years, getting released early due to a technicality.

I couldn't believe it. Miguel Rodriguez, released early, and now possibly tied to Victor Mandez. The puzzle pieces were starting to fit together. A rush of adrenaline surged through me as a memory clicked into place—Captain Simmons had led that case several years before I joined the force. I could still recall how furious he had been when Rodriguez got out early. He would definitely want to see this new information.

As I printed off the property details, I snagged the Mendez file and beelined it to Captian Simmons's office. His door was slightly ajar, revealing a dimly lit room with a single beam of sunlight casting shadows across his desk. He sat hunched over his computer screen, his grizzled jaw tight with focus. I knocked on the door.

"Officer Moore," he said in a curt tone, all business. "What can I do for you?"

I stepped forward, my hand gripping the property report along with the file. "I have something that I think you're going to want to see."

Captian Simmons narrowed his eyes, taking in the urgency in my voice. He motioned for me to come closer, gesturing for me to sit. "What is it, Moore?"

I took a deep breath, trying to gather my thoughts before I spoke. "The other day, I received an anonymous phone call with a tip regarding the Mendez case."

"An anonymous call?" he asked with a raised eyebrow.

"At first, I wasn't sure about it. Ramirez and I checked out the house. It looked squeaky clean, but there was a nagging sense in my gut that told me to keep digging, and this is what I found." I placed the property report on his desk, making sure he had a clear view of it. "The legal owner of the Brinnon house is listed as Miguel Rodriguez."

"Miguel Rodriguez?" Simmons grabbed his reading glasses from his desk and studied the paper intently, his jaw setting with determination. As he scanned the report, his fingers traced over the name. "Miguel Rodriguez. Damn. That's a blast from the past," he muttered, letting out a low whistle.

Simmons sat back in his chair, the well-worn leather creaking under his weight. He looked at me with a newfound seriousness in his demeanor. He steepled his fingers, carefully considering the information. "You know, Moore, Rodriguez was supposed to be in prison for the better part of a decade. But he got out early on a technicality."

I nodded, eyebrows knitted together in a firm line. "Sir, between the anonymous call and Rodriguez's possible connection to Mendez, I believe we should start surveillance at this address and get to the bottom of it."

Simmons gave me a thoughtful look, his fingers still steepled together. The silence in the room was deep enough that I could his computer buzz. After a minute or two, he finally broke it, letting out a deep breath. "That's quite a leap, Moore. You're aware of the resources that it takes. It's not just overtime; it's paperwork, manpower, strained budgets, stretched teams. Are you certain this is necessary based on an anonymous tip and mere property ownership?"

I braced myself for his questioning, knowing he was right. Surveillance was a big step, but the stakes were equally high. I wasn't here for the paycheck or paperwork—I was here for justice, to protect our community from criminals like Rodriguez and Mendez. To keep loved ones safe.

"With all due respect, sir, I do." I met his gaze head-on. "I wouldn't have suggested it if I didn't think it was crucial. This case goes beyond just drug-related crimes."

He rolled his glasses between thumb and forefinger, a thoughtful frown creasing his forehead.

"I'm talking about lives here, sir." Dakota came before my vision then and everything she suffered because of people like Mendez and Rodrigez. "It's about ruined lives and a circle of destruction that doesn't stop with him."

Simmons watched me silently. I could almost see the gears turning in his head, weighing my words against the mountain of responsibilities we already had. The seconds ticked on, an eternity in the pressure-cooker atmosphere of the cluttered room. Finally, he sighed. "I don't know, Officer Moore... Do you understand the kind of danger you're walking into? Rodriguez...he's no run-of-the-mill crook. He's a shark in a sea. I knew that years ago when I nailed him the first time."

My stomach twisted at his question. Of course, I knew. "Look at these." I pulled out photographs from the Mendez case file—snapshots of trembling women, emaciated children, and hollow-eyed men—victims of this deadly game hidden behind the veil of suburbia. One by one, I laid them out on his desk.

He picked up each photograph with care, studying them intently, his expression growing wearier with each one.

"These aren't just names on a page. They're human beings with lives and families. They deserve our very best—even if it means putting ourselves on the line."

Simmons' gaze eventually moved from the photos back to me, a silent understanding passing between us. He knew I wasn't just talking out of idealism. I was driven by the raw, grim reality of the job. After a moment that hung in the air like a charged cloud, he nodded almost imperceptibly.

"Alright," Simmons said. "Set up your surveillance. But, Moore, do it by the book. We can't afford slip-ups—not with Rodriguez."

I felt a victorious surge within me, but it was tempered by an acute awareness of the gravity of his concession. "Thank you, sir."

Simmons reached for his phone with a sigh that spoke of battles past and those yet to come. "I'll call in some favors, get you the equipment you need. But keep me informed, Moore. Every step of the way." "Understood." I gathered the photos and slipped them into the file, their images burned into my memory, a haunting motivation.

As I stepped out of Simmons' office, I could feel the weight of the task ahead settling firmly on my shoulders. The air in the hallway seemed lighter, less oppressive, but it did nothing to ease the knots in my stomach. A surveillance operation on Rodriguez wasn't just another stakeout. It was a chess game where humans were the pawns and the board was littered with traps.

CHAPTER 38

February 20, 7:25 p.m.

DAKOTA

The sun dipped low on the horizon, casting a warm orange glow over the highway as I drove through the outskirts of Olympia. It was hard to believe an entire week had passed since our time in Ocean Shores. And over two weeks since I'd heard a word from Justin and Avery. Each day slipped by quickly, consumed by work and errands, but the quiet moments brought a nagging fear. Would they ask me to do something else for them? Something worse? Yet with each passing day, their absence lulled me into a false sense of security.

Maybe it was just a one-time thing. Just one measly drop and in their minds, whatever debt I owed them was paid in full. Probably wishful thinking, but lately, I'd felt more hopeful.

My phone dinged as I pulled into the parking lot of the Cascadia Grille. I grabbed it from the cup holder and glanced at the screen. It was a text from Tamara. *I got us a table and ordered us an appetizer. I'm starved.*

I quickly parked the car and hurried inside, not wanting to keep Tamara waiting. She had called mid-week and told me that even though we'd seen each other last weekend, she could really use some sister time. With everything Tamara had done for me, there was no way I could refuse her. And if I was being honest, I could use a bit more sister time in my life too. Besides, with Tim working nights, I didn't have much else going on.

As soon as I stepped inside the Cascadia Grille, a warm and savory aroma wafted from the kitchen and filled my senses. The sizzle of steaks on the grill, and the creamy scent of mashed potatoes mingling together made my mouth water.

Spotting Tamara at a booth by the window, with her phone to her ear, I paused at the entrance. She was deep in conversation, her lips drawn into a tight line, her forehead creased with worry.

I weaved through the bustling crowd of families, couples, and friends gathered around their meals. Upon reaching the table, I took a seat across from her, just as she was ending her call. "Keep me posted," she said and paused for a moment. "Love you too, bro."

She hung up, her hand lingering on her phone as though she was reluctant to let it go. Her worried gaze met mine across the table, and I felt a knot tighten in my stomach.

"You okay, sis?"

"Yeah." She sighed, rubbing her forehead. "That was Josiah. He's been talking to Dad, trying to help him stay accountable with getting sober. But he got a call from Mom today..." Tamara trailed off, and she looked at her hands, twisting her wedding band on her finger. I felt a pang of sympathy for her; she was always looking out for others, even when it threatened to break her.

"Mom keeps finding empty booze bottles hidden around the house," she finally continued. Her eyes were steady on her hands, the diamond of her wedding band catching the low light of the restaurant. "She's scared ... and honestly, so am I."

"Dad's a fighter, Tamara," I said firmly, the words more for me than for her. "You know how he is. He's stubborn, and that stubbornness will see him through this. He's overcome so much already."

"You're right," she said with a half-smile, but I could still feel her doubt. Or maybe that was just my own. I knew how deep addiction ran through our family... Hopefully, Dad would find the same strength I had to fight that vicious demon.

"I just don't want to lose him." The words tumbled out in a vulnerable whisper, her usual strength momentarily eclipsed by the fear of our father's mortality.

I reached across the table and took both her hands in mine, giving them a reassuring squeeze.

A waitress approached with mozzarella sticks, offering a brief distraction from our heavy conversation. She nodded at us, her notepad ready in hand. "What can I get you ladies?"

Tamara eyed the menu, running a hand over her swollen belly before settling on the chicken salad. I was not as decisive, my eyes skimming over the list of sandwiches and sides. "I'll have the club sandwich with fries, please."

The waitress scribbled down our order and moved away, disappearing into the kitchen.

As the waitress retreated, Tamara grabbed a mozzarella stick and dipped it in the marinara sauce. "Josiah has been a real support over the last few weeks, but he can only do so much being so far away."

I nodded, wishing I hadn't been so consumed with my own problems that I hadn't been there for her more.

"Between Dad's failing liver and Nathan's failing marriage, it's just a lot to handle," Tamara whispered.

I leaned in, my heart aching for her. "I'm so sorry, sis," I said sincerely. "How can I help?"

"You being here helps. Thanks for meeting me tonight. Sorry for being so heavy."

I shook my head. "Never have to apologize for needing support. You've been there for me too many times to count. Being here is the least I could do."

She gave me a wobbly smile, her expression reflecting gratitude and relief.

Our food arrived, breaking our emotional exchange. The waitress set our plates on the table with a soft clatter, the aroma of freshly grilled chicken and crispy bacon filling the air around us.

Tamara focused on her salad, stirring the mixture of lettuce, grilled chicken and croutons absent-mindedly. "So how has your week been?" she asked, her tone light as she tried to shift the atmosphere to a more positive side.

I thought about Valentine's Day with Tim and despite the recent setbacks, our relationship had grown deeper. I found myself opening up to him in ways I hadn't thought possible.

"I've been...good," I replied, grabbing a fry and twirling it in the pool of ketchup on my plate.

She tilted her head to the side and raised an eyebrow. "Just... good?" she probed, the mischievous twinkle in her features, reminding me so much of Nathan.

I laughed softly, my attention drawn to a speck of ketchup on my thumb. "Better than I ever thought possible..."

She nodded knowingly. "I'm glad, Dakota. Have you thought any more about your wedding details?"

My cheeks warmed as a smile crept up my face, thinking about how I'd grown in my capacity to love him right. I had always thought if we did get married, it would be at a courthouse, but I never really thought about what he wanted. I would never be able to bear a large wedding, but perhaps a small ceremony in our backyard, surrounded by our families. "Well," I said, finally sorting out my thoughts. "I'm warming to a small ceremony."

"Really?" Tamara's eyes sparkled with delight, the weight of our earlier conversation momentarily forgotten. "That's wonderful, Dakota!"

I laughed at her enthusiasm and shrugged. "Well, we haven't planned anything yet. But yeah, I think..." I thought about my future with Tim, nestled comfortably in the small haven we'd created together. "I think a small ceremony at home, surrounded by our family, would be perfect for us."

Tamara's grin was infectious, and I found myself returning it full measure.

"It sounds absolutely beautiful," she said dreamily. "Do you think you'll wear white?"

My nose scrunched in distaste at the thought of a traditional wedding gown. "Oh, definitely not," I declared with a chuckle. "I was actually thinking a simple sundress, something light and airy. Maybe even with some color to it."

"That would be perfect," she said, delight filling her voice. "With the sun setting behind you two as you say your vows? It would be such a beautiful moment to capture!"

I laughed out loud at her excitement. "Girl, I think you're more excited for my wedding than I am."

Tamara shrugged. "What can I say? I'm a hopeless romantic."

We both chuckled at that, the tension melting away as we fell into lighthearted banter about wedding plans and Tamara's over-the-top ideas for decorations. We were still laughing when our server came to take our empty plates.

We relaxed in our booth, cradling warm cups of decaf coffee and allowing the hum of conversation around us to blend into the background. I glanced at Tamara, her dark hair haloed by the soft lighting of the restaurant. Her face was lit up with joy as she remembered past moments of family celebrations and shared stories about Lillie's latest antics. The cloud of worry that had hung over her earlier seemed to lift slightly in the face of shared memories and anticipation for the future.

Even as we were lost in recollections and laughter, I couldn't help but feel the echo of our earlier conversation. The quiet undercurrent of worry had receded, yet it remained in the set of her shoulders, in the fleeting shadows behind her eyes. I knew the scales were now teetering on a precarious balance—our shared hopefulness tugging on one end and the unsaid fears weighing on the other.

"I should head home," Tamara finally said, her voice soft against the hush that had fallen over the diner.

"Duty calls?" I asked with a teasing smile.

She laughed, but there was a tiredness to it that had not been there before. "More like pillow calls," she corrected, wrapping her scarf around her neck. "It's past my bedtime."

I watched as she left, waving at me through the glass window before disappearing into the night. I sat alone in the restaurant for a few more moments, my thoughts slowly circling back to the wedding.

A wedding at home—it was certainly unlike me but it felt... right. A deep sense of peace washed over me at the thought of celebrating our union in a place that symbolized us so well. The quiet, intimate space where we cooked together on weekends, argued over silly things and made up later in the warmth of our shared bed, laughed and cried and loved—our little world steeped in memories and comfort.

CHAPTER 39

February 20, 6:27 p.m.

TIM

The unmarked van glided smoothly into position, the purr of its engine barely audible over the sound of rain tapping against the car windows. My partner and I parked across from the Rodrigez house, nestled on a quiet, dimly lit street in Brinnon. A knot of tension formed in my stomach as we settled into our stakeout, the distant rumble of thunder adding to the growing unease that hung in the air. Despite having done this countless times before, a feeling lingered that tonight was different—that something big was about to happen. And we needed to be ready for it.

"This place looks like the Waltons reside here," Ramirez said with a small laugh, peering through the rain-streaked windshield.

"Right?" I chuckled. "But who knew what creepy stuff really happened at the Waltons behind closed doors?"

"In this day and age, you never freaking know," Ramirez said, her chuckle dying down to a murmur. She pulled out her binoculars and scanned the house. "Let's just hope we can catch these scumbags tonight." She began unpacking our surveillance equipment with swift efficiency while I searched for any hint of suspicious activity in the area. The rain continued to fall steadily, creating an eerie soundtrack to our mission.

"Agreed."

With that, I reached into the bag at my feet, the warmth and enticing scent of freshly grilled burgers offering a brief but welcome distraction from the task at hand. "Dinner time," I announced, passing one of the parcels to Ramirez. Despite the tension in the air, there was something comforting about this shared routine.

She accepted it with a grateful nod, peeling away the wrapper to reveal a perfectly assembled beef patty, crowned with melting cheese and sandwiched between two fluffy buns.

"You know," she began thoughtfully, taking a bite and letting out a satisfied sigh, "this reminds me of that one time in Port Townsend. Remember?"

"Ah...the meth lab debacle," I said with a wry grin.

She laughed softly as she nodded. "Yes! That was a complete disaster."

The memory sparked a chuckle between us, a shared moment that thinned the tension in the air. I took my own bite, the taste of the burger filling me: savory grilled meat, sharp cheddar cheese, a tang of pickles that I'd asked them to add.

"We've come a long way since then," I muttered, glancing at the Rodriguez house. It was now completely dark, save for the faint light filtering through the water-streaked windows. There was no telling what awaited us inside that seemingly ordinary suburban home.

"True story," Ramirez said, raising her burger in a toast before taking another hearty bite.

When our meal was finished, I took out my coursebooks from the backpack I had brought along. It would be hard to see with the low light from the street lamp, but I'd make it work. "Mind if I get a little studying done?" I asked Ramirez, pulling out the one with a vibrant cover titled *Restorative Justice*.

Ramirez threw a glance at my direction. "Restorative Justice? I remember that class."

"Yeah? What did you think?"

A thoughtful expression lingered on her face. "It's tough, ya know. I get the concept and think that our current system needs some reforming, but sometimes people don't have the will or desire to change," she said, turning her attention to the windows of the Rodriguez house.

"Like trying to reform a terrorist or a serial killer," I replied, flipping the pages.

"Or a psychopathic drug lord," Ramirez said, jerking her head toward the house. "But at the same time, shouldn't we offer a second chance to people who have made serious mistakes and are willing to change?"

"But how can we make that call? Like, how do we know if people really want to change?"

"That's the million-dollar question, isn't it?" She slouched in her seat, her gaze drifting from the house to the open skies above.

I pondered on her words, thinking about Dakota while my eyes remained glued to the textbook. She had made mistakes as well, mistakes that had put her in the crosshairs of dangerous people. But she was trying to change, to make amends for her past. Wasn't that worth something? To me it was.

"I suppose we can only work with what we're given. And hope for the best."

"For the most part, that's all we can do. But you go study, I got this for now."

With that assurance, I found a spot in the corner of our van, leaned against the cold metal wall, and began to study. For the next hour, Ramirez maintained her watchful vigilance over the house while I flipped through the pages, continuing to struggle a bit with the course material.

"Tim," Ramirez said after a while, her voice quiet and serious. "Do you ever wonder if we're making a difference?"

I closed the textbook and took a seat next to her. "Sometimes I do," I admitted my thoughts drifting to Dakota. "But then I think about the people we've helped, the lives we've changed. And I know that what we do matters."

"Even when it feels like we're just putting out fires?" She turned to me, her eyes searching mine for reassurance.

"Especially then," I replied firmly. "Because that's when our actions have the most impact—when we can save someone from getting hurt or protect those who can't protect themselves."

"You're right," she said after a long pause. "It's just hard sometimes, you know? Balancing the job with our personal lives... it takes its toll."

I couldn't argue with that. Ever since Dakota had reentered my life, every day was a balancing act. Between trying to be there for her as she healed and maintaining my job as a cop—it was an uphill battle. But it was a battle that I had willingly chosen to fight. Because for Dakota, I would do anything. I felt something stir inside me at the thought of her, a mixture of worry and a fierce protectiveness I couldn't quite explain.

"Believe me, I know," I said softly, giving her a sympathetic smile. "But at the end of the day, we're making the world a safer place—one case at a time."

She nodded and turned her attention to the house. "I know you're right, but sometimes, especially on nights like this." She motioned toward the quiet house. "It just seems like we're spinning our wheels."

"But that's the thing about our job," I said, following her gaze to the house. Its silhouette, stark against the inky night sky, seemed to hold a thousand dark secrets we were yet to uncover. "It's not always about catching the bad guys or busting drug rings. It's about being there when it counts, even if that means spending countless hours staking out a suburban home."

She was quiet for a moment. "You make it sound so noble."

"Isn't it?" I asked. "We're offering justice and protection, even when it's inconvenient or dangerous for us."

She studied my face for a moment and then nodded. "I guess when you put it that way, it does sound pretty noble."

I grinned at her, trying to lighten the tense atmosphere. "Well,

Ramirez, we're not exactly filing paperwork in an office building. We're out here, making a difference."

She chuckled wryly. "With as slow as things are going tonight, it's as boring as filing paperwork."

"Perhaps," I agreed, "but remember, patience is key in our line of work. Plus, can you imagine us being office drones? No adrenaline rush, no excitement."

She smirked and shook her head, looking back out the window. "Not a chance. I'd go stir-crazy within a week."

I laughed, knowing full well how true that was. Carla Ramirez thrived on the excitement and unpredictability of our job. We both did.

The hours rolled by as we watched the house, exchanging theories about the Rodriguez family and their possible involvements in the underground drug trade. The night was still and quiet, save for our banter and the occasional hooting of an owl nearby. We kep vigilance, scanning the surrounding area for any signs of suspicious activity.

"At least the weather is nice," Ramirez said, cracking a small smile as the rain pelted against the windshield. Her hand stretched out to the dashboard, double-checking the radio we had set to chatter with base.

"Right?" I replied, glancing towards the sky. The rain was a steady shower, each drop hitting the van roof with a soft drumming rhythm. It was soothing, almost peaceful—a sharp contrast to the tension-filled environment inside my mind.

"Hope we're not out here all night," Carla murmured, her words barely piercing the symphony of raindrops. Her gaze remained fixed on the house, darting around vigilantly, catching every shadow and rustle behind the curtain.

"Yeah, here's hoping," I said as an unexplainable sense of unease crept over me. Something was not right about this whole situation.

We fell into silence again, lost in our thoughts and bracing ourselves for another extended length of surveillance. As much as

I had tried to convince Carla earlier about the nobility of our job, there were moments, like this, when the tediousness of it truly gnawed at me. But I remained steadfast, counting every droplet of rain that hit the window as a reminder of my commitment to justice and peace. As the evening drug on, everything continued to be obnoxiously quiet. By the time our replacement team showed up, I began to think that my anonymous tip was nothing more than Mendez and Rodrigez yanking my chain. Only time would tell, but time never seemed to be on my side.

CHAPTER 40

February 22, 10:32 a.m.

DAKOTA

Tim and I were nestled into the deep cushions of our old couch, legs entwined, the scent of freshly brewed coffee mingling with the faint musk of his cologne. Tim's heartbeat was a steady rhythm against my ear, a reminder that I was here, anchored in a reality far kinder than any I had known before.

I'd had the same nightmare last night—the one of me being forced to relapse—but being here in Tim's arms on our rare day off together was enough to chase the fear away. I looked up at him. His brown eyes were soft with affection, yet always alert, always vigilant. It was the cop in him, the guardian who never truly rested.

His fingers caressed a path down my arm, sending goosebumps spiraling outward, in tiny ripples of sensation against my skin.

"Dakota," he said, his voice simmering with warmth.

"Yes?" The word caught in my throat, a soft sigh against the quiet sounds of the morning.

"Remember when we were kids," he said, a hint of nostalgia creeping into his tone. "And we would build forts out of blankets and pillows? We swore they were impenetrable."

I couldn't help but smile at the memory, my mind conjuring

images of our younger selves huddled under a chaotic fortress of sheets and cushions, our giggles echoing in the makeshift canopy. "Yeah, and then your mom came in with snacks, and we pretended she was the invading army."

"Best invasion ever." He chuckled, his chest rumbling beneath me.

"Right," I agreed, my laughter mingling with his.

I nuzzled deeper into his chest, remembering those times during our childhood. Those were the times I felt the most safe, most shielded from the world that would later prove to be so cruel and relentless.

"Back then, I thought nothing could ever hurt us in there," I whispered, the last words catching in my throat, a rising wave of emotion threatening to break free. I thought of the nightmare from last night. Avery's sick laughter as he blew the smoke from the glass pipe in my mouth.

Tim's arm tightened around me, as if trying to shield me from my own thoughts. "Nothing can hurt us here either, Dakota. I'm right here. Always."

His reassurance was a tangible thing, wrapping around me like the throw blanket nestled on our laps. His warmth seeped into my skin, and for a moment, the world outside our small cocoon ceased to exist.

I clung to him, letting his familiar scent and faint hint of coffee grounds comfort me. Tim's hand moved in slow, soothing circles on my skin as he held me close. No words were needed in these quiet moments together. The cadence of our breathing fell into sync, and time seemed to slow.

The stillness of our shared morning broke with the sudden chime of Tim's watch. He glanced at it, then at me. "Dakota," he said with a hint of mischief. "How do you feel about a little adventure today?"

"Adventure?" I questioned, my brows knitting together in confusion.

"Yes." He pulled away from me, flashing a smile that reminded me of a younger Tim. The one who I used to run free with in the woods behind the trailer park. "Something... unexpected awaits."

As he disappeared down the hallway, I sat motionless for a moment, the fabric of the couch still warm from where he'd been. A part of me wanted to stay with him here in the comfort of our home together all day. He seemed so excited though ... I stood and padded toward the bedroom, curiosity pushing me forward.

The wooden floorboards felt cool under my bare feet as I walked. I rifled through my closet, selecting a comfortable pair of jeans and a soft sweater. "Where are we going?"

"Port Townsend," Tim announced from the other side of the door, his voice holding a note of excitement that made me pause mid-button on my jeans. "That's all I'm saying for now."

"Tim..." My protest died on my lips as I considered the town —a place etched with history, sea salt in the air, and a picturesque beauty that could almost make one forget their demons.

Within minutes, we were heading out the door and then driving out of our driveway. As we drove, the landscape transformed the greens, making them more vibrant, and the sky took on a deeper shade of blue. Tim's hand found mine across the center console, his fingers wrapping around mine in a gentle yet firm grip.

I watched the trees blur past as the road stretched out before us, a ribbon tying together the present and an unforeseen destination. "Tim, why all the secrecy?"

His gaze flickered to mine, then back onto the road. "Because"—he paused, his lips curling into a crooked grin —"Sometimes the most beautiful moments in life come wrapped in surprise."

I laughed despite myself. His words, his tone, his grip on my hand—it was all so adorably Tim.

I looked over at him, his profile lit by the dappled sunlight filtering through the trees. His eyes were steady on the road, but he spared a quick glance towards me, his smile reassuring.

We drove in comfortable silence, the hum of the engine

providing a steady soundtrack for our journey. Soon the lush greens began to fade into the rich blues and grays of Port Townsend. Its rustic buildings, weathered by salt and time, hinted at stories from another era. We drove through the quaint town center, dotted with boutique shops and eateries that exuded an old-world charm. The hustle bustle of the townsfolk carrying about their daily tasks lent a certain vibrancy to the otherwise serene environment. We rounded a corner, went up a hill and then Tim pulled in front of The Uptown Theater.

I glanced at Tim, my brow furrowed in bewilderment. "Are we... watching a movie?" My voice was tinged with incredulity, the idea too mundane for the secrecy and promised adventure.

"Something like that." He exited the car and walked around it to open my door for me. "My lady," he said with a bow, reaching to help me out of the car.

I laughed and took hold of his hand. "You're being really weird."

His lips twitched as he led me to the sidewalk. The air was crisp, the scent of sea salt weaving through the streets. He opened the theater door for me and gave me a wide gesture to go inside, keeping that same silly smirk on his handsome face.

The lobby was steeped in shadows, the silence punctuated by the soft hum of anticipation that seemed to resonate from the walls themselves. Posters of bygone films adorned the space, their colors muted but their stories alive, whispering to me of heroes and heartbreak—a backdrop far removed from the starkness of my own narrative.

"Okay, Tim. Time to spill it. What in the world are we doing here?"

"Well," he said with a chuckle, pulling me in close to him. "I thought we could end our marathon the right way," he said and then opened the door he had led me to. The room unfolded into a private sanctuary, a projector ready to illuminate the darkness. And there, on the screen, awaited the title crawl of *Return of the Jedi*, the final episode of our childhood saga.

"Tim, you didn't..." My words trailed off as the realization sank in.

"I did," he said, pride lacing his voice.

A laugh bubbled up within me, mingling with the tears that pricked my eyes. It was absurd, wonderful, and utterly unexpected.

"Thank you," I whispered, allowing the moment to envelop me in its warmth.

The room dimmed to a hushed reverence as we sat, and the iconic fanfare burst forth. I leaned into Tim's side, my senses sharpened by the larger-than-life images flickering across the screen. The familiar scroll of yellow text receded into the starry abyss, grounding me in a narrative etched into my very soul.

"I always loved how they just threw you right into the action," Tim whispered, his breath warm against my ear.

"Like life," I murmured back, "no time for hesitation."

My gaze followed the plight of the heroes with an intensity I hadn't felt in years. Each quip from Han Solo drew a chuckle from deep within me, and Leia's unwavering strength filled me with a sense of kinship and aspiration. I marveled at their resilience, these lighter characters who refused to be extinguished by the darkness that swirled around them.

I watched as Skywalker faced the Emperor, the ultimate test not just of his power but of his character. My own struggles, though galaxies apart, resonated with the tension on the screen. Redemption wasn't just for fallen Jedi—it was for people like me too, facing the shadows of their past.

There was a palpable triumph when Vader—no, Anakin—redeemed himself. A tear escaped, tracing a hot path down my cheek. "Maybe there's hope for everyone," I whispered more to myself than to Tim.

"Always," he affirmed, his thumb brushing away the tear.

As the Ewoks celebrated and the ghosts of Jedi past appeared, offering silent benediction to the living, I found myself captivated by the idea that this could indeed be the pinnacle of the saga.

"Tim... I think this might actually be my favorite," I confessed, my words dancing on the edge of sacrilege given my longstanding allegiance to *Revenge of the Sith*.

"Really?" His eyebrows arched in playful surprise.

"Really. There's something about how it all comes together—the battles, the growth, the closure..." My voice trailed off as I grappled with the realization that perhaps what I craved most was that same sense of completion.

"Endings are important," he said, eyes not leaving the screen. "They give meaning to the journey."

"Exactly," I agreed, feeling the pull of resolution in my own life—a closing of chapters long left open.

As the final credits rolled, the soft glow of the projector light held us in a timeless embrace. The theater slowly brightened, coaxing us to reality, but we lingered in our seats, reluctant to sever the connection to the universe we had just inhabited.

"That's you, Coda. Like my nickname for you implies, I know you are the ending of many things in your family line. You overcoming what you have will end the pain of future generations," he said as he held my gaze.

"Thank you, Tim," I said again, this time with the weight of a deeper understanding pressing against the words. "For sharing this with me—for bringing me back here."

"Anytime, Dakota. Anytime." He smiled, and together we rose and headed out to the car.

"Tim," I ventured, my voice a soft murmur against the vacuum of the ending credits. "Do you think there could ever be more? More stories?" The possibility of extending the journey tugged at me—a craving for more of this magic that had somehow stitched together the torn pieces of my past.

He turned toward me. "More movies?" he asked, and there was a note of caution in his voice, as if even voicing the thought might fracture the perfection of what we'd witnessed.

"I mean, it feels... unfinished, doesn't it? Like there's more to tell." My hands fidgeted with the frayed edge of my sleeve as I waited for his response.

Tim's hand found mine, stilling the restless motion. "Dakota," he said, his tone gentle yet resolute, "sometimes the most powerful thing a story can do is end."

"But just think of the possibilities," I pressed, leaning into the warmth of his touch. "New adventures, new characters."

"Sure, there are possibilities," he conceded as we stepped outside. "I would like to see if they could find a way to balance the force, like merging the best parts of the dark side with the light side."

"You mean balancing evil with good?"

"No no, not like that. I have been thinking about this for a while. I don't really see the dark side as evil, but instead a bunch of people full of intense emotions with no way to process them. And the stoic self-righteous Jedis on the light side aren't helping one bit. They seem afraid of emotions, afraid of the mess, so they just say stupid things like 'fear leads to the dark side.' But what if it doesn't have to? What if they could have helped people like Anakin process through his fear and pain instead of just abandoning him? I'm not so sure he would have chosen the dark side."

"I like that idea," I replied, intrigued. "A lot actually."

Tim laughed as he held the opened car door. "Spoken like a true Star Wars nerd."

"You really do bring out my dork side." I chuckled and slipped into the car.

"That's why you love me. Join me on the dorkside," he teased, shutting the car door gently behind me. I rolled my eyes as he jogged around to the driver's side and slid into the seat beside me.

My focus stayed on the theater as we drove away. "It's just hard when a good story ends. It's hard to say goodbye, you know? To something that feels like a part of you."

"Goodbyes are tough," Tim said, keeping his gaze steady on the road. "But remember, every ending is a chance for a new beginning. Our own story isn't written in opening crawls or bounded by trilogies. We get to choose the next chapter."

I let that sink in, his words bringing comfort. I stared out the window as the city lights blurred past, lost in thought. Tim was right; we had the power to write our own stories, carve our path— our destiny.

"Thanks, Tim," I said, a smile breaking through as I envisioned our own saga continuing outside the confines of the theater, the joy and the pain, the laughter and the tears, every single moment that had defined us paving the way for everything yet to come.

CHAPTER 41

March 1, 1:26 p.m.

TAMARA

The scent of lemon-infused polish wafted through the air as I wiped it over the mahogany coffee table, erasing dust motes that danced in the slanted beams of afternoon sunlight. My movements were rhythmic, a domestic dance to the soundtrack of Lillie's giggles and the cheerful tunes emanating from the television where animated vegetables reenacted biblical stories.

"Mama, peas sing!" Lillie squealed, her tiny fingers pointing at the screen where a tomato and cucumber bopped in unison.

I set the cloth on the counter, my heart swelling with a soft warmth. "Alright, sweetie," I replied, my voice joining the melodic chorus of "Veggie Tales." "God is bigger than the boogeyman."

Lillie clapped her hands, her curly hair bouncing as she mimicked the movements of her favorite characters. I marveled at her innocence, how her world was so small and pure, encapsulated within these four walls where we could shut out the shadows lurking beyond.

My gaze drifted across our living room, landing on the family photos that lined the mantle. Each frame was a captured moment, a snippet of time where smiles were genuine, and eyes sparkled without the weight of secrets or sorrow. My brother Josiah and Lindsay, his wife with their precious daughter Mia, donned in matching Christmas sweaters, looked at the camera with beaming smiles. Then Nathan and Amanda with their beautiful family of three, their expression filled with joy and pride. I sighed, thumbing the edge of the wooden frame and hoping things were going better for Nathan at home. The tension between him and Amanda had been palpable the last time we'd seen them.

Lillie sang, punctuating her song with a triumphant stomp of her little foot. Her laughter pierced through the veil of my encroaching thoughts, tethering me to the present.

"Very good, baby girl," I praised and scooped her into my arms. Her joy was infectious, banishing the shadows from my mind as I twirled her around, making her squeal with delight. For a moment, the worries of health issues and divorce dimmed into the background, dissipating under the golden glow of Lillie's laughter. Her innocence was pure armor, impervious to the world's perils.

I nestled her against my shoulder, swaying gently back and forth as we hummed together in unison.

Out the front window, Joe approached the front door, his normally light countenance darkened and weighed down. What was wrong with him?

The front door creaked open, and Joe stepped into the room, closing the door behind him with an intentional softness that seemed out of place.

His hazel eyes met mine, a storm brewing in their depths. His jaw was tight, the tension evident in the way he held himself. My heart pounded hard, the rhythm quickening with apprehension. Putting Lillie gently down, I moved towards him.

"Joe?" I said, trying to steady my voice, to keep it light. "You're home early."

"Tamara, we need to talk," Joe said, his voice measured but heavy, as if each word carried a weight, he wished he didn't have to bear. Lillie noticed the tension and clung to my leg. I bent down to lift her into my arms, her small body a comforting warmth against the cold dread that was starting to settle in my stomach.

Joe's gaze flicked to Lillie before returning to me, his expression pained. The sight of him—so often my rock in the storm—now as troubled as a tempest was deeply unsettling.

I nodded, swallowing hard. "Is everything okay?" The question felt foolish even as it left my lips, because nothing about his entrance spoke of 'okay.'

"Let's go to the kitchen," he suggested, a clear sign that whatever news he carried wasn't meant for little ears. Nodding, I found a new episode of Lillie's favorite cartoon and placed her on the couch, tucking a soft blanket around her.

Once she was settled, I followed Joe into the kitchen. "What is it, Joe?" I asked as he leaned against the counter. The hum of the refrigerator became oddly deafening, filling the silence as I waited for him to speak.

"It's about Nathan... and Amanda," he finally began, his eyes not meeting mine. He leaned heavily against the countertop as though the burden of his next words might topple him. "I think she's having an affair."

"What?" The word slipped out of my mouth like a gasp, a harsh sound against the quiet hum of the kitchen. My hands found the edge of the counter, seeking something solid in a suddenly shifting world. An affair? Nathan's Amanda? My sweet sister-in-law, who felt more like a sister to me than my brother's wife.

"Are you sure?" I pressed, my voice shaking with disbelief vying with a surge of protectiveness for my younger brother. Nathan, with his easy laughter and love that he wore so openly for Amanda. How could this be? I needed him to be wrong, to have misunderstood something.

Joe let out a long, slow exhale. "I saw her with another man. It didn't look innocent, Tamara." His voice, usually so steady and sure, wavered with a rawness that tugged at my heart. All I could do was gape at him in shock. Poor Nathan. What would this do to him? How would our family weather such a betrayal?

"Tamara?" Joe's hand reached out and brushed against mine.

"Sorry, I just..." The sentence trailed off, unfinished. I clasped his hand to draw strength from its familiarity. A million questions buzzed at the edges of my consciousness, but for now, they remained unvoiced. Right now, all I could do was stand there, holding onto Joe, bracing for the aftershocks of this revelation.

The cheerful chirping of "Veggie Tales" seemed distant now, an ironic soundtrack to the heavy silence that held Joe and me captive. Lillie gave a delighted giggle from the other room, jarring against the somber undertone of our conversation.

"Joe," I whispered, my voice barely above the hum of the television. "Tell me everything. What did you see?"

He hesitated before drawing in a deep breath. "This afternoon in Olympia, after shopping for the stuff I needed for the B&B, I stopped by Anthony's Homeport Restaurant for lunch and there she was with some guy. They were tucked away in a corner booth, far from prying eyes." He paused, swallowing hard. "His hand covered hers in an intimate gesture, and they seemed deep in conversation. He looked at her like she was the only person in the room. And she stared back at him in the same way."

My heart pounded against my rib cage, each beat echoing Nathan's name. I pictured him, his mischievous smile that could light up a room, now dimmed by shadows of pain and betrayal. "Did they see you?" A sickening knot formed in my stomach at the thought.

"No, I don't think so." His hand found mine again, squeezing gently.

"But what if it's a misunderstanding?" I asked, desperate for any shred of hope. "Maybe he's a friend or a colleague; they might have been talking about work."

"Tamara." He sighed. "I've seen plenty of business meetings, and they never looked like that. It was intimate, personal."

I bit my lip, struggling against the tears threatening to spill. "What are we going to do, Joe?

"I don't know..."

"How can she do this?" My fingers curled into fists, nails

digging into my palms. "She's going to break his heart. I know that Nathan has his issues, but he doesn't deserve this. It will crush him."

"Tamara." Joe's voice cracked with empathy. "I'm so sorry."

I stood motionless, the familiar textures and colors of my living room blurring into insignificance. Lillie's innocent melody from the TV played on, oblivious to the tectonic shifts happening around her.

"Joe, how do we tell Nathan? How do we even begin to break his world apart?" The words were thick with fear and sorrow, weighted with the responsibility of shattering illusions and mending broken hearts.

"I'm honestly not sure, but we need to be careful."

"Of course, careful," I repeated hollowly. The room felt too small, as though the walls were inching closer, suffocating me with the gravity of what lies ahead.

"Joe," I started again, my voice barely an echo, "we should confront Amanda first. Before we take this to Nathan."

He nodded solemnly, his gaze mirroring my own sense of dread. "You're right. But we can't accuse her outright, Tamara. We need to give her a chance to explain herself."

I let out a quiet sigh and hung my head in resignation. Part of me wanted to storm over to their house and demand answers from Amanda, but I knew that Joe was right, as he usually was in these situations. We had to tread with caution. The stakes were too high.

"Tamara?" Joe came close, put his finger under my chin, and pulled my face toward his. "Whatever happens, we'll get through this. Nathan's strong, and he's not alone."

"So, when do we talk to her?" My voice sounded small, vulnerable even, lost in the magnitude of the situation that unfolded before us.

"Soon," he replied with a sigh. "We just need to make sure our hearts are in the right space when we do."

"Okay," I said, a knot twisting in my stomach at his words.

Dealing with this matter delicately was paramount, but we couldn't wait too long either.

From the corner of my eye, I saw Lillie coming toward us, a small frame bouncing with the sort of childlike innocence that usually brought me comfort. But now, it only made me feel more desolate.

I forced a smile as I turned to her, scooping her into my arms.

As I held her close, my fingers running through her soft curls, I whispered another prayer for strength. The unspoken promise of love and protection that a mother makes to her child seemed even more poignant now. My heart ached at the thought of Nathan's world crumbling.

Lillie's chubby hands touched my cheeks that were now wet with tears. I hastily swiped at my tears that had slipped unnoticed down my cheeks. "Mommy's okay, baby. Just a little sad."

I glanced towards Joe, who gave me an understanding nod before turning his attention to Lillie. "Hey, princess," he said, using his usual nickname for her. "How about we go watch some more cartoons?"

She reached for him with bright eyes, and he took her from me.

Joe offered me one last reassuring glance as he balanced Lillie on his hip, her small hand already reaching out to press buttons on the remote.

For a moment, I took in my daughter's innocence as she and Joe played together in front of the TV. Then emotions overtook me, and I headed upstairs for some quiet time. Once inside the sanctuary of my room, I reached for my Bible and my journal and sat on my bed, burdened for my family, not only Nathan and Amanda, but my dad and Dakota too. The past few months and all that had happened swirled around me as I sat and prayed.

I prayed for Nathan to have the strength to withstand whatever blow fate was about to deal him. I prayed for Amanda too, despite the cold anger seeping into my veins.

As I poured my heart out in prayer, I could still hear Lillie's giggles and Joe's comforting voice downstairs, a sweet counterpoint to the bitter storm brewing in my mind. A sense of peace settled over me, as I opened my journal and began to write, chronicling the raw emotions and thoughts swirling inside me. My pen moved swiftly across the page, the ink forming words, sentences, a stream of consciousness that helped to lessen the weight in my heart.

Peace I leave with you, my peace I give unto you.

These words I'd read time and time again from the book of John welled up inside my being, wrapping around me, overwhelming me with a deep feeling of peace.

I wasn't sure what to do with this new information, this awful truth that threatened to tear Nathan's world apart. But it was out of my control. Perhaps there was an explanation—a reason that would make this entire situation less devastating. Or maybe I was just grasping at straws, unwilling to accept the truth that lay bare in front of us. For now, all I could do was trust that God would show me how to navigate through these dark and treacherous waters. I settled into my bed and released this burden to God as I basked in the peace that the Holy Spirit was pouring over me in that moment. I thought of Jesus in the boat with his disciples, asleep in the back while the storm threatened to consume them. In my mind's eye, I joined Jesus in the back of the boat. There wasn't a thing I could do to change the people in my life and the poor decisions they were making, but I could choose to rest my head on my savior's chest and rest in him until the storm passed.

CHAPTER 42

March 1, 2:55 p.m.

DAKOTA

Tim and I both left for work at the same time, a rare occurrence but now that he had been assigned to the night shift, it would happen more frequently. I followed closely behind him as he locked the front door. We strolled side by side to our respective cars, and then he drew me into a warm embrace and gave me a gentle kiss.

"Stay safe out there tonight."

"Always do," he said, pulling away.

I watched him leave the driveway while messing with the radio knobs, searching for a good song to start my workday.

As the glow of his taillights receded, I felt an odd pang in my chest—some sort of foreboding that I couldn't quite place. Turning up the radio, I backed out of the driveway and hit the road. On the way to work, I smoked a cigarette and prepared my mind for another boring day at the covienteint store. I was only halfway done with my smoke when I parked my car behind the store.

As I exited the car, I exhaled rebelliously, the smokey tendrils curling into the air around me. Flicking the remnants of the cigarette onto the gravel below, I watched as the glowing ember died a quick death, much like my enthusiasm for yet another night shift. Coughing lightly, I trudged toward the back entrance of the gas station. The air was cool, carrying the scent of damp earth and petrol, a strangely comforting cocktail of aromas that I had grown accustomed to. I could see Silas, the day shift guy, through the dingy windows, stacking packs of chips and candy bars near the counter.

"Hey, Dakota," He looked up and waved as I walked in, the chime above the door tinkling as it swung open. "You ready for another fun-filled night?"

I rolled my eyes, taking off my coat to hang on the hook by the door. "Oh, you know it," I responded sarcastically.

Silas flashed me a wry smile before gathering his belongings, eager to flee this place and bask in the freedom of his time off. I couldn't say I blamed him. Starting where he left off, I stacked cartons of cigarettes behind the counter.

My shift at the gas station was generally uneventful—mostly locals passing through to buy a six pack or some smokes. Sometimes the occasional drunk would stumble in from Lenny's Bar across the road and make a ruckus, demanding more booze. I'd have to play the part of security, tossing them onto the street while they hollered a string of incoherent profanities. Tonight seemed like it would be another one of those quiet nights, just me and the monotonous whirring of the cash register.

To my surprise, the shift passed quickly, with a steady stream of customers ebbing and flowing. Caffeine seekers, weary travelers, and the occasional local who lingered too long by the snack aisle. As the clock neared the end of my shift, the pace slowed, giving way to a silence that allowed my thoughts to wander. I went through my end of shift routine of cleaning the bathrooms, sweeping and mopping and then finally counting the till. When the clock turned 11:00 pm, I ran to the door, and locked it quickly, then I gathered all the garbage, changed out all the bags and ran to the back door. This one final chore, and I'd be done for the night. I locked the door behind me and turned toward the dumpster. I pitch the first bag into the dumpster and then the second. The roar of an engine cut through the air, sending a surge of fear through me.

My breath hitched as I slowly turned. There, parked with predatory stillness, was the blue Mustang.

"Hey, Dakota," Justin said in a mock friendly voice as he climbed out of the passenger side of the car.

"Damn it!" I cursed under my breath. This couldn't be happening—not now, not when I'd come so far. The familiar sense of dread knotted in my stomach.

Avery stepped out from the shadows as well.

"Long time no see," Avery drawled, his cocky grin.

"Not long enough," I said under my breath as I backed up slowly.

"We have another job for you," Justin continued, the danger in his voice thinly veiled by his casual demeanor.

I straightened up, forcing myself to stand tall despite the pounding in my chest. "No! Absolutely not! I'm done with this little game you're playing,"

Justin's predatory grin stretched wider, a cruel mockery of human warmth. "I thought we made things clear the other night. We own you."

"I don't belong to anyone!" I shot back, clenching my fists and stepping back. "I'm not your pawn anymore."

Avery chuckled darkly, circling me like I was some sort of prey. "Love the spirit, Dakota. It's a shame it'll be broken soon enough." Justin advanced, the silhouette of his bulky figure closing in.

"Go to hell!" I turned to run but found Avery blocking my path, his sinister grin growing wider.

I tried to break free, but he seized my wrist in an iron grip, his fingertips digging cruelly into my flesh.

"Let me go!" I hissed, trying to yank my wrist free, but his grip only tightened. "I'm done!"

Justin locked his large hand around my throat and pushed me against the dumpster. "The hell you are!"

The musty smell of damp garbage filled my nostrils as I gasped for air, my vision starting to blur from the lack of oxygen. "We. Are. Not. Done!" Justin snarled, his breath reeking of stale beer. Each word was emphasized with a sickening thud of my back against the cold metal of the dumpster.

"Go to hell!" I choked out again.

Avery punched me in the rib, knocking the air out of my lungs. "You will do what we say or there will be consequences."

"I'd rather die than be your pawn."

Justin pulled out a switch blade and pressed against my cheekbone. "We would gladly oblige, but first we'd go after your cop boyfriend and hack him to pieces in front of you."

Behind us, a car door slammed. "That's enough." Ricky came across the parking lot and ripped Justin off of me.

Justin stumbled backwards as Ricky loomed over him.

"What do you think you're doing?" Ricky growled, his hands clenched into fists.

"I was just doing what Victor told me to do!" Justin seethed defensively, his gaze darting to the switchblade lying ominously on the ground. Avery stood silently, a smug grin creeping onto his face.

"These were not your orders!" Ricky shouted. "Victor said to get the job done, not to rough her up!" He turned to look at me, concern written all over his face. "Are you alright?"

I nodded but didn't trust myself to speak. The sharp sting of the blade against my cheek had etched itself into my memory, a sick reminder of what these men were capable of.

Avery slipped past Ricky and moved towards the car. "This isn't over, Dakota," he sneered.

I slid down the side of the dumpster, my trembling hands clutching my aching ribs as I forced oxygen into my lungs. Ricky knelt beside me, his brows furrowed with worry.

"Dakota," he started but seemed at a loss for words. "I'm so sorry you got pulled back into this. I hate it. I've tried to go to bat for you, but Victor he's.... Anyway, I'm trying, but we need you to run one more package."

I stared at him, a bitter laugh escaping my lips. "One more package? It's never just one more. This stops now, Ricky!" I snapped, pushing myself off the ground. "I'm out! I can't do this. I can't keep lying to Tim. I will lose him."

Desperation clouded Ricky's expression. "If you don't do this, Victor will put a hit out on Tim."

I felt my stomach drop at his words, the color draining from my face. My pulse pounded in my ears, drowning out the ambient noise of crickets and the faint hum of the gas station's neon signs. They were not threatening just hurting Tim, but actually taking his life.

Ricky's hand found mine, his fingers threading through mine in an attempt at reassurance. "I know it's hard, Dakota. God knows I wish there were another way," he said quietly, honesty radiating from him. "But there isn't. I can't protect Tim if you don't follow Victor's orders."

A wave of nausea hit me as I squeezed my eyes shut, willing the world to stop spinning. My heart pounded against my chest, each beat echoing the same word over and over. Tim. Tim. Tim.

"You know what we are up against," Ricky continued, a solemn note in his voice. "I will do everything I can to help, but right now, we need to do this. Then, we find a way out."

"Okay," I said, feeling a piece of my soul darken. "I'll do it."

The relief that swept through Ricky was painfully palpable. He pulled me into a fierce embrace, murmuring an apology into the crook of my neck. It took every ounce of willpower not to break down right then and there. But I had to stay strong. For Tim, for me.

CHAPTER 43
March 7, 8:36 p.m.

TAMARA

My stomach tightened around the baby growing inside me as I settled into the couch next to Joe, sending a sharp pain through my abdomen. I winced, one hand moving to cradle my swollen belly.

"Are you okay, T?" Joe asked with concern.

I breathed in deep and rubbed my belly until the pain subsided. "It's just a Braxton-Hicks contraction." I assured him. This wasn't my first rodeo. Braxton-Hicks were a normal part of pregnancy. It was just my body getting ready to give birth. This one did seem a bit more intense than others, but I brushed the thought away, attributing it to nerves.

Joe placed a gentle hand on my stomach and leant in, pressing a soft kiss to my forehead. Then brought his face to my stomach and whispered, "Hey, little guy, we're all anxious to meet you, but it's not quite time for you to come yet."

I laughed softly, my free hand coming to rest on his head, fingers threading through his dark hair. "He's got your impatience," I murmured.

Joe chuckled, placing another kiss on my belly before sitting up. He intertwined our hands, his thumb gently stroking over my knuckles.

A knock at the door stole our attention. Joe untangled our hands and rose to answer the door.

Nathan stood there, his dark hair a bit disheveled and pain clouding his features. The usually heart-and-soul-of-the-party Nathan looked like he hadn't had a good night's sleep for days. My heart crashed into my stomach. Six days ago, Joe had seen Amanda with another man. Since then, I'd wanted to talk to him, to tell him, but every time I prayed about it, I felt to wait and trust. Seeing him now, though, with the pain etched deep in his countenance, I was almost positive he knew.

"Hi, Nathan," Joe said and then gestured to him to come in. Then Joe turned his attention to me and I could tell he was thinking the same thing I was. Internally, I prayed for strength, for the right words to say, for a way to help Nathan through this.

"Sorry for just showing up like this," he said, stepping inside. "I just... I didn't know where else to go."

"No need to apologize, Nathan. You're always welcome here." I struggled to stand, my pregnant belly making it difficult. Then I crossed the room and pulled Nathan into my arms and enveloped him in a tight hug. He stiffened at first, but then his shoulders slumped, and he let out a heavy sigh, wrapping his arms around me.

"It feels like everything's falling apart," he admitted as he pulled away.

I gave a sympathetic nod and gestured toward the couch for him to sit down. Joe and I exchanged another look, and I hoped he could sense that I needed him to lead this conversation. I felt lost in the moment. Not knowing what to say or if I should let on if I knew anything.

"Talk to us, Nate," Joe said as Nathan sank onto the couch.

"Amanda and I, we're"—he paused, swallowing hard—"we're done. She...she's leaving me."

A painful silence hung in the room as his words landed with a sobering thud. "Oh, Nathan," I murmured, my voice thick with unshed tears. Taking a seat next to him, I reached for his hand. "I'm so sorry."

Joe placed his hand on his shoulder and gave it a firm squeeze, but he stayed silent, giving him space to share his pain.

"You remember the jar of sand on the mantle from our wedding?" Nathan's voice choked with impending tears. "I told her that as long as those grains of sand remained intertwined in that jar, I would never give up on our vows."

Waves of despair seemed to roll off him. "Then in the middle of our fight, she poured out the sand on the table in the study, and she's been working on separating the sand ever since," he choked out, trying to hold back tears.

"Oh, Nathan," I uttered again.

"I'm trying. God, I've been trying. But it feels like..." His voice cracked on the words as he spoke. "It feels like I'm chasing shadows in the dark."

A painful silence settled once again, the room devoid of all else but the sound of our breaths and Nathan's soft sniffles. I glanced at Joe. His expression reflected a depth of sorrow akin to my own.

"Last night she told me she had an emotional affair," Nathan's voice was a mere whisper, like he was afraid the words would shatter the already fragile space around us. "With Ivy's first-grade teacher."

Wow. I already knew about the affair. But with Ivy's teacher?

Joe breathed out, the lines of his face hardening with empathy. "I'm so sorry, man."

I gave his hand another reassuring squeez. "We're here for you, Nate." My voice was shaky but steady, filled with the assurance that his pain was ours too.

"Nathan," Joe said, his voice firm but kind, "this may seem like an insurmountable mountain now, but remember, life always provides us with the tools we need to ascend our toughest peaks. I won't lie to you. It's going to be hard. But we're here for you." He paused, letting his words sink in, then continued, "And there's something else you need to know. The flames of pain you're experiancing now? They're fierce, and they burn, but they also purify. From their ashes rises a stronger spirit, tempered by heartache."

Nathan's eyes flickered to Joe, a wariness mingling with the raw vulnerability in his gaze.

"I just don't want to lose my family," Nathan whispered, his voice strained as if he were hanging onto the edge of a precipice. "Amanda and what she did. The emotional affair. It hurts like hell, but I'd still be willing to work through things with her, but she seems so damned determined to leave me."

Despite his words, something didn't quite add up. The whole situation felt off, and I struggled to reconcile it with the Amanda I knew.

"This all seems so unlike her. I've only known her for a couple of years, but it simply doesn't fit with who I know she is."

"I know," Nathan said and then buried his face in his hands.

"I can't even imagine how much this hurts," I said, placing my hand on his back. "But have you tried seeing it from Amanda's perspective? Maybe she feels lost too."

"Lost?" He looked at me.

"Yes," I responded gently. "Lost. Because people don't just wake up one day and decide to rip their family apart. There must be something she's dealing with, something she can't or won't share. It's usually something that builds slowly over time, like secrets buried under snow. Perhaps she felt trapped, or uncertain, or even afraid. And that fear might have driven her to take drastic actions."

"Trapped?" he asked with a grimace, his tone harsh. "We've built a life together. A home, a family—"

"Believe me, I understand." I looked at Joe for support, and he gave me a nod, his expression a mix of sympathy and understanding. "I'm not trying to justify her actions nor argue their fairness. But understanding is the first step towards healing."

Nathan shifted in his seat, staring at his fidgeting hands, seemingly lost in a turbulent sea of thought.

"I don't know if this is my place to say, but when she was at girls' night with us the other night, she confided in us how lonely she was feeling in your marriage. She was asking a lot of questions about our history. Like she was really trying to understand you better."

"Lonely?" Nathan questioned, the word was foreign to him, something he hadn't even considered.

"Yes, and she mentioned your drinking." I didn't want to kick a man while he was down, but if there was any hope of mending his marriage, he needed to face the reality.

"My drinking?" His face paled as the gravity of the situation sunk in.

"She said it had gotten really bad," I added, hesitating slightly.

Joe leaned forward, his hand resting hesitantly on his shoulder. "It's not an easy thing to face," he said. "But it seems Amanda felt all this time she was fighting a battle alone. A battle against the bottle, against your indifference."

He sat there, frozen as the color drained from his face. I watched him slowly try to digest my words, his hand absently rubbing the nape of his neck.

"Remember, this is how Amanda perceived things. Perception tends to warp reality."

Nathan swallowed hard and looked around the room as if searching for answers. "This...this changes everything." His voice trembled, heavy with regret. "I'm the villain in my own story. I pushed Amanda away. My drinking, my indifference—they pushed her away."

Joe and I exchanged glances but said nothing, choosing instead to let Nathan grapple with the hard realities we'd laid out before him.

"I have to make it right," he said with determination. "I owe it to Amanda and my kids to try."

"Addiction is a relentless beast, man," Joe said. "I know that firsthand. It ripped my life to shreds until I made the decision to fight it, once and for all. You have a long journey ahead."

"But remember, Nathan," I added softly, "you won't be walking that road alone."

Nathan nodded, his hands clenching and unclenching in his lap. It was clear to see the internal battle already raging within him.

"And maybe," I said, infusing my tone with hope. "Maybe when you come out on the other side, Amanda might be able to see that man she fell in love with again."

"But what if it is too late?" he asked, his voice filled with so much fear and uncertainty that it tugged at my heart.

"The bitter truth is it may very well be too late to save your marriage, but in this moment, you can't think about that," Joe replied solemnly. "At the core, this is a disease, a disease that has affected your wellbeing. You have to do this for you. And the first step in getting better is admitting you have a problem, and you want to change."

"And the next?" he asked.

"Understanding your problem is unmanageable, then surrendering your life to a Higher Power," Joe replied.

"Higher power?" Nathan repeated with a skeptical lift of an eyebrow.

Joe's eyes glistened as he spoke. "I struggled with the concept for years. I was raised with a strong faith, but when my mom died, I couldn't see how a loving God could take her from me. I spiraled, indulging in sex in alcohol, thinking it would numb the pain. But you know what? It didn't. Instead, it consumed me, until there was nothing left but the hollow shell of who I once was."

"And how did you find Him again?" Nathan asked.

Joe looked at me, his expression contemplative. "It was more like he found me."

"He leaves the ninety-nine for the one," I whispered, reminiscing on my own personal encounter with God.

Joe paused and looked at me with a thoughtful expression. "It was actually in the middle of a break-up with your sister. I was so devastated, but as I let go and surrendered to Him, He brought healing to my soul and the strength to move forward. I was shattered. But surrendering to God and acknowledging my own weakness, that was the first step towards rebuilding myself."

Nathan seemed to take in Joe's words with a quiet seriousness that I hadn't seen in him before. His expression, usually filled with laughter and mischief, now held a glint of determination and resolve.

Joe stood, left the room and returned carrying a book, its deep-brown and red cover well-worn as if it had been read hundreds of times. "There are so many keys in this book that have helped me through my deepest struggles." He handed it to Nathan. "Take it. I hope it helps you as much as it helped me."

Nathan took hold of it gently, as if he was holding something fragile. He stared at the title, *The Heart of Addiction,* for a long moment. "Thank you."

I gave him a small, encouraging smile as Joe patted his back. "We are all fighting our own battles," Joe said quietly. "But remember, you're not alone in this."

"We're with you every step of the way, Nathan," I promised.

Nathan nodded, his eyes still on the book.

"Tomorrow is a new day," Joe said. "Start there. You don't have to figure it all out tonight."

"Start small," I suggested. "Remember, it's not about sweeping declarations—it's about consistent, daily choices."

"Like showing up for your kids and being present," Joe added. "They need their dad."

"Tomorrow," he declared with newfound resolve, "I start anew. Not just for them, but for me too."

"That's all anyone can do, take it day by day," I reiterated, hoping the words would provide some comfort.

Nathan stood, the book clutched tightly in one hand.

"Thank you both. For everything."

"Anytime, brother," Joe's voice held the sturdiness of an anchor. "We're always here for you."

Nathan turned then and made his way to the door, pausing before he walked out. He didn't look at us, but he didn't need to. His gratitude was silent but palpable—as tangible as the suspended breath of a moment before dawn.

After he left, Joe and I sat in silence for a while, each lost in our own thoughts. "We should pray for him," I suggested, breaking the silence. The room was filled with the heaviness that hung around after intense conversations—like the aftermath of a storm. Joe nodded and pulled me closer to him, weaving his fingers through mine.

As I clasped his hand, we bowed our heads. The words that flowed from Joe's lips were sincere, carrying a weight that filled the room. They hung in the air, an invisible cloud of compassion, hope, and earnest desperation for my brother's plight.

I thought of Dakota and my dad too, silently giving God the burden of them once more. Tears fell down my cheeks and as I worked to find peace, my stomach clenched tight another Braxton Hicks contraction bearing down on my body. And I hoped against hope that in the middle of all this stress, my baby would be okay.

CHAPTER 44

March 9, 9:00 p.m.

DAKOTA

A chill ran through me as I laced my familiar worn-out sneakers to get ready for tonight's NA meeting. I checked the thermostat, but it was set at its normal seventy-three degrees. The house always felt a little colder when Tim was gone. I threw on a hoodie and then hurried outside to my car. Just as I slipped into the driver's seat, my phone vibrated with a notification.

"The package is ready. Meet me at the Quilcene house ASAP."

"Dammit, Ricky," I whispered under my breath. The Quilcene house. I knew this text was coming, but I still wasn't ready for it.

What I needed was the NA meeting. I needed it like I needed air, a constant reminder to breathe, to stay afloat in a sea that threatened to swallow me whole.

Tim's face flashed before me, his brown hair and steady gaze that always seemed to see right through me to the person I was beneath the scars and the shame. He believed in me—fought for me when I was too weak to fight for myself. I hated betraying his trust once again. But what choice did I have? *If you don't do this, Victor will put a hit out on Tim.*

Ricky's words played through my head like a scratched CD, a haunting melody of despair and desperation. I gripped the

265

steering wheel tighter, my knuckles turning white under the streetlamp's soft glow. As I drove away from the safety of my little sanctuary, the road stretched out before me like a dark ribbon, leading me to a place I'd sworn I'd never return to. There was no turning back now, not with Tim's life hanging in the balance.

As I drove, the darkness outside matched the turmoil within me.

It was a twisted game of chess I was playing: the kingpin against the pawn. And tonight, I was to be the sacrificial lamb one more time.

Once at the Quilcene house, I parked a block away, not wanting to draw attention. The old house stood in silhouette under the ghost in the moonlight, a vivid reminder of our sordid past.

My heart pounded against my ribs as I approached the trap house, each beat a protest against this dark path that I found myself on. It was a place heavy with memories best forgotten, a place where shadows clung to the walls and whispered secrets you wished you'd never heard.

I glanced at my phone again, the message from Ricky staring at me like a death sentence. As I pocketed the device, the crunch of gravel underfoot seemed so loud in the stillness, and I winced at the sound. Each breath felt like inhaling shards of glass, sharp and painful.

"Please forgive me," I prayed silently, not quite sure to whom I was speaking—to Tim or to God.

The wind whistled a lonely note as I reached out and knocked on the weather-beaten door. The door opened; Ricky stood there, his expression the same as the other night, regret mixed with a silent plea for forgiveness.

The air in the room was stale and musty, carrying the faint scent of dried blood mixed with the lingering smell of alcohol. Justin sat huddled in the corner of the room, his posture rigid and his expression blank. A large bruise covered his left eye that was starting to darken. Avery sat next to him on the worn couch, his swollen lip telling a story of pain and violence, yet his face remained emotionless.

What in the hell had happened to them? Had Victor roughed them up for the way they had treated me?

My skin crawled as Ricky stepped toward me, a small, nondescript package in his grasp.

"Sorry you got dragged into this, Dakota," he said softly. "I know what you've been trying to do for yourself...and I'm sorry."

My fingers brushed against his as I took the parcel, the paper cool and slick. His touch should have comforted me, a human connection in this den of ghosts, but it only tightened the dread coiling in my gut.

The paper was coarse, an unpleasant contrast to the cold sweat that had formed on my palms.

"Be careful, Dakota," he added softly, and for a moment, I thought I saw the old Ricky, the one who used to dream of a life beyond all this chaos.

"Always am," I lied, tucking the package under my arm. The weight of it felt like a shackle, dragging me further into the abyss that yawned open beneath my feet.

With every step I took away from them, away from the Quilcene house, the tightness in my chest wound tighter.

As I pulled away from the curb with the package in the driver's seat, the darkness of the road ahead mirrored the dread twisting in my gut. I drove on autopilot, the hum of the tires against the road a steady drone in the background of my tumultuous thoughts.

Each mile I covered, the more fervent my internal monologue became—a litany of fears and what-ifs. What if this package was the end of the line?

What if it contained my doom and sealed my fate? What if I was trapped, bound by the tenuous threads of loyalty and fear? The more I pondered, the more immense the weight became, pressing down on me like a malevolent darkness.

Each passing moment, I felt the noose of potential

consequences tightening around my neck, suffocating me with the weight of choices made and those yet to come.

The road stretched endlessly before me, an abyss of uncertainty that seemed to consume all light and hope. My headlights were feeble beacons, struggling to pierce the oppressive darkness that enveloped the car.

"Tim would find a way out of this," I reasoned aloud, trying to draw strength from his unwavering sense of duty. "He'd know what to do."

But I wasn't Tim—I was Dakota Jensen, the girl with a fractured past and a penchant for finding trouble. And right now, trouble was sitting shotgun, an uninvited passenger on a journey to a destination unknown.

The miles ticked by, marked by the rhythmic passing of faded road signs and the relentless drumming of my heart. With each one, the fear for Tim's safety sharpened into a keen edge, cutting deeper into my resolve.

"Almost there," I whispered, the Brinnon house looming on the horizon like a harbinger of reckoning. The gravel crunched under the tires as I edged closer to the house. My breaths came in short, ragged gasps, mirroring the erratic thumping of my heart.

I killed the headlights as I neared the property, cloaking my arrival in darkness. My car rolled to a stop, and I sat there for a moment, listening to the engine's quiet ticking as it cooled.

"Tim..." His name escaped my lips like a prayer, a plea for strength I wasn't sure I possessed.

I slid out of the car, the night air biting at my skin, and walked towards the ominous front door. The package felt heavier now. Every step was a battle against the fear clawing at my throat. It didn't matter though; the only thing that mattered now was Tim. I would keep him safe, no matter how much it cost me.

CHAPTER 45

March 9, 9:55 p.m.

TIM

Everything was set. The video was constantly rolling to record any information that Ramirez and I could possibly miss. There was no way we could mess this up. Victor Mendez's game was over. It was just a matter of time. It may have been a dangerous game but one that I was determined to win. After everything Ryan had done to Dakota, it was the least I could do to bring his boss—the puppet master—down for good. Personally, I rather kill him with my bare hands, causing him a slow agonizing death, but this would have to do.

Ramirez had walked to the local gas station to get some coffee, leaving me alone to keep an eye on the house and the constant buzz of the surveillance equipment.

I wasn't sure what it was exactly, but I had a feeling about tonight. The air was thick and tasted like anxiety. I tried to calm my nerves with the rhythmic hum of the equipment and soft music from the oldies station, but the mix of excitement and fear couldn't be quenched.

Through my binoculars, I could see a slight frame walk up the sidewalk, with a package in their hand. Her hair fell down her mid-back, blowing in the wind. This was it. What she carried in her hand could be enough to blow this case wide open. She turned to scan the area, and my heart dropped.

It was Dakota! Her face was hidden by the shadows, but I knew that silhouette anywhere. Her long dark hair flowing in the wind, her walk, the way she held herself—it was her. What. The. Hell? Dakota? Panic clawed at my insides as a dozen questions raced through my mind.

What the actual hell was she doing here? How could she possibly be involved with this? Confusion and devastation stole my breath. How could Dakota do this after everything we'd been through?

I thought she'd been sober for the last year and a half, and now she was showing up with a package full of drugs? My pulse raced; if Dakota got caught on my tape, then things would be bad all around. Without hesitation, I shut off the feed, hopefully in time before she walked into the scene.

The van suddenly plunged into darkness as the monitors went black. The steady rhythm of my heartbeat pounding in my ears was the soundtrack to my worst nightmare unfolding. The silence in the van was deafening, broken only by my ragged breathing. I was gasping for air as if I'd been sucker-punched in the gut.

I could still see Dakota, oblivious and walking towards Mendez's house. The night veiled her from the rest of the world, but I could see her clearly through the binoculars—as if she was under a spotlight meant only for me. It was like a sick, twisted play—one where the love interest turns out to be a villain.

I wanted to run across the street and shake her. I wanted to scream at her and beg her to stop at the same time. My fingers clenched on the binoculars, my knuckles straining white against the darkness. I knew I couldn't risk blowing my cover, not now when we were so close...

The door on the house opened, and a man with dark hair, in his mid-twenties stood there—one of Victor's cronies no doubt. She handed him the box, and he handed her a small baggie of what looked like drugs in return.

Damn it, Dakota! All this for your drugs? The crushing weight of despair pressed down on my chest. I dropped the binoculars, too shocked to keep looking. The image of Dakota, trading a box for a packet of drugs, was seared into my brain.

She was willing to throw us away for the next high? I reeled in the suffocating darkness, my mind spinning in a whirl of disbelief and betrayal. I felt sick to my stomach, the bitter taste of disappointment burning my throat. All of our promises... shattered in the blink of an eye.

Dakota clutched the small baggie in her hands, hurried to her car, and sped off into the night, leaving me alone in my surveillance van. I could still see her taillights, glowing like two red eyes looking at me in the rearview mirror until they disappeared around the bend.

On the other side of the street, Ramirez approached the vehicle carrying two cups of coffee, oblivious to what had just happened.

Pull yourself together, Tim. Ramirez could not know about this. I flipped the surveillance equipment back on and did my best to shove my emotions deep into a corner of my heart, hoping they wouldn't bleed through my voice.

A few moments later, she opened the door and climbed in, holding a coffee cup toward me. "Did I miss anything?" she asked with an eager grin.

"No, nothing much," I murmured, taking the coffee cup from her hands and forcing a half-hearted smile. The hot liquid scalded my tongue as I took a sip and blinked hard, trying to erase the image of Dakota trading for drugs. But it was stuck there, etched into my mind like a painful tattoo that wouldn't fade. I swallowed hard, the heat from the coffee doing nothing to quell the icy dread that coated my insides.

Ramirez was rattling off something about leads and informers, her voice a mere buzz in my ears as I struggled to focus on her words. I nodded mechanically every now and then focused on the dimly lit street outside. All I could think about was

Dakota, her choices, the downward spiral that was her life. And even still how much I loved her.

My grip around the coffee cup tightened, its heat seeping into my skin, as her face swam in my mind's eye, filled with a terrible desperation I had hoped to never see again. Anger washed over me, a red-hot fury that threatened to consume me. I clenched my jaw and took a deep breath, releasing it slowly in an attempt to calm my racing heart. I wasn't sure what the next right step was. All I knew was that this mission had just taken a complicated turn, and I needed to tread carefully, not just for the operation but for Dakota too. We had a lot to sort out, but for now, I had to focus on taking down Victor, and pray that no one reviewed the footage and started asking questions. Because tampering with evidence was a felony just as much as running drugs.

CHAPTER 46

March 9, 10:05 p.m.

DAKOTA

The baggie was clenched tightly in my fist as I drove away from the house, the lights receding in the rearview mirror. I opened my hand and stared at it in the dim glow of the car's dashboard, studying the tiny pills. My payment, they said. But the weight felt wrong, dirty. With a swift motion, I tossed it into the glove compartment. The clunk of it hitting the plastic felt like a gavel coming down on my past life—a judgment I'd have to live with. I resisted the siren call of old habits and slammed the compartment shut. I bit the inside of my cheek hard enough to taste metal, my heart racing, battling between the haunting allure of addiction and the future I desperately wanted with Tim.

"Tim." His name was a prayer, a beacon in the storm of my thoughts as I drove. Guilt gnawed at my insides, a relentless rat that wouldn't stop until it chewed through my resolve. Relief, however, flowed through my veins like a reprieve from a death sentence. It was done. I was done.

"Never again," I whispered to myself, the words a fragile vow floating in the confined space of my car. I would find a way out of this. I couldn't see how at the moment, but I would find a way. I gunned the gas pedal, speeding home to clear my head from this awful night.

The roads were empty, and the soft purr of the tires against the rough pavement was the only sound that filled my ears, a soothing rhythm that drowned out the clamoring chaos inside my head. I forced myself to focus on the road ahead, the beams of my headlights cutting through the darkness like a pair of glowing eyes in the black abyss. I could feel the pull towards home, drawing me like the tide. The drive seemed to drone on forever, the winding roads a labyrinth of choices and consequences. The night pressed around my car, heavy and suffocating, brooding like the thoughts that churned in my head.

When I finally pulled into our driveway, I felt restless and anxious, like a hunted animal finally reaching its den. I thought about the pills in the glove box, my mind taking me on a dark road for a few merciless seconds. But I pushed the thought away as if it were a venomous snake, ready to sink its teeth into my vulnerable flesh. The house stood before me, a beacon of safety within the ever-growing storm.

Once inside, though it was late, I busied myself straightening cushions, dusting surfaces, and sweeping floors—each action a step toward normalcy. Each stroke of the broom swept away a piece of my trepidation. And then I thought of Tim, picturing his smile, the way his brown hair would fall just over his forehead when he was tired. He deserved more than this—more than a fiancée with a rap sheet for a past and secrets that skulked in the corners.

In the kitchen, I reached for the box of cereal. The rattle of flakes against cardboard was oddly comforting. I poured them into a bowl, the cascade a staccato rhythm to the quiet of the room. But when I opened the fridge, the milk carton felt too light in my hand. A sniff confirmed my suspicion: sour, spoiled, gone off.

"Crap," I muttered, scrunching my nose. The spoiled milk was a catalyst, driving me to purge the refrigerator of anything that mirrored my own potential for ruin. I tore through it, chucking expired items into the trash with more force than necessary. My movements were frantic, as if by cleaning I could scrub away the dirt from my soul. I wished it was this easy to clean my soul of the lies I told and a past that never seemed to let go no matter how hard I tried. I lined the shelves neatly, replaced everything that was good, that was pure.

The serenity of the tidied home surrounded me, but it couldn't quite reach the tremors of unease that still lived in my bones. The silence of the house stretched before me, a vast and empty ocean that seemed to sit heavy in my chest.

The sound of Tim's car pulling into the driveway split the silence, and a few moments later the front door creaked open.

Tim stepped inside, his figure a silhouette against the dim light filtering through the entrance. There was something wrong in his face—a hardness in his expression that instantly set my pulse racing. His usually soft, warm gaze had been replaced with a steel-cold stare, as if he had just seen a ghost, or worse yet, the truth. A shiver of apprehension ran through me.

"Where is it, Dakota?"

"Where is what?"

His features twisted into an accusing scowl as he stalked into the kitchen. "Don't play innocent with me." He yanked open each kitchen drawer one by one, muttering curse words under his breath.

"Where are the drugs, Dakota?" he barked, the tendons in his neck taut with barely restrained fury. He ran into the living room and flung the couch cushions aside with a violent desperation that seemed to shake the very walls around us. His hand paused over the final cushion, and then, with a roar of frustration, he flung it aside.

I followed him helplessly, my heart pounding against my rib cage like a wild animal in a trap. How could he possibly know? Was he following me? "Tim... I..." The words were a choked whisper. He continued his crazed search, ignoring me, his form trembling with raw anger and betrayal.

"No more lies, Dakota!" he spat out, tearing through our

ELISHEBA HAXBY & JESSE VINCENT

home, upending furniture and scattering our possessions. Finally, he turned toward me, out of breath. His eyes were bloodshot and full of pain—the kind of profound hurt that could permanently damage a man's soul.

For a long moment, I held his gaze, the truth clinging to my tongue like bitter poison.

"I saw you at the Brinnon house tonight, trading that package for drugs." He towered over me, his athletic frame rigid with accusation.

"You know I wouldn't—" I choked on the words, fear constricting my throat as I searched his face for the man I loved.

"Wouldn't what? Fall back into old habits? Make deals with drug dealers?" His questions were like daggers, each one aimed with precision at my weakest spots.

"Tim, please," I pleaded, my hands outstretched as if I could physically push away his assumptions. "It's not what it looks like."

"Save it, Dakota. I saw everything." His dismissal was a cold slap, making my skin prickle with despair.

My mind raced, images flashing—leaving the house in Brinnon, the weight of the drugs in the glove compartment, a ghost of my past self-whispering temptations.

"Look at me, Tim. I promise you, it's not what it looks like." My voice broke, the edges sharp with desperation.

"I can't look at you, Dakota! It hurts too damn much." His voice cracked, his anger tumbling into a pit of anguish. He ran a hand through his hair, staring at the ground as if it could provide answers.

I reached for him, my fingers trembling, but he jerked away from my touch. "I trusted you," he murmured, his words barely audible. "And you played me for a fool."

His words were like punches to the gut, each syllable twisting a tighter knot in my stomach. "Tim," I began, my voice ragged with emotion. "I didn't—"

"But you did!" he interrupted. "Because you haven't changed, have you? You're still that same junkie who can't resist a score!"

Tim's words were like shrapnel, tearing through the fragile peace I'd built around myself.

His accusation hit with the force of a physical blow, and I staggered against the kitchen counter. The cold granite beneath my palms was real, solid—so unlike the ground beneath my feet, which seemed to tremor with each syllable he hurled at me.

"Is that what you think? You think I'm nothing more than a junkie?" My own voice sounded foreign, as if it belonged to someone else—a version of me teetering on the edge of a precipice I'd fought so hard to climb.

I could see the battle behind his features. The man who loved me, who'd promised to stand by my side through thick and thin, wrestled with the man witnessing the resurrection of my old self.

"That's not what I meant," he said, his voice softer now. But it held a finality that squeezed at my lungs. His gaze had a faraway look, as if he was seeing past me, seeing the past years of our shared history unspooling like a film reel. The childhood memories. The late-night talks under the stars. The shared dreams. And then, the shared nightmares.

"Then what did you mean, Tim?" I asked, struggling to keep my voice steady. "Because it sure as hell sounded pretty clear."

His silence was deafening. He didn't refute my words, didn't try to offer an apology or an explanation—nothing but dead air and the ticking clock in the background.

I clung to the counter, my knuckles white against the cool granite. Hee opened and closed his mouth, the words dying before they could take flight.

"What do you want me to say?" His eyes bore into mine, the raw hurt in them sending a shiver through me. "That it's all okay? That everything will go back to normal?"

"I..." I stammered, choking on my own words. The weight of his stare and the heavy silence in the room threatened to crush me. He didn't understand. I wasn't that person anymore, couldn't be that person anymore.

"No," I said finally, straightening up, forcing myself to meet his gaze head-on. "I want you to believe me."

He scoffed at that, a bitter laugh that echoed around the quiet room. "Believe you?" He muttered incredulously. "How can I believe you when every word out of your mouth reeks of lies?"

"That... That's not fair." My heart broke under his accusatory glare.

"Fair?" Tim echoed my word with a bitterness that twisted my stomach. "You want to talk about fair? Was it fair when you stood there lying to my face all this time? Was it fair that I defended you, time and again, to my family, to my mother, while you were sneaking around behind my back?"

His words were a torrent, each syllable a bludgeon that shattered the remnants of our relationship. I winced under their weight, feeling the sting of his accusations even as I knew they were based on false pretenses.

"I never lied to you," I whispered against the storm of his anger. His eyes blazed with pain and betrayal, and I could see every shred of trust he'd had in me crumbling away.

"You did!" he roared.

"I was just delivering! I never used," I spat back, finally finding some sliver of courage to defend myself. "I was trying to protect you!"

"Protect me? How noble! By becoming a drug mule?"

I flinched at his words. "It isn't like that. You know me."

"Know you?" He stepped close, his breath hot on my face, his presence an oppressive weight. "I don't recognize you, Dakota. Maybe I never did."

The engagement ring on my finger—a band of white gold set with a modest diamond, a symbol of promises and shared dreams—burned against my skin. It was a reminder of a future we'd planned, now dissolving into the acrid air between us.

"Is this what you want?" I tugged at the ring, a desperate bid to salvage something from the wreckage. "To believe the worst in me?"

"Want?" he scoffed, his face contorting with anger. "I wanted a partner, someone I can trust—not a criminal!"

That word 'criminal' ignited something within me—a fury born of pain and dashed hopes. With a swift motion, I yanked the ring off, its cool metal slipping from my trembling fingers. I threw it at him with a force that felt almost cathartic, watching as it bounced off his chest and clattered to the silent floor. The sound rang out like a death knell for all we had been to each other.

"Then consider yourself free of one!" I yelled, the taste of bitterness coating my tongue.

He caught his breath, the harsh lines of his face reflecting the glinting metal on the floor. Then he looked up at me, his eyes clouded with a mixture of pain and anger. His fingers clenched into tight fists at his sides.

Gut twisting, I turned and stormed towards the door, each step fueled by a swirling maelstrom of emotion. Anger, fear, but most of all, an overwhelming sense of loss that threatened to consume me whole.

"Where do you think you're going?" Tim called after me, his voice a blend of rage and desperation.

"Anywhere but here!" I shot back, my hand closing around the doorknob. As I wrenched it open, the cold night air rushed in, wrapping around me like a reprieve from the stifling heat of our shattered home.

"Damn it, Dakota!" His voice cracked like a whip, but it couldn't snare me—not any longer.

I crossed the threshold, leaving behind the man who had once been my anchor in a tempestuous sea. Now, he was just another storm I had to escape. The slam of the door echoed in my ears, a final note in the symphony of our discord.

The chill of the outside world embraced me, and I welcomed its bite. For now, it was enough to keep the encroaching darkness at bay, enough to let me breathe without the weight of accusations crushing my chest. The gravel crunched beneath my fleeing steps, each stone a sharp reminder of the fractured pieces I left behind. The night air was thick with the scent of impending rain, and it mingled with the salt of my tears.

"Dakota!" Tim yelled after me. "Please don't do this."

But how could I not? He had shown his true thoughts of who he thought I was, just a damaged junkie. I didn't turn back, but I heard the soft thud of the front door closing and the crunch of his footsteps on the gravel as he pursued me. "Dakota!" he yelled again, his voice stretched thin with desperation.

For a moment, I considered stopping, giving in to the familiar pull of his voice, of what we used to have. But his accusations repeated in my mind, drowning out my wavering resolve. "Leave it, Tim!" I shouted over my shoulder without breaking stride. My legs were heavy, leaden with the weight of my own heartbreak. Yet I willed them to carry me further away from him, from us.

CHAPTER 47

March 9, 11:47 p.m.

TIM

My body refused to stay still, my feet pacing back and forth across the living room floor. Each step was a reminder of my fight with Dakota. My fingers dug into my scalp, trying to alleviate the tension that was consuming me from within. The sound of our argument replayed in my mind, each word clawing deeper into my already wounded heart.

I couldn't rid myself of the images that plagued me—her walking up to the Rodrigez house, carrying a package, then accepting drugs in return. "Why, Dakota?" I whispered, knowing there was no one around to hear my cries for answers. The silence amplified the emptiness I felt inside, as if her absence had carved a Dakota-shaped hole in my chest.

I bit down on my lip with enough force to taste blood, a futile attempt at numbing the pain.

As I continued to pace, the anger slowly dissipated and was replaced by fear and doubt. What if she was telling the truth? What if it really wasn't what it looked like? *Believe it or not, Tim... I was trying to protect you.* Her words resounded in the suffocating quiet like a haunting refrain, bouncing around the corners of my mind, mingling with the throbbing silence. My gut churned with uncertainty and confusion.

The desperation in her eyes as she'd said the words. The rawness in her voice. The sincerity was palpable, yet so was the deceit.

Protect me from what? The thought of her being involved in such a dangerous game was enough to make my blood turn to ice. I slumped onto the couch, my breath hitching as her tear-streaked face materialized in my mind once more—her pale skin under the dim lights of our living room, her long brown hair falling over her face like a curtain trying to hide her tears.

The desire to hold her, comfort her was overwhelming, but so was the sense of betrayal. My vision caught a glint on the floor. The engagement ring, that little band of gold and diamond meant forever, yet there it lay—cast aside, just like our promises to each other.

My fingers, usually steady, trembled as I reached for the ring. It was cold to the touch, the metal unforgiving. I rolled it between my thumb and forefinger, the weight disproportionate to its size. That tiny circle held everything—hope, love, the future we'd planned. Allies forever. And now what? What did it represent but a gaping chasm between us?

I closed my fist around the ring, the edges pressing into my palm. Dakota's words sounded in my head once more. *I was trying to protect you.* The words clung to the charged air of the empty room—a stubborn ghost that I couldn't exercise. Could there have been truth laced within her cryptic confession? A reason shrouded in secrets she felt too burdened to share? I thought back to the night she had come home so late, and the story she had told about Avery and Justin. When I had found them that day, they were at one of Victor's houses. Had she somehow become a pawn in Victor's game?

Dread settled in the pit of my gut like a stone sinking to the bottom of a murky lake. I'd been a cop long enough to know when things didn't add up, and right now, my world was a jigsaw puzzle with too many missing pieces.

The ring in my hand felt heavier with every second, as if it absorbed the gravity of our situation. *Believe it or not, Tim... I was trying to protect you.* And in that moment, I acknowledged the sincerity in her desperate words. She'd been trying to shield us, and I'd only seen betrayal.

I set the ring on the coffee table, my fist unclenching as if I was releasing the burden of blame. I stared at it for a long moment, taking in its stillness. It remained there, undisturbed, just as my love for Dakota endured despite the tumult. A flame that refused to be snuffed out even in the face of a chilling storm.

Suddenly, I knew what I had to do. I pushed to my feet, my determination steeling my resolve. I needed to find her—to understand, to protect, to fix whatever fissure had cracked open between us. No more pacing, no more hesitating. I ran to the door and yanked it open so forcefully it banged against the inner wall.

My breath came in short bursts, hot against the chill of the evening air. It tasted like desperation. My heartbeat was a rhythm against my ribs, a drumbeat urging me onward. Dakota was out there somewhere, alone and likely as scared as I was. I bounded down the steps toward my car, shoes slapping against the concrete with each stride.

I climbed in the car, turned the key in the ignition and the engine roared to life. As I pulled away from the curb, my hands gripped the steering wheel with purpose. The streets were empty as I sped through red lights and stop signs, each ignored signal a testament to my desperation.

My thoughts careened to Dakota's haunted eyes, the way they could shift from storms to still waters in a heartbeat. The memory cut through the panic, sharpening my focus. She was fighting demons, just like me—only hers were so deeply personal that sometimes I felt powerless in their wake.

"Damn it, Dakota, why didn't you trust me to help?" The dashboard was silent, offering no answers, only reflecting my furrowed brow in the dim glow of the streetlights. The night air whistled through a crack in the window, carrying with it the scent of impending rain.

The looming shadows no longer held me captive, but instead served as a reminder of the danger that surrounded me.

"Where are you, Dakota?" I racked my brain, trying to come up with something. But I was at a loss. All of her usual haunts would be closed at this time of night. Could she have called Tamara and taken off to Ocean Shores? My fingers scrolled through my phone until I found Tamara's number. It didn't matter that it was well past midnight; I needed to know.

CHAPTER 48

March 10, 12:05 a.m.

TAMARA

The sound of my phone's loud ringtone filled the quiet darkness of my bedroom and I jolted awake. Adrenaline coursed through me as I fumbled for my phone. Who would be calling at this hour?

Tim's name lit the caller ID. Dread spiked in my veins as I swiped to answer.

"Tim?" I answered, voice groggy from sleep.

"Tamara!" Tim's voice crackled with desperation on the other end.

"Have you heard from Dakota?"

I sat up in bed and turned on the light as fear drilled through my foggy realm of half sleep. Something was terribly wrong. I could feel it. "Not since we had dinner the other night. What's going on?"

Joe stirred in bed next to me at the disturbance. His eyes flickered open, sleepily glancing over at me with concern etched across his handsome face.

Tim's breathing was heavy on the other end of the line, and I could tell he was trying to keep his emotions in check. "We got into a huge fight, and she stormed off. Please, Tamara, pray for her. I think she's in trouble."

I swallowed hard, pressing the phone tighter to my ear as if physically bridging the distance between us could somehow offer comfort. "What kind of trouble?"

"I saw her dropping off a package at a house that I've been surveilling."

I thought of the night Tim proposed to Dakota. She had said Ryan was always there to bring retribution. "Are they connected to Ryan?"

Joe scooted closer to me as if trying to bring comfort. "Tim can't find Dakota," I whispered to him.

His face paled at that, but he didn't interrupt.

"It's highly likely," Tim said, his words full of dread.

"Tim, I never told you this, but on the night you proposed to her, she called me and said that her past would always catch up to her, and that Ryan would never stop bringing retribution."

Tim cursed under his breath, the anger in his voice crackling through the phone line. "Why would she keep that from me? I could have protected her."

"I don't know, Tim," I whispered, tears blurring my vision.

Joe reached over, gently taking the phone from my trembling hand. His voice was steady, a rock amidst the churning sea of fear. "Tim, we're here for you, man," he said, clicking on the speaker phone. "What do you need us to do?"

A long silence followed as Tim seemed to crumple under the weight of the situation. "For now, just sit tight and call me if she gets a hold of you," he finally said, "and please pray for her safety. And...and for my quick thinking. I need to find her."

His gaze was filled with pity, and it made my heart clench in my chest. "We will, Tim,"

"Thank you," Tim said. "I'll be in touch."

With those final words, the call ended, leaving us accompanied by a heavy silence. I began to pray for Dakota with a desperation I had never felt before. My words, raw and urgent, filled the room as Joe held me close. Tears streamed down my face as I begged for my sister's safety, for Tim's strength. When I ran out of words Joe took over, his deep voice a comforting hum in the otherwise somber room. His prayers were heartfelt and sincere, a sound lullaby to the storm raging inside me.

I thought about the night that Dakota and I had almost died at the hands of Ryan. God had intervened that night, sending Joe at just the right time. I found myself hoping for another miracle now, clinging to the belief that God would protect my sister once more. His hands had worked miracles before, and I prayed they would again.

CHAPTER 49

March 10, 12:17 a.m.

TIM

The town was a blur, a living canvas painted with shadows and streaks of light as I searched for Dakota. Tamara's words on the phone played through my mind again and again as I scoured the city. This whole thing had gone all the way back to the night of our engagement? But what exactly happened? And how did she get sucked into this? She'd said she'd been trying to protect me, but what had that meant?

As the engine hummed beneath me, determination settled in my chest like armor. I would find her. I would bring her home. I thought of the harsh words I said during our fight. I had hurt her, and that knowledge gnawed at me as I drove on.

My eyes darted from one street to the next, searching for a hint, a sign, anything that might lead me to Dakota. The steering wheel felt cold and slick under my palms, yet I gripped it like a lifeline.

"Think, Tim," I murmured to myself, staring out into the night. The city was asleep, its inhabitants tucked away in their homes while Dakota's whereabouts remained unknown. Every shadowy corner seemed to promise answers yet offered only more questions.

289

And then, as if summoned by sheer desperation, there was someone who possibly had answers—Ricky. He was leaving a convenient store with a pack of cigarettes in his hands, his face partially obscured by a low-slung baseball cap. I slammed on the brakes and pulled into the parking lot.

"Ricky!" The urgency in my voice clawed its way out, raw and unfiltered as I stumbled out of the car. "Have you seen Dakota?"

Something flickered in his eyes, but he shook his head. "I haven't. What's going on?"

"Don't screw with me, Ricky. If you know something, tell me."

"Look, man, I don't know where she is. I swear." But there was a tension in his voice, a slight tremor that suggested he wasn't entirely truthful.

"Ricky, please, " I began, closing the distance between us. "We had a fight, and she took off. She said something about keeping us safe, but—I don't know, man, it doesn't make sense." My words tumbled over one another, tripping in their haste.

His face crumpled, a show of true concern replacing his usual poker face. "I swear, Tim. I don't know where she is, but I'll help you find her."

Relief washed over me, but it was tinged with anxiety.

"Okay."

Ricky had always been a bit of a wildcard, but he also knew a lot of the same people Dakota used to run with. "I covered most of Chimacum. How about you head toward Quilcene while I sweep through Hadlock?"

"I'm on it," he said, rushing to his car. "I'll text you if I see her." With that, he climbed into his blue Mustang and peeled out of the parking lot.

I watched him leave, the squeal of his tires echoing long after he'd disappeared from sight. The abandoned street suddenly felt all too quiet, the silence deepening my worry. "Dakota," I whispered into the void, my voice barely audible against the night.

With a heavy sigh, I returned to my car. Churning with

adrenaline, I took off for Hadlock. The quiet streets felt eerie in their stillness as if they were holding their breath alongside me. I twisted through the suburban maze, passing familiar landmarks and houses shrouded in darkness—unaware of the anxiety coursing through my veins.

CHAPTER 50

March 10, 12:36 a.m.

DAKOTA

The shadows clung to the corners of Logger's Landing like cobwebs, and I sat in their embrace, a solitary figure on a worn barstool. The dim light barely chased away the gloom that weighed heavily in the room, as heavy as the sorrow pressing on my chest. The smell of alcohol hung thick in the air, mingling with the acrid scent of stale cigarettes. It was the kind of place where despair blended seamlessly with the ambiance, and tonight, it matched the color of my thoughts perfectly.

"Another," I murmured, my voice barely carrying over the low hum of muffled conversations and the occasional clink of glasses. It was a familiar symphony, one that had been the soundtrack to too many nights like this. The bartender, a middle-aged man with a grizzled beard and a permanent frown etched into his weathered face, nodded without a word.

As the shot glass landed in front of me, I caught sight of my hands. They were trembling, betraying the turmoil that raged within as Tim's words cut through my mind again and again, reminding me of the truth I'd never escape no matter how hard I tried. *You're still that same junkie who can't resist the score.* The echo of his voice was a poison, seeping into every crevice of my mind, leaving no room for doubt or denial. If Tim thought this of me, it must have been true.

The man knew me inside and out. He'd seen every ugly corner of my soul. His words were a damning sentence, cutting deeper than any knife.

My eyes lingered on the amber liquid inside the glass, a feeble lighthouse in the storm of my thoughts. I watched as it sloshed gently with my trembling hands, the liquid fire promising oblivion. "To forgetting," I whispered to no one in particular, because there was no one. As the burn of alcohol seared my throat, a bitter taste of self-loathing followed. Tears threatened to come, but I wouldn't let them. I couldn't. Not here. Not where the walls might whisper my weakness to any prying ear. My fingers tightened around the empty glass, seeking strength in its fragile clarity.

"Hey, you okay?" The bartender's voice cut through my reverie, his concern barely concealing the weariness behind his eyes.

"Fine," I lied, offering him a sarcastic grin.

He grunted something that sounded like agreement and moved away, leaving me to stew in the bitter broth of my own thoughts. True love had been a fairy tale, and fear was the dragon I could never slay. I signaled for another shot, knowing full well it was a temporary salve on a wound that ran bone-deep. But tonight, temporary would have to be enough. Tonight, I just needed to forget. I thought about the pills in my pocket, the ones that they handed me in exchange for the package. I wasn't sure what they were, but I was sure they were stronger than the whiskey and would offer me a deeper relief.

The world spun on its axis, the dim light flirting with my hazy vision and then retreating as though shy. I could feel the rhythm of my heavy heart clear as a pulsating rhythm in my ears, matching pace with the slow tick of the dusty clock hung over the bar. For now, I took another shot and heaved myself off of the barstool and headed to the jukebox in the corner, each step hesitant, like wading through water or dreams. The wooden floor tilted beneath my feet, and I caught myself on a table before reaching the musical relic. I searched the music machine, my fingers hovering over the buttons like a pianist before the first note. I chose a song that used to be ours—the one Tim and I would play back when love was a secret written in smiles and stolen glances. Now, it was just a ghostly melody that twisted in my chest, every chord a reminder of what I had lost.

As the singer crooned, I closed my eyes, letting the lyrics pierce me. Each word was a thorn, each verse a tightening vice around the remnants of my shattered emotions.

"Hey, Dakota!" Ricky's familiar voice called out behind me, pulling me from my trance.

I flinched at the sound of my name, not wanting to tether myself to reality just yet. I turned toward the noise and, Ricky stood there—his handsome face marred by concern and something darker, a guilt that didn't belong to him alone. His presence was unexpected, unwelcome—a stark reminder of the world I was trying to escape.

"Tim's lookin' for ya," he said, his voice laced with urgency. "He's worried sick."

"Is he?" My reply was flat, drained of any inflection that might betray the chaos within. I turned away from him, focusing on the jukebox once more. "Since when does he worry about a junkie?"

"Dakota, come on. You know that's not fair." Ricky reached out, but I stepped back, unwilling to be touched or consoled.

"Fair?" I scoffed, the word tasting bitter. "Tell me about fair, Ricky. Tell me how fair it feels to have your heart ripped out and then be told you're nothing but a junkie."

Ricky's features softened. He wanted to help, I could see that much, but what could he do? He reached for me again, wrapping a strong arm around me, leading me to a nearby table. "Let's have a drink, Dakota. I'm buying."

I sat while he ordered us two long island ice teas.

His gaze met mine then, and there was a haunted, desperate

look in them. "I cannot begin to say how sorry I am about you getting dragged into this."

I studied him, taking in his sincerity. He was sorry. But that didn't change anything. It didn't take away the pain or give me back the life I had once loved so dearly.

"They did the same thing to me." His voice was quiet now, barely audible above the bluesy melody that filled the bar. "They dragged me right back into the hell I thought I'd escaped."

I looked at him, really looked at him, for the first time. A deep sadness shone in his eyes, a shadow that mirrored my own. His strong jawline was etched with tension, and his features were marred by lines of regret. I saw in him not an enemy, but a fellow survivor—a comrade in the war we had both been consigned to fight.

The bartender came and placed our drinks in front of us.

"But why? Why couldn't they just leave us alone? " I asked quietly, my curiosity piqued despite the numbness that still threatened to consume me.

Ricky leaned in his chair, a bitter smile twisting his lips. "For me, it was the family I was born into. With a name like Cooke, they thought I'd be the perfect replacement for Ryan."

Nausea tore through me at the mention of Ryan's name and the years of torment that followed the night he killed my brother Gabriel passed before my vision. It didn't matter that Ryan was dead; his name would always strike terror in the pit of my guts. "But you're nothing like Ryan."

Ricky snorted, the sound devoid of any real humor. "It doesn't matter. They needed a new mule in the area, and they had enough on me to get what they wanted. Enough to destroy any remnants of the future I dreamed of."

I tilted my head to the side, studying this man who I'd known for years, but at the same time, never really knew at all. The music from the jukebox played on, filling the silence between us—a melancholic soundtrack to our shared pain.

His gaze bore into mine with an intensity that was almost

tangible. There was a desperation there—a yearning for understanding, for empathy. Ricky had been torn apart by the same monsters that haunted my own nightmares. I felt a strange sense of camaraderie with him, a connection that transcended our shared pain and loss.

"Ricky... " The words floated out, forming from the fog that had enveloped my mind. "I'm... I'm so sorry."

"They promised me a way out if I did their dirty work. If I became their puppet. A chance to leave behind the filth and grime of this life." His features glazed over with a distant sorrow. "Turns out, it was just another cruel joke."

"So, guess that's it then? We're just stuck in this empty life without any way out? Victims to whatever they command?" My mind drifted back to the drugs in my pocket, and then to Tim's betrayal and harsh words. This wasn't a life I wanted to live. "I gotta go to the bathroom." I stood and left Ricky to his drink as I stumbled to the bathroom, mind in a daze. Thoughts of my brother's life being taken away from him at the hands of that psychopath and now my life taken from me, my freewill stolen by men who only wanted to bring me harm. And now Tim thought of me as a junkie, someone unworthy of trust, someone unworthy of his love.

Once in the bathroom, I dug out the baggie that carried two small pills. If Tim thought I was a junkie, and I was stuck in this sick drug world anyway, why did it matter? I shook the two pills into my hands and without another thought, I put them in my mouth and swallowed them dry, the bitter taste lingering on my tongue. There was a strange comfort in knowing that I was firmly in control of this specific moment, no matter how painful and terrifying it was.

CHAPTER 51
March 10, 1:06 a.m.

TIM

I sped towards Quilcene, my mind on the text Ricky had sent seven minutes ago. *Found her. Logger's Landing. She's been drinking. Get her asap.*

That meant she really had relapsed. Our fight, my harsh words had pushed her over the edge. My jaw clenched as self loathing rippled through me. Dakota, my beautiful, stubborn Dakota, crumbling under the weight of her demons, and I had been the one to give them power. I just hoped I got to her before she went down darker roads. I thought of the drugs I'd seen them given her when she'd delivered the package, and my foot pushed harder on the gas pedal. Quilcene was a twenty-minute drive when going the speed limit, but I was going 85 in a 55.

The world outside was black and unforgiving as I tore through it, my headlights barely slashing through the thick layers of darkness.

I gunned the accelerator. Panic sat on my chest like a heavy weight, threatening to crush me as I navigated the narrow, winding roads. I could taste fear at the back of my throat; it was a bitter tang of adrenaline and regrets.

My phone lit up with Ricky's number blinking urgently on

the screen. A cold sweat prickled at my brow as I snatched it up, swiping to take the call.

"Tim," Ricky's voice came through, strained and hurried. "Where are you?"

"Halfway to Quilcene," I grunted, throwing the car into a vicious curve as I hugged the phone to my ear.

"Just hurry, man," Ricky grimaced over the line. "Something feels off. She's in the bathroom right now, but she's been in there a little too long."

My heart missed a beat, a painful throb thudding in my chest as the implication of his words sunk in. I thought of the drugs again. Was she in there taking them?

"Dammit," I hissed through gritted teeth. The wheels screeched beneath me as I took a sharp turn, bringing the vehicle back onto the road. "Go check on her, Ricky, now!"

His only response was a curt, "On it," before the line went dead.

I flipped on my flashing lights and pushed the car to 100 miles per hour. I wasn't supposed to use them while off-duty, but rules be damned—not when Dakota's life could be on the line.

CHAPTER 52

March 10, 1:08 a.m.

DAKOTA

The world around me seemed to tilt and sway as my body reacted to the potent drugs, each breath drawn becoming more labored than the last. My reflection became hazy in the dingy bathroom mirror as the edges of the room blurred. My legs faltered beneath me, finding it harder to support the weight they had been so used to carrying. As my knees buckled, I felt a strange sense of peace comfort me. Despite the room spinning and my heart pounding like a jackhammer in my chest, I was serene. Here I was, teetering on the precipice of oblivion, and all I could think about was how grateful I was for this moment of stillness amidst the chaos.

I sunk to the cold tile floor beneath me, back braced against the edge of the sink as I let myself descend further into this welcomed abyss. The last coherent thought that passed through my foggy mind was that maybe this would be it—the end, the grand finale to my tragic story. A fitting curtain call for a life that had spiraled out from under my control, governed by forces far stronger than I could ever contend with. The darkness in the corners of my vision crept inward now, enveloping me in its embrace as my thoughts became muddled and disjointed.

In the dim confines of the bathroom, as my consciousness started slipping away, I felt oddly comforted. These last moments were not filled with terror or regret, but with a profound sense of relief. No more running, no more hiding, no more being a pawn in someone else's game.

As my body continued its descent, a peculiar warmth spread from the pit of my stomach, radiating outward through my limbs. The cold tiles beneath me no longer felt harsh against my skin; instead, they melded into a soft pillow cradling me ever so gently. My senses seemed to be heightened. I could now clearly hear the rhythmic drip-drip of the leaking faucet, each drop echoing like a solemn toll in the silence of the room. The air smelled faintly of bleach and mildew, a scent normally unpleasant, but in this moment, it brought a strange sense of reality to this surreal experience—a tangible connection to the world I was leaving behind. I thought of Tim and then of Tamara. The two people I loved most in this world. I didn't want to leave them. I didn't want to hurt them like this, but it wasn't enough to make me fight through the tendrils of darkness that had wrapped around me.

The darkness lapped at the edges of my mind now, pulling me gently towards its inviting abyss. It wasn't a hostile force but rather a strangely seductive entity. It crooned sweet promises in my ear, whispering of an end to the chaos, of peace that stretched into eternity. I welcomed it, this darkness. I had been running from it for so long, but now, I was too tired to resist. Too weary to fight. Too broken to gather the fragments of my shattered self.

My mind, unbound by physical constraints, seemed to expand, reaching out towards the silent darkness with a sense of curiosity and acceptance.

A sudden flash of memories flooded forward then—not just my own, but others too—as if the veil between life and death was thinning, offering glimpses into other lives, other hearts, other pains. I saw my mother in her youth, her hair wild in the breeze as she laughed with a man I assumed to be my father. There was a flash of children playing in a field, their laughter ringing clear as bells. Then, a sudden shift into anguish, an elderly man on his deathbed surrounded by a weeping family, a little girl weeping over her lost doll, a soldier bleeding out on a battlefield far from home. Scenes from other lives spilled forth like an outpouring river, each one both alien and intimately familiar. Then came a series of familiar faces—the trembling lips of Tim as he confessed his love for me, the fierce determination in Tamara's eyes as she fought her own battles, the proud smile of Joe as he cradled Lillie for the first time, the furrowed brow of my father as he managed his business, the gentle nurturing gaze of my mother. Each memory, each face, was a piece of a profound mosaic that was life.

A frantic knocking pounded through the bathroom, slicing through the peaceful haze that had enveloped me.

"Dakota!"

I recognized that voice. Ricky? Panic laced each syllable of my name as he pounded on the door.

It didn't matter though as I gave into the weightlessness taking over my body as if every cell was being lifted on a wave of tranquility. I realized then, this was not an ending but a transition, a crossing over into a different state of existence. As my consciousness began to merge with the light, the edges of my reality started to blur. More flashes came. A man's gaze so loving and pure, then Jesus being nailed to a cross The visions wavered, a kaleidoscope of suffering and love, of peace and pain. A certain calmness took over, making my heart resonate with a rhythm it had never known. I saw it then. Despite my mistakes, despite my failures, I was perfectly loved. Jesus touched the center of my a love greater than anything I'd experienced filled me

Ricky's voice became more frantic, his pounding on the door more desperate. But I couldn't answer him, couldn't reach out to tell him that everything was okay.

The images slowed gradually, fading until there was only darkness again. And then, quite unexpectedly, a new sensation blossomed within me. A soft light appeared in the distance, its warmth reaching out towards me, drawing me closer. I was no longer alone in my descent. My brother Gabriel, stood beside me, his soft blue eyes full of the same pure love I'd just experienced.

His lips moved, but his voice sounded as if he was speaking from underwater—distant yet clear.

The light gradually brightened around us, becoming a luminescent halo that pulsed in rhythm with my own heartbeat. Gabriel's grip on my hand tightened gently, his reassurance anchoring me in this surreal vortex between life and death. With each pulse, I felt myself being drawn towards the light — away from the world of cold tiles and bleach smells, away from the crushing weight of reality and towards a realm that projected serenity and warmth. The boundaries of my being began to dissolve, blending with the luminescent glow that surrounded us.

CHAPTER 53

March 10, 1:11 a.m.

TIM

As the outskirts of Quilcene rushed to greet me, my phone dinged from the passenger seat. Without taking my focus off the road, I snatched it up, thumb swiping the screen with an urgency that bordered on panic.

"Get here now. 911!"

Ricky's plea was sharp, a digital scream that filled my chest with ice. My foot slammed on the accelerator, the needle on the speedometer lurching past one hundred. The stop sign at the intersection was a blur—just another obstacle in a night full of them—as I shot through without a second thought.

Lights from the convenient store flickered as I passed, the neon beer signs in the bar's windows streaked across my vision as I tore through town.

The parking lot of Logger's Landing loomed ahead, an oasis of gravel and asphalt. I yanked the handbrake, the cruiser fishtailing into a dramatic slide that ate up the remaining distance. Gravel pinged against the undercarriage like gunfire as I skidded to a halt, throwing the door open before the car even stopped moving.

With Ricky's text flaring in my mind, I grabbed my Narcan kit before I jumped out of the car, praying I wouldn't need it. My

305

boots crunched on the gravel, the smell of damp earth and engine oil filling my nostrils as I sprinted toward the entrance of Logger's Landing.

Inside, the atmosphere was thick with despair and stale beer, a sense of foreboding hanging over the dated decor like a storm cloud. The usual laughter and clinking glasses were absent, replaced by a hush that clung to my skin.

"Dakota!" I called out, my voice cracking with the strain of suppressed terror. "Dakota!"

I shoved past tables and chairs, scanning the faces of patrons frozen mid-sip or mid-sentence, their eyes wide with shock or something darker.

"Please," I begged the universe, to anyone listening, "let her be okay."

A tremor shook through me as fear and helplessness crushed against my chest. "Dakota!" I yelled again as her image gathered in my mind—my childhood best friend, the girl who held my heart in her haunted eyes. She had to be okay. I couldn't lose her. Not now. Not ever.

Panic coursed through my veins as I sprinted down the hallway. The sound of my feet hitting the cold linoleum echoed through the empty corridors. My mind raced with fear and dread as I approached the bathroom, but when I saw Dakota lying lifeless on the ground, my world stopped spinning. Ricky was hunched over her, one hand folded over the other, compressing against her chest. Her once vibrant lips were not a haunting shade of purple and her skin a sickening shade of blue. My breath hitched in my throat, bringing me to a staggering halt. Ricky glanced over his shoulder, his gaze filled with raw, untamed horror that mirrored my own.

"Dakota!" I choked out her name again, stumbling towards her body. My fingers trembled as I checked for any signs of life, a pulse, a fluttering eyelid—something that could assure me that she wasn't gone.

Ricky continued his desperate ministrations, sweat dripping

from his forehead as he pumped his hands against her chest rhythmically, counting under his breath.

"Tim! Narcan, now!" Ricky's command cut through the paralysis gripping me. His hands moved with practiced urgency, breathing life into lungs that refused to draw air.

I stumbled backward, my legs nearly giving out. This wasn't supposed to be her story—not after clawing her way out of the darkness that had ensnared her for so long.

"Tim, damn it! Narcan!"

Ricky's voice was a lifeline thrown into the churning sea of my thoughts. I grabbed the Narcan with fumbling hands and tore off the packaging.

"Come on, come on." I barely recognized the motions of preparation, the muscle memory from countless hours of training guiding me as my mind screamed in protest.

"Please," I whispered, pushing the plunger down, delivering the first dose of Narcan into Dakota's still form. Her body remained unresponsive, the seconds stretching into agonizing eternities. My hands shook, my breath caught in my throat, as I willed the drug to work its miracle.

"Fight, Dakota. Fight," I urged, my voice a desperate plea to the void. There was no flutter of eyelids, no coughing, no sudden intake of breath—only silence. I could feel the seconds slipping through my fingers, each one a cruel phantom of possibility.

"Please," I whispered again, a prayer. "Don't take her from me."

The room faded, the sounds and sights blurring into insignificance. All that existed was Dakota's pale face, the rise and fall of Ricky's shoulders as he refused to yield, and the crushing weight of fear that this might be the moment where hope died.

"Stay with me, Dakota," I murmured, my voice cracking. But she remained still, the room so quiet I could hear the beat of my own heart pounding against my chest.

Outside, the distant wail of sirens began to rise, a symphony of despair and hope, intertwining. But for me, time stood still, holding my breath as we waited for Dakota to take hers.

"Tim, the other dose—now!" Ricky's voice, ragged from exertion, cleaved through the fog in my mind. My hands, slick with sweat and trembling with an adrenaline cocktail of fear and desperation, fumbled for the second Narcan kit.

With a shaking hand, I grasped the second kit, ripped it open and pulled out the plunger. With shaky hands, I put it up to her nose and released it. The world seemed to dim around me as I focused entirely on the task at hand. The sirens grew louder with each heartbeat that Dakota didn't share.

"Come on, Dakota. Don't leave me," I begged under my breath, my voice barely audible over the wailing sirens that were now so close, their red and blue lights likely painting the night sky just outside Logger's Landing.

I watched her face intently, searching for any sign of life—a twitch, a shudder, anything to indicate she was coming back to us. The seconds ticked by, weighted with the gravity of a lifetime, each one heavy enough to crush the fragile hope I still harbored.

"Fight, Dakota!" I urged again, this time a command born of both love and terror. "Don't let go."

The ambulance sirens continued their relentless approach, promising help but also reminding me of the grim reality we faced. Each wail seemed to echo my own fears, the possibility of loss amplifying until it was almost too loud to bear.

"God, please," I prayed, my normally secular heart finding religion in the face of Dakota's stillness. The room spun around me, the walls closing in, yet all I could see was her—the woman who had my heart since we were kids playing hide-and-seek in the woods. "Stay with me, Coda," I murmured. "You've never backed down from a fight. Don't start now."

Suddenly, a sharp intake of breath sliced through the stifling tension like a beacon. Dakota's chest rose abruptly, her body convulsing slightly as a rush of air filled her lungs. It was the most beautiful sound I'd ever heard—a gasp that sang of life clawing its way back from the abyss.

"Dakota?" My voice cracked, raw with the surge of emotions that flooded through me—relief, love, fear all melding into an overwhelming torrent. Her eyelids fluttered, the haunted darkness of her gaze obscured by the struggle to re-engage with the world.

"Tim?" Her voice was barely a whisper, but it roared in my ears like a victory cry. Her hand twitched in mine, a tentative grasp that held all the strength and fragility of her spirit.

"Stay with me. You're doing great," I encouraged, gently squeezing her hand.

Ricky let out a choked noise, part laugh and part sob, relief etched deeply into the lines of his face. "Paramedics are here," he announced, his voice steadying as he stepped away to let the professionals take over. But I couldn't move, couldn't think beyond the moment.

The medics bustled around us, their swift efficiency a blur as they stabilized Dakota, prepping her for the journey ahead. But in that bubble of time, it was just Dakota and me— two souls tethered amidst a swirl of chaos. The harsh, artificial light cast long, haunting shadows across her face, transforming the familiar features I held dear into harsh landscapes of struggle and survival. But beneath the apprehension and dread, there was also a flicker of defiance—a spirit that refused to be extinguished.

The paramedics moved with a rhythm born out of numerous crisis situations, transferring her body onto a stretcher, their gloved hands tender yet firm as they secured her for transport. The paramedics loaded her onto the stretcher, and allowed me to ride with her to the hospital. The journey through the dark streets was a blur, flashing lights illuminating fragments of reality that I barely noticed. All my focus was drawn to Dakota, to her fragile breaths and paler-than-moonlight complexion.

CHAPTER 54

March 10, 1:26 a.m.

DAKOTA

Tim's hand never let go of mine when they lifted me onto the gurney and then into the ambulance. It was the one thing I was fully aware of as I felt the tug of that other realm, pulling me back toward it. I was partially conscious of my world around me. I closed my eyes, giving into the intoxicating pull of the darkness.

"Stay with me, Dakota," Tim whispered, gripping my hand harder, as if he could somehow tether me to this world with his touch alone.

The siren from the ambulance was a dim echo in my ears, the lights an annoying flicker behind my eyelids. I opened my eyes and looked at Tim. His face was pinched, worry lines etched into his forehead. My eyes were too heavy though, and breathing felt like an impossible task. I let my eyes close again, the darkness coming back in waves.

"You can't leave me, Dakota." Tim's words were barely a whisper over the blaring sirens, his voice full of desperation. But it was easier to sink into the abyss than fight against the relentless pull.

I felt myself drift further away, the voices becoming whispers, my body numb and weightless. But then I felt Tim's hand squeeze mine again, harder this time, as if trying to anchor me in the stormy sea of consciousness.

I didn't want to hurt him, but I wasn't sure I could keep fighting, not when the most beautiful peace beckoned me—more alluring than any drug.

"Give us space. She's crashing," someone said with urgency, but it was hard to hear as the darkness descended over me.

"Dakota, please stay with me," Tim's desperate voice was muted, sounding far away.

Gabriel appeared before my vision once more, his loving presence a beacon guiding me through the symphony of light. The memory of pain, of suffering, it was all dissipating like smoke in the wind. Each ragged breath I had taken in the world I left behind now replaced it with an ethereal serenity. My consciousness seemed to extend infinitely, merging seamlessly with everything around me—the light, Gabriel and something more profound, something ancient and timeless.

His face was in front of me, full of vibrancy. He spoke, and this time I could hear him. "It's not your fault, Dakota." His words washed over various fractures in my heart, sealing them with an ineffable warmth. In those words, I felt the weight of his forgiveness, safety, and depth of his understanding.

He hadn't judged me for his death. I did not have to pay for my past mistakes. I could let it all go. He took my hand, and the warmth of his touch infused me with a sense of peace that radiated through my entire being. His smile mirrored my own, one that held not only love but understanding and acceptance. There was no more pain between us, no more anger over what he had done to me and no more guilt over his passing.

The tension, the remorse that had been gnawing at me for years, suddenly didn't matter anymore. I was forgiven, I was loved. This was beyond mere redemption—it was absolution.

I reached out, my fingers brushing against the edges of his ethereal form. His smile widened, a shimmering ripple spreading across the light that enveloped him. His whisper touched my consciousness again, "I'm okay, Dakota, and so are you."

"Dakota, please," Tim's voice broke through the serene moment, shattering the peace like a stone thrown at a window. His voice was full of agony, filling me with a sense of guilt that rivaled the tranquility I had just experienced.

For a moment, I wavered between both worlds—between Tim's desperate plea and Gabriel's calming presence. The pull from both sides was strong, like a relentless tug of war between past and present, guilt and absolution, life and death.

"Fight, Dakota," Tim's said again, more urgent this time, the words piercing through the veil that separated me from my imperfect reality.

My eyelids fluttered open, and I was instantly hit by the blinding brightness of the ambulance lights, making me wince. As the haze lifted from my eyes, I saw Tim's face in front of mine—his features full of raw emotions, brimming with worry and relief. I realized then how much he cared for me, and how much he'd been through because of me.

"Tim," I whispered, my throat feeling raw.

"I'm right here." His free hand reached out and gently brushed a loose lock of hair away from my face. "And you are going to be okay," he said fiercely, his hand cradling mine with an unyielding grip. It was more than a mere physical act. It was a tether, an anchor that kept me grounded in a world I was so close to leaving. His words were not just hollow promises but declarations of faith. They resounded in my foggy consciousness, slowly piecing together the shattered remnants of my willpower.

I tried to smile, but my lips felt heavy, as if they were made of lead.

"Never doubted you," he said, choking back tears as he caressed my face. "You're the strongest person I know."

His words stirred something inside me, a small spark of stubborn resolve that refused to be extinguished entirely. I squeezed Tim's hand in response, a weak but determined confirmation of my will to hold on.

He leaned closer, pressing his forehead against mine. "That's it, Dakota," he encouraged softly, "You're doing great."

I nodded, gazing into his brimming eyes. It was a small act, barely a twitch of my muscles, but it felt monumental. I was still here. I was still fighting. No matter how much the darkness beckoned, no matter how soothing the call of oblivion felt, I wouldn't let it take me. Not while Tim held onto me so desperately.

CHAPTER 55

March 10, 6:00 a.m.

TIM

For hours, Dakota fought for her life on the hospital bed in front of me, her chest rising and falling with a mechanical rhythm that belied the stillness of her form. Her dark hair spilled across the pillow like an ink stain on pristine white, and under the harsh glare of fluorescent lights, her pallor was that of marble—cold and unnervingly perfect. The beeps of the heart monitor were a grim metronome to my vigil. I reached out with a trembling hand, the warmth of her skin a crisp variance to the chill that had taken up residence in my bones. In that touch, there was gratitude—an overwhelming surge of it—that she was still here, still breathing. But beneath the relief, suspicion coiled in my gut like a restless serpent, ready to strike. I'd sat with her all night, staying close, willing her to pull through, nodding off occasionally, leaning my head on her bed.

Throughout the night, the weight of what had happened threatened to crush me. If Ricky hadn't found her when he had, if he hadn't known what to do, if I hadn't had the Narcan. There were so many variables that would have changed this night into one I wasn't sure I would have survived. I thought of my conversation with Tamara earlier and how I had asked her to pray. I'd never been a religious man, but tonight, with Dakota by my side, alive, I couldn't help but thank God for the miracle that lay beside me. God had saved Dakota tonight, and in doing so, he had saved me.

My phone lit up. It was Tamara. After all the chaos subsided, I had managed to send her a message saying I found Dakota. I wanted to reassure her without waking her. She was over eight months pregnant. She needed her rest to deal with whatever the day would hold with Dakota.

"Tim?" she said, her voice tired and concerned. "Is she safe?"

"Yes," I answered and paused, emotions rising in my throat at the memory of finding Dakota lifeless on the floor, Ricky fighting to resuscitate her. "But, Tamara, she's in the hospital. Jefferson General."

There was a sharp intake of breath on the other end—a pause that stretched long enough to fill me with regret for having to deliver such news.

"What happened?"

"She overdosed." I clenched my jaw, willing the tremble from my words as I watched Dakota's chest rise and fall. "She's stable now. The doctors say she'll pull through."

"Thank God." Tamara exhaled, the relief palpable in her voice. "I'll be there as fast as I can."

"Thank you." The words seemed inadequate to express the depth of gratitude I felt as I ended the call. I sank into the chair. Gritty-eyed from lack of sleep, I focused on Dakota's peaceful face, yearning for some sign of life beyond the mechanical rhythm of her breathing. My mind replayed every moment leading to this, scouring for missed signs, for clues I should've caught. Whatever sinister plot had ensnared Dakota, I would unravel it thread by thread. My hand found Dakota's, her skin cool and fragile beneath my touch.

I interlaced our fingers like interlocking puzzle pieces, hoping that the simple gesture would somehow anchor her to this world. My thumb traced gentle patterns her hand.

"Tim?" she mumbled.

A surge of relief washed over me at the sound of her voice, weak and feeble, yet music to my ears. "Dakota," I said, squeezing her hand in response.

Her eyelids fluttered. Slowly, very slowly, her eyes opened, and the sight nearly brought me to my knees. "Tim?" she repeated, her voice a mere wisp of air carrying a question. Her gaze wandered to our entwined hands and then to my face.

"Yeah, it's me."

She frowned, scrutinizing my face as if trying to commit it to memory, then slowly nodded. "You... you're here," she murmured.

"Always," I replied.

She scanned the sterile room around us until her focus landed on the heart monitor. The green line danced in rhythm with her heartbeats. Her brows furrowed, the gentle creases in her forehead indicating a struggle to comprehend. Her fingers gripped mine tighter.

I spoke in a soft tone, careful not to startle her as I delivered the harsh truth. "We're in the hospital, Dakota. You overdosed." The words hung heavy in the air, and I watched as they slowly registered on her face. Her eyes clouded over with a mix of emotions—disbelief, regret, shame—as memories flooded back to her. It was like watching a storm pass by in slow motion, each one crashing into the next until all that was left was a sense of overwhelming sadness.

"I... I... " Her voice trembled as she attempted to articulate her thoughts, but the words seemed stuck in her throat. She looked away, and a single tear trickled down her pale cheek.

"We're going to get through this, Dakota," I said, trying to reassure her. "You're not alone."

"I'm so sorry, Tim," she whispered, turning to look at me. Her gaze was full of regret and shame.

I leaned in close and gingerly cupped her face in my hands. "I love you so much, Dakota."

She trembled as she began to cry.

"I would have died if something happened to you." I confessed, tears ran down my face and landed on her cheeks.

"I'm so sorry," she whispered again, her voice hitched by sobs.

"It's okay, Dakota. I'm sorry too." I leaned searched her face. "I should have listened to you instead of jumping to conclusions."

Sadness overwhelmed her countenance as she scanned my face. "Listen?" she asked, her voice falling to a soft whisper.

"When I saw you with the package. When you told me you were trying to keep me safe."

Her gaze was locked on mine, brimming with fear and hope alike. "I was."

"And I said things... things that I should never have said."

"You were angry," she said, her voice barely above a whisper. "You had every right to be."

"No, Dakota." I shook my head, choking back my own tears. "I should have slowed down. I should have heard you out."

Her features softened and she extended her free hand to tenderly wipe the tears from my cheeks. It was a simple, gentle motion, yet it held so much meaning.

"I can't go back to who I was, Tim." Her voice was a broken whisper, all the fight drained out of her. "I can't be that person anymore."

"You're not that person anymore," I said as I reached into my pocket, fingers closing around the small band that she had thrown at me last night in the middle of our fight—the symbol of our commitment—a commitment that had been tested by fire. The engagement ring, a simple band crowned with a modest diamond, had once promised a future free of the darkness that stalked us. Now, it felt more like a vow—a vow to fight for that future, come what may.

Gently, I held her left hand, bringing it up to my lips. She watched my every move, her eyes reflecting a river of emotions. Uncertainty, confusion, hope... it was all there. I took the ring from my pocket and gently placed it on her finger.

She stared at the ring, silent tears cascading off her cheeks. Her fingers trembled as she touched the ring, tracing its outline as though savoring its existence. "I thought I had lost you," she said finally. "I thought that Victor had won."

At the mention of his name, anger flared within me. I didn't want to talk about this now. I wanted to tend her wounds and love her back to health until she was fully the Dakota that I knew and loved. But the questions that had plagued my mind earlier came rushing to the forefront. What had she meant when she said she was trying to keep me safe? Was she trying to keep me safe from Victor?

"Victor Mendez?" I found my voice and repeated her words.

Her gaze dropped to our hands, now tangled together on the worn-out hospital blanket. Her lip trembled as she took a shaky breath, a sign that the truth wasn't going to come easy. "Yes."

My cop's mind kicked into overdrive, trying to piece together fragments of conversations, reactions, odd moments but it still didn't make sense. "Dakota, please, help me understand."

She hesitated, her eyes flickering with the struggle between fear and trust. She took a deep breath as if to gather her scattered courage, and then she spoke, her voice still trembling but no less determined. "It all started the day you proposed to me. Just as I was leaving work, Justin and Avery showed up. They said Victor sent them. That he was calling in a favor because of Ryan's death. They said I owed them."

Because of Ryan? I suddenly wanted to punch something. Victor was calling in a favor because of Ryan's death? Ryan had tormented Dakota for years. Tamara's words from last night clicked into place as the puzzle pieces fell together. Dakota had told her Ryan was always there, threatening retribution. "What kind of favor?" I said, pulse thrumming, a drumbeat of anger and protectiveness.

"Running a package." The words spilled out, laced with shame and desperation. "I tried to refuse. I didn't want anything to do with it after all the work I'd done to stay clean, but they threatened you—said they'd hurt you if I didn't do it."

319

"Damn it!" Fury crackled beneath my skin, a storm ready to break.

"Tim, I tried to refuse. I did." Her voice cracked. "But they made it clear there was no choice. I know what they are capable of."

The pain I felt was unbearable, like a dagger in my stomach twisting with each word she spoke. How had I not seen the signs? Especially after the night she told me she almost relapsed. "Why didn't you tell me?"

"I couldn't risk something happening to you." Her raw answer stripped me bare, revealing just how deeply this woman loved me, even if it meant sacrificing herself.

Hot coals burned in my stomach. Victor used Dakota's love and loyalty toward me to drag her into his twisted circle. But why? Did he relish the idea of destroying people's lives? Was this fun for him? "Dakota, in order to beat this, I need to know everything."

Her mouth tightened. "I thought it was over, Tim. I thought after that first package, Victor would leave us alone."

I adjusted the stiff plastic chair closer to her bed, every muscle in my body tensed, ready for battle. "But he didn't."

Her eyes, mirroring the storm that had become our lives, locked onto mine. "Justin and Avery came back. I put up a fight. I told them I wouldn't do it. They roughed me up pretty good."

My fists clenched involuntarily, the nails biting into my skin. The notion of anyone laying a hand on Dakota ignited a fury in me so intense that I worried I might break down the walls of the hospital room. "They hurt you?"

"They did," she whispered. "But Ricky was there. He defended me."

"Ricky?" It was hard to keep the surprise from my tone. Ricky was in on this too?

"Ricky told them to back off. Then stood between us like a shield. But then." She hesitated as she seemed to sink into the painful memory. "Ricky told me that if I didn't do what Victor wanted"—she swallowed hard as sadness overtook her expression —"Victor would put a hit out on you."

"A hit on me?" The words echoed in my mind, ringing like a funeral toll as they sank in. A cold chill ran down my spine, the reality of Victor's threat crashing into me like a torrential wave of icy fear. I could handle threats against me—I had taken plenty of them in stride throughout my career in law enforcement—but this was different.

This wasn't just a threat against my life—it was a threat against Dakota's peace. She'd already lost so much, sacrificed too much, and now she was being blackmailed into risking everything for me.

"I couldn't let that happen. I couldn't risk your life, Tim." Dakota said, her voice strained with anguish. "So, I...I did what Victor wanted."

Dakota had relapsed because of Victor's manipulation, because she'd been terrified for my life. My heart clenched painfully at the thought, my mind spinning with the horrifying realization.

The walls of the hospital room shrunk around me, my pulse thrumming in my ears. I took a moment, trying to control my breathing. I needed to stay calm, focused. "Do you know what was in those packages?" I asked, forcing myself to keep my voice steady.

"No," she whispered, her attention dropping to our entwined hands. "I didn't want to know. I just wanted it to be over." The pain in her voice was palpable, a raw wound spread out for the world to see. My chest tightened at the sight of her so broken, so defeated. Dakota had always been a fighter, someone who never backed down. To see her this way was devastating.

"And Ricky?" I pressed, needing to understand the full scope of the situation.

"He was helping Victor, but he hated it. He confided in me when we were at Logger's." She sniffed, swiping at her cheek.

"Victor is doing the same thing to Ricky that he did to me. Using whatever leverage he could to force him to do his dirty work."

The sickening realization twisted my gut. I had known Victor was a manipulative prick, but this... this was something else entirely. "What do they have on Ricky?" I asked, a bitter taste reaching the back of my tongue.

She shook her head, weariness overtaking her beautiful face. "I don't know. Ricky just said they were after him because of his family ties. Victor thought he'd be a good replacement for Ryan."

My mind raced with the implications. Ricky, like Dakota, was a pawn in Victor's brutal game. The thought sickened me. This whole situation was spiraling out of control and the stakes were too high—lives were on the line.

A tide of rage washed over me, turning my vision red as I grappled with the scorching anger in my chest. "I'm going to end this, Dakota." I looked at her with a renewed determination. "I'm not going to let Victor play with our lives anymore. I'm going to bring him down if it's the last thing I do."

Fear flickered in her expression, but there was something else. There was trust.

"Please, just... don't lose yourself in this revenge," she pleaded, her gaze searching mine for the reassurance only I could provide.

"Revenge isn't what drives me, Dakota. It's justice. For you. For us." I brushed a stray lock of hair from her forehead, the action tender yet laced with an unspoken promise of retribution.

A heavy silence hung between us, filled with the unsaid words and promises. The beeping of the machines tethered us to this world, but our hearts were navigating the murky waters of a future fraught with peril.

Her eyes closed, and I watched the tension ease from her features as she drew comfort from our entwined hands. I kissed her forehead gently, sealing our pact with the brush of my lips against her skin.

As she drifted into the fitful sleep of the wounded, I sat there, her hand clasped in mine, feeling the weight of the ring on her finger.

The darkness outside the hospital window seemed to press against the glass, a reminder of the shadows that lurked, waiting for us. But within these walls, with Dakota by my side, I found a sense of purpose that turned the simmering fear in my veins into a resolve as sharp as a blade.

"Rest now, Dakota" I whispered to her sleeping form. "I've got a war to wage."

And with that silent vow hanging in the air, I steeled myself for the confrontation to come. Justin and Avery, and yes, Ricky too—they would all answer for what they'd done.

CHAPTER 56
March 10, 9:15 a.m.
TAMARA

Joe maneuvered the jeep through the bustling streets of Port Townsend Washington and parked it in front of Jefferson County Hospital. The building loomed in front of us, its brick façade stark against the blush painted sky of the early morning. He cut the engine, and the jeep shuddered to a halt. "Ready?" Joe asked, looking over at me.

I nodded, holding tightly to the peace that I'd fought for all the way here. On the three-hour drive, I played worship music and rehearsed the scripture God had given me last week while praying for my family. *My peace I leave with you, my peace I give unto you.* I knew then that the peace he gave to me had little to do with circumstances and everything to do with the fact that he was with me inside the storm. And last night he'd answered my prayers once more by saving Dakota's life. I had to trust that he would bring us through whatever trials lay ahead.

I pulled out my phone with trembling hands and texted Tim, "We're here." Almost immediately, the brisk ding of a reply pushed against the silence in my head: "Meet you outside."

"Tim's coming out," I told Joe.

In the back seat, Lillie played with a picture book, babbling at a picture, oblivious to the storm swirling around her.

"Alright, let's pray he has good news." His hand came to rest on my knee, with a warm and tight squeeze, his silent way of reassuring me.

Tim emerged like a sentinel, his short-cropped brown hair tousled by the wind, the lines of worry etched into his youthful features.

I climbed out of the car to meet him. Joe circled the car and grabbed Lillie from her car seat as Tim crossed the parking lot.

"Hey," he greeted us, his voice carrying a tiredness that mirrored my own.

"Tim," I said, swallowing the knot that had taken residence in my throat. "How is she?"

"Been in and out of consciousness," he said, his gaze steady but I could tell it was a struggle to maintain. "She's sleeping now, but the doctors say she's going to pull through."

Relief washed through me, a warm wave that seemed to bring color into the world. Joe exhaled sharply next to me, his grip tightening around our daughter as he nodded to Tim.

Tim sighed and nodded, running a hand through his hair. "It's better than what it could've been," he said finally. Light seeped from the horizon, casting long shadows over Tim's face. He looked so much older than he was—weary from the strain of watching someone he loved fight a battle they might not win.

Lillie's chubby arms reached out eagerly for her soon-to-be Uncle Tim. Her face lit with excitement, and she bounced in Joe's arms, eager to capture his attention. Did she sense the sadness inside him? Without hesitation, Tim scooped her up into a tight hug, finding comfort in the innocent embrace of a child.

Tim finally spoke again. "Listen. I wanted to thank you so much for your prayers last night." He shook his head. "I can't explain it... I'm not even sure if I believe it. But it's a miracle that Dakota is still with us."

I nodded as tears burned my eyes. "Our prayers are with you both, Tim. We're one call away anytime."

He nodded his gratitude, his gaze drifting towards the

hospital's entrance as a rush of medical personnel came pouring out. The sight appeared disturbingly normal, the chaos of the hospital's daily operations seemingly in contrast with our own world that had come to a standstill.

As if sensing the shift in the atmosphere, Lillie's laughter faded away. Her tiny fingers curled around the collar of Tim's shirt, her young face mirroring the worry lines etched on ours. "We definitely need your continued prayers. I can't go into detail, but it seems that Dakota had been targeted and purposefully manipulated to drag her back into her old life."

I sucked in a sharp breath, my mind whirling. Dakota had fought so hard to step away from her past of drugs and addiction. The thought of someone using her vulnerabilities against her was devastating.

"Deliberately?" I questioned the implications sinking in. I looked at Joe. His hand found mine, entwining our fingers together, giving my hand a firm squeeze.

Tim shook his head, expression solemn. "I need to go and dig deeper into all this. It's good you are here because I don't want to leave Dakota alone."

"We're here now." Joe said, his voice assuring.

"And we're not going anywhere soon," I agreed.

"Thank you both. I can't tell you how much it means to have you here." With a final squeeze of Lillie's hand, he handed her off to me before making his way toward his police cruiser. We watched him drive away and then Joe turned to me. "Sounds like we might be here for a while. Why don't you go and spend time with your sister while Lillie and I find a hotel for the next few nights."

I nodded, though a part of me didn't want to face what was in the hospital room alone. Joe was right though, and bringing in an energetic toddler into Dakota's room while she was resting didn't seem like a good idea either. Joe pulled me into a group hug with him and Lillie and whispered a quick prayer.

"I'll be back soon," he said, his confidence lending me

strength. Then he loaded Lillie into her car seat, and they were off, leaving me alone in front of the hospital building.

I watched their car disappear around a corner before steeling myself, taking a deep breath and walking towards the entrance.

CHAPTER 57

March 10, 9:30 a.m.

TIM

The morning outside was bitter cold as I drove, a reflection of the icy fury within me. Overhead the clouds painted the town in the shades of gray of the coming storm, the silence interrupted only by the distant hum of traffic. I thought about Victor and his twisted pawns that did his bidding. Victor seemed out of reach at the moment, but Justin, Avery and Ricky would be easy enough to find.

Every turn I made was one closer to them, one more step down a path I knew was dark and dangerous. But somewhere along the line, fear had turned into resolve. Today, for Dakota's sake, I would find a way to serve justice to those who had inflicted so much pain upon her.

Justin, with his sick smile and expression as cold as ice. Avery, his willing accomplice, all bluster and bravado with just a hint of fear in his eyes. And then there was Ricky. I wasn't sure what to think about him. In Victor's eye, he was Ryan's replacement, and he had been culpable in Dakota's torment, yet he had saved her. If he hadn't helped me find her. If he hadn't of been there, Dakota would have died. The thoughts of her lifeless body, cold purple lips and the sick bluish hue to her skin would forever haunt me.

The pathways of my heart ran cold, but the embers of resolve flared hot at the forefront of my mind, igniting a flame that could burn worlds.

My phone rang, piercing through the silence with its insistent tone. It was my partner Ramirez. But why was she calling me now? We weren't scheduled to work for hours. I answered hesitantly, trying to keep my voice steady. I couldn't let her get involved in this dangerous situation until I knew the full extent of what I was facing.

"Ramirez," I answered smoothly, "What's up?" There was a pause before she responded, her voice tinged with worry, "Hey, something's come up. Captain Simmons wants to see you."

A cold pit settled in my stomach. "Is there a reason why?" I asked, my tone casual despite the sudden rush of anxiety. Ramirez sighed into the phone, her voice lowering to a whisper. "He's been reviewing the tapes. Seven minutes are missing and it coincides with my coffee break."

Fear rushed through me. In the moment that I had stopped that tape, I hadn't even thought about the repercussions, I just acted on basic fear and the need to protect Dakota.

"He just questioned me about it, but I didn't know what to say. I was gone and you can hear me leaving on the tapes."

A cold sweat broke out across my skin as the implications of her words sunk in.

Once I stopped recording last night in order to protect Dakota, I was aware that this could become a problem. But right now, I wasn't prepared to deal with the consequences of my hasty decision. "Thanks for letting me know, Ramirez," I muttered, my mind already spinning with possibilities of how to navigate this conversation with Simmons. "I'll handle it."

"Tim," she started, her voice faltering a bit. "This is serious, you know? Simmons...he won't let this go."

I swallowed hard, my throat dry. "I know." The gravity of the situation was not lost on me. I was all too aware that Simmons was a hound when it came to sniffing out discrepancies.

"I know. I'll figure something out. Don't worry about it." But even as I said those words, my mind was a whirlwind of fear and uncertainty. What if Simmons already suspected something was off? What if he brought Internal Affairs into this? Damn. The tiniest slip, the smallest discrepancy, could send my career spiraling.

"I'll head to the station right away." I hung up the phone and turned the car around, my pulse pounding in my veins. As I drove to the police station, I could only think of one thing—Dakota. The fear that rose with in me had nothing to do with my potential career suicide or the prospect of an IA investigation. No, my fears were all for her. If Simmons found out about the missing footage, then it wouldn't be long before he discovered what I was trying to hide.

CHAPTER 58

March 10, 9:45 a.m.

TAMARA

Nurses rushed down the hallways, doctors conferred in hushed voices over charts, and the pervasive scent of disinfectant hung heavy in the air. The receptionist finally handed me a visitor's badge, her sympathetic smile doing little to halt the unease twisting in my stomach. With a nod of thanks, I found the elevator and pressed the button for the fourth floor.

Inside me, a tempest brewed—a fierce concoction of dread and determination. With each thud of my heart, I felt the weight of what we faced. In the quiet corners of my mind, prayers mingled with fears, forming a silent vigil for Dakota's safety, for Tim's return.

Pushing open the door to Dakota's room, a gasp escaped my lips. There she was—my little sister, lying so still on the hospital bed, a ghostly pale shadow of her vibrant self. Her dark hair fanned out across the pillow, and the steady beep of the heart monitor played counterpoint to the ragged rhythm of my breathing.

I walked across the room with careful steps to the chair next to her bed and gently took hold of her hand, fighting tears.

My thumb stroked her hand, each caress a wordless prayer. I imagined infusing her with life, with the warmth she needed to chase away the chill of this place. The soft sound of her breath brought me a measure of comfort, a reminder that where there is breath, there is hope.

Dakota stirred slightly, her eyelids fluttering. I held my breath, wondering if she would wake, but she settled once more into sleep's embrace.

In that cold, liminal space between wakefulness and dreams, I clung to her hand and prayed for a miracle. Prayed for Tim's safety. Prayed for the redemption we were all seeking. And somewhere, deep within me, fear gnawed at the edges of my resolve. But I pushed it away, buried it beneath layers of faith and love, because that was what Dakota needed from me now.

The coldness of the chair seeped into my bones as I sat vigil, Dakota's hand clutched in mine, her skin pale against the stark white sheets.

"Tim," her voice rasped, so faint I thought I imagined it.

I jerked upright, my attention snapping to Dakota's face. Her eyelids were parting, revealing the haunted pools of her eyes, now clouded with confusion and pain.

"He went to work, sweetie," I said softly, stroking her hair away from her forehead. "But he'll be back soon."

Dakota's brow furrowed, her lips trembling as she tried to speak. "I'm scared, Tamara." She looked at me then, the lines of fear etched deeply into her youthful face. The admission twisted my gut, and I fought to keep my face neutral as I squeezed her hand reassuringly.

"I know, Dakota, I know," I admitted. "But you're not alone. "I'm right here."

"But Tim..." Her voice was a barely audible whisper, each word wheezing its way out of her lips.

"Don't worry about Tim," I said, my voice more solid than I felt. "He's safe, and he's doing what he's good at. Trust him."

She nodded slowly, as if she took strength from my words, but the fear in her features didn't entirely fade. My heart ached for her.

"The only thing you have to worry about right now is getting better," I told her, swallowing the lump in my throat. "Just focus on that. Nothing else."

Dakota exhaled a shaky breath and nodded again, her hand weakly squeezing mine back. "I'm so sorry, Tamara. I didn't mean..." Her voice cracked and she trailed off.

"It's okay," I whispered, my fingerstroking the stray tendrils of hair on her forehead. "I know."

Tears streamed down her face as her gaze locked onto mine—haunted, yet full of a determination that clenched at my heart. It was the look of someone who had been to the edge and stared into the abyss, only to return with a newfound resolve. It was painful and beautiful all at once. It was Dakota.

"Did Tim tell you"—she hesitated and swallowed hard—"that I died?"

I blinked, taken aback by her words. Of course, I knew about the overdose, but hearing her phrase it like that stole my breath. "He said you overdosed."

Dakota's lips parted in a breathless whisper. "I died, Tam. They brought me back, but for a moment... I was gone."

The harsh reality of it was too much to bear. My baby sister, the one I held when she was just a newborn, the one I'd protected and cared for, had brushed against death's cool fingertips. My throat constricted, and my vision blurred with tears.

"The thing is, I wasn't afraid. Your Jesus was there, and for the first time in my life, I felt truly and deeply loved, no matter how much I'd messed up." She paused, looking upward as if searching the shadows on the ceiling for words. "It was the purest form of love you could imagine."

A tear slipped down my face as her words settled in my heart. Such profound peace in the face of such profound darkness was a juxtaposition that left me breathless. I thought of Joe and me praying for her last night when we got the call from Tim that he couldn't find her. Jesus had shown up for Dakota in her darkest hour. He had heard my prayer and met her in the abyss. The thought humbled me and stirred something deep within.

"And then I saw Gabriel," Dakota whispered.

My breath caught in my throat. Gabriel? Our late brother. He'd been such a source of pain in Dakota's life...

"He was so peaceful and vibrant, more alive and real than you could imagine," Dakota continued, her voice a fragile murmur that sliced through the silence of the hospital room. "He healed something between us, Tamara." Tears welled in her eyes again, before spilling over.

The memories of our brother flooded back—his laughing eyes, his wide grin, the sound of his voice. And the many times he'd taken the beating for us when he was a kid.

"He told me it wasn't my fault that he died." Her voice broke, making a jagged sound that felt like it was tearing through my soul.

I closed my eyes against the wave of emotion that crashed into me. Gabriel's words were a balm to the wounds etched deep in Dakota's soul—scars that had festered and bled for far too long. Our brother was at peace, and he'd given Dakota something far more valuable than anything this world could offer—the truth. The truth to set her free from the suffocating guilt that had followed her like a relentless shadow. What a gift in the middle of this insane storm.

I blinked away my own tears and was quiet for a while, just holding her hand and letting the enormity of her words settle around us like a comforting blanket. Finally, I found my voice.

"Dakota," I whispered. I could barely comprehend what she had just said. The potential for that revelation to transform her life was overwhelming. "That's absolutely wonderful." My voice choked up. "It's time to fully let go of the past and let yourself live. Seeing Gabriel was a gift. And you coming back..." I stopped, my voice catching in my throat. "You coming back is your chance for a fresh start. To move forward with Tim and create a new life. A life that's free from guilt, fear, and the shadows of the past."

"Tim..." she whispered, biting her lower lip. "I'm really scared for him. They threatened to kill him if I didn't make the drops for them. And now Tim knows everything."

The confusing statement sent a chill down my spine, spreading unease and fear throughout my body. I leaned closer, hoping to understand her troubled words. "Who, Dakota? Who threatened Tim?"

Her features filled with a palpable fear that made my chest constrict. "Victor, Avery, Justin... There's too many of them. And I'm afraid that Tim will take matters into his own hands after this."

"Hey, it's okay," I reassured her. "He's strong, and he's smart. He knows what he's doing. And more than that, my Jesus, the one you met last night, he's watching over Tim, too. "

Dakota remained silent, her gaze distant and hand tighter as if drawing strength from the contact. A silent agreement hung heavily in the air between us. In the stillness that followed, I held onto her hand like a lifeline, letting the silent prayers for redemption and safety rise within me. Fear prowled at the edges of my consciousness, an icy phantom threatening to consume me whole. But I pushed it back, filling my mind with fervent prayers, letting the peace that God given me as a shield be the thing I focused on as I prayed for Tim, for Dakota and for everyone tangled in this dangerous web.

CHAPTER 59

March 10, 9:55 a.m.

TIM

The city streets blurred into a monochrome tunnel as I accelerated, the car's engine growling in response. I couldn't believe this. My messy attempt to protect Dakota could be my downfall. All my work in the police force could be thrown away because of one mistake. Tampering with evidence could cost me more than just my badge; it could land me in prison from two to ten.

I hit the steering wheel. How was I going to talk myself out of this mess? Should I tell Simmons that Dakota was in the hospital? No, because he would find out it was because of an overdose and then it would be too easy to put the pieces together as to the reason for the missing footage.

I had always been good at improvising, but this... this was something else entirely. Each turn of the steering wheel felt like a heavy, damning decision. Every streetlight I passed under was a glaring spotlight, highlighting my guilt.

When I reached the precinct, I had no more of a plan than I did before. I made my way through the familiar hallways, each step harder than the last. The soft chatter of daytime officers and the mechanical hum of computers seemed louder than ever. I

ELISHEBA HAXBY & JESSE VINCENT

tried to keep a poker face, even managing a weak smile at Jenkins as I passed by his desk.

Reaching Captain Simmons' office, I took a deep breath and knocked on the door. His voice boomed, a deep baritone that seemed to resonate with authority. "Come in!"

I pushed the door open and stepped in, taking in the map-lined walls and dark mahogany desk littered with papers and coffee mugs. He looked up from the file he was reading, his brow furrowing into deep lines.

"Detective," he began, his voice gruff as he gestured towards the chair opposite his desk. "Have a seat."

I did as instructed, my senses alert to every minute detail. The scent of his black coffee wafting in the air mingled with old paper and ink, creating an atmosphere of impending doom.

"You know how invested I am in the Mendez-Rodrigez case."

"I do, sir," I managed to say, keeping my gaze firmly on him.

He shifted in his chair, rested his elbows on the surface of his desk, and laced his fingers together. "Every day since I got surveillance approved, I've been studying the tapes."

My heartrate spiked at the weight he put on the mention of the tapes.

"But," he continued, a frown casting a shadow over his face, "the feed from last night went black. For seven minutes."

I felt my stomach drop. "Seven minutes?"

"Seven minutes," Simmons repeated, watching me intently. "And it somehow happened when Officer Ramirez slipped out to get you coffee."

"That's... strange." I coughed, trying to keep my voice steady.

"Strange indeed," he repeated as his fingers drummed a steady rhythm on the worn wood of his desk.

"I don't understand," I said, keeping my eyes locked on his, hoping he would read sincerity in them. "Maybe there was a glitch in the system."

The Captain sighed and rubbed his temples, an obvious sign

of his growing frustration and impatience. "Perhaps. Call it a hunch if you will, but something feels off to me."

The room fell into a tense silence, my mind like a whirlpool of thoughts—each one darker than the last. Finally, I managed to muster a response, swallowing hard against the dryness in my throat. "I have no idea what would be off, sir. It's been pretty uneventful since Ramirez and I have been surveilling the Rodrigez house. And last night was no different."

He rose from his chair and began pacing slowly, his hands clasped behind his back. "I want to believe you, Tim," he said after a moment, his tone weary. He stopped in front of me, leaning against his desk, and for the first time since I walked into his office I saw doubt in his eyes. "But I need to know—is there something you're hiding?"

My heart pounded like a desperate prisoner as I searched for the best response. "You know me, sir. What would I possibly be hiding?"

"You're right. I do know you," he said solemnly. "You are one of the best officers we have in Jefferson County. I also know that you're human. You make mistakes. And sometimes, you let your personal feelings get in the way of your job. And I do also know that Victor Mendez has the uncanny ability to turn even the best people to his side, through manipulation, force, or blackmail."

Simmons' gaze was piercing, as if he could see straight through my façade, straight to the very secret that now threatened to unravel my career and potentially, my life. I held his gaze with all the fortitude I could muster, my jaw set in a firm line. I had always been headstrong and intuitive, but my loyalty and protective nature had landed me in hot water more times than I cared to admit. But never this hot of water.

"I understand your concerns, Captain," I said, hoping my calm demeanor would mask the turmoil raging within me. "But I assure you, last night was uneventful. Perhaps it's time to upgrade our system."

I knew it was a stretch to blame our old surveillance system, but it was plausible enough at the moment.

"There may be truth to that." He crossed his arms over his chest. "But until I have a chance to complete my investigation into this, you and Ramirez are off the Mendez case."

"Understood, Captain," I said.

"So you are okay with me just removing you like that? Haven't you put a lot of work into this case?"

I swallowed hard. "Yes, sir, but I trust you have your reasons."

The captain eyed me for longer than I would have liked, then finally broke the stare with a nod. "Okay then. Moore, you are dismissed."

"Yes, sir," I said as I rose from the chair. .

As I moved towards the door, Simmons spoke again, his voice surprisingly soft. "Moore," he started, causing me to pause and look back towards him. "You're a good officer, but in my years I have seen good officers go down bad paths because they got in too deep. If Victor has anything over you, you can let us know. I would hate it if anything happened to you. "

"Thank you, sir, I will," I said and then left his office. My head spun from the strain of maintaining my composure during our conversation.

Leaning against the cool concrete of the precinct's outer wall, I tried to regain my bearings. My usual confidence was quickly being replaced by a gnawing sense of dread that threatened to consume me. But I couldn't let it go. Dakota needed to be safe, and that meant ridding the streets of Justin and Avery. If I did it right, it could be swift and clean. I just needed to act fast.

CHAPTER 60
March 10, 10:55 a.m.

TAMARA

Dakota sat in her hospital bed, absentmindedly picking at the unappetizing lunch provided to her. I watched as she pushed the peas around her plate, not really eating anything. Her long dark hair hung around her face, and her body was drawn and fragile beneath the crisp white hospital sheets.

Suddenly, a sharp pang shot through my lower stomach. Another Braxton-Hicks contraction, but they seemed to be getting more intense. Anxiety crept up my spine like a spider, its cold legs leaving a trail of dread in their wake. In the midst of everything, the baby could not come now. It was too early.

"Tamara?" Dakota's voice was a frail thread in the air.

"Yes?" I turned my attention to her, brushing off my anxiety.

"Do you think it's possible for me to ever have a normal life?"

I blinked at her, the simmering pain of the contraction momentarily forgotten. My heart hurt for her as I thought of the many trials she'd been through. The abuse we grew up with, her being molested, her slow decline into addiction, her watching Gabriel die. She had been through so much, but the last few years, she had fought her way through her addiction and had built a life with Tim.

"Absolutely," I said emphatically. "You've fought harder than

343

anyone I know. This is just a setback. You'll get through it and come back stronger."

"I hope you're right."

A distant memory flashed before me. We were children again, running through the woods near the old trailer park, our laughter echoing through the trees. Dakota was always the faster runner, the fiercer competitor.

"Remember when we used to play tag in the woods behind the trailer park?" I started, hoping to lighten her spirit. Her lips twitched into an almost-smile as she looked at me with a forlorn nostalgia. "You always outran me, Dakota. You were unstoppable."

Dakota's gaze shifted from me to the window, where a lonely sparrow pecked at the sill, oblivious of our world. "Those were simpler times," she murmured, her voice a mere whisper in the fluorescent-lit room.

"Don't you see?" I asked. "The one who outran me in those woods, the one who was unstoppable...that's still you. You're still that girl, and she's still inside you, waiting to outrun this too."

She looked at me, a hint of warmth creeping into her expression. But it was replaced quickly with the same hollowness that had been there all morning.

"I don't know, sis, I think the demons that have been chasing me, they've finally caught up. They're too fast, too strong."

I wanted so badly to reassure her more, to promise her that everything would be okay, but the words felt hollow. "Maybe you just need to get out of here. You could come stay with Joe and me and rest for a while."

"I don't want to impose on you and Joe," she whispered. "You have your own life...your own family."

"Dakota, you're my sister," I said with a quiet intensity. "You're my family too."

Dakota's features sank into a thoughtful expression. She remained silent for so long that I feared she might have drifted off again. "I wouldn't want to be that far away from Tim."

"Tim is always welcome too. We have plenty of room."

Silence swept over us again, thick and heavy. The sharp tick-tock of the wall clock punctuated the quiet, reminding us of the time that was slipping away.

"Excuse me." A nurse's voice punctuated the moment with its clinical cheer. She peeked around the curtain, clipboard in hand. "Your parents are in the lobby to see you."

"Thank you," I said and stood to leave. The hospital only allowed two visitors at once in this wing of the hospital.

"We'll finish this conversation later. Just think about it."

She nodded, pressing her lips tightly before grabbing my hand, a fresh dread overshadowing her features. "I'm not sure if I can handle our parents' disappointment right now."

"Dakota. They're not here to judge you. They're here because they care, because they love you."

Dakota nodded and wiped a stray tear. I pulled her into a tight hug despite the forest of tubes and wires around us. "I'll be back soon," I promised and let her go.

The hallway was a river of activity—doctors, nurses, patients all flowing past in a current of life that did not cease for anyone's heartache. I found Mom and Dad waiting, their faces drawn, each wearing an expression of concern.

"Mom, Dad," I greeted, my voice steady even as another sharp pain hit me, this time in my lower back. Another wave of anxiety ran through me, and I prayed silently that everything was okay with the baby.

"Tamara." Dad's voice was gravelly. "How is she?"

"She's scared," I admitted, "but trying to be strong. She's worried about disappointing you two."

A ghost of relief washed over their tired faces at the words. Mom reached out for my hand, her grip trembling yet firm. "Your sister has always been a fighter," she said slowly. "We just need to remind her of that."

"How could this have happened? I thought she was doing so

well," Dad mumbled, his voice echoing the heaviness of defeat. There were no easy answers to his question.

"It's complicated." I sighed, rubbing my neck with aching fingers. "She has been doing well. This was just a setback." They didn't need to know the true horrors behind this fall.

"Dakota...she has a lot of demons," I continued. "Demons from her past that she's having a hard time putting to rest. I'm trying to talk her into staying with Joe and me for a bit, to heal, to get away from it all."

Dad's eyebrows furrowed in dismay while Mom's hands covered her mouth.

"I need to see her," Mom said urgently, her voice a shaky whisper.

"Of course. Just be gentle with her," I said, looking between the two of them. "It's hard for her, that she disappointed you both again."

They exchanged glances, and I saw a mutual understanding pass between them. Mom was the first to break the silence. "We'll be there for her, Tamara. No matter how many times she stumbles."

With that, they moved toward Dakota's room, their apprehensive strides echoing on the linoleum floor of the hospital wing. I watched them disappear behind the curtains, a whirlpool of anxiety twisting in my gut.

Closing my eyes, I leaned against the cool wall and rested my hand protectively on my swollen belly, feeling a bit strange, like something was off, but I couldn't put my finger on it. My phone vibrated, and I pulled it from my pocket. Tim's name lit the screen. I hit the green icon and spoke to him as I walked toward the exit of the hospital, needing fresh air. I told him that Dakota was doing physically better, though she seemed to be wrestling through the shame of the relapse. "Mom and Dad are in with her now," I told him.

"Okay, well, I have a few more things to take care of. I'll be back as soon as I can. Tell Dakota I love her, and please keep praying."

"I will, Tim." I said and ended the call. Stepping outside, I breathed in the crisp clean air and took a moment to soak in the silence. The hospital bustle was replaced with the calm hum of distant traffic and occasional bird calls. I sank onto a nearby bench, the cold metal seeping through my clothes but doing little to cool my nerves. I rested my hands on the curve of my belly once more, tracing idle patterns.

My phone vibrated again, pulling me from my quiet moment. Joe's picture lit the screen. "Joe, hey, I'm glad you called."

"How is she doing? And how are you holding up?"

I sighed, letting my head fall against the bench as I looked at the stretching expanse of sky above me. "It's hard to tell," I admitted. "She's scared. And she feels like she's let us all down again."

Joe was silent for a moment, then responded in his gentle, understanding tone. "We all stumble and fall, T. Dakota just needs to see that no one is giving up on her. What she needs right now is support and understanding—not judgment and disappointment."

"I know." I gave a weary sigh. "That's what I've been trying to tell her. But it seems like she can only see her mistakes right now."

"I'll be over soon," he said. "I'm just letting Lillie play for a bit. I got us a room at Manresa Castle, and Lillie—she's having the time of her life pretending to be a princess in those grand halls."

I could almost see our curly-haired wonder, exploring the nooks that history had whispered secrets into. A chuckle escaped me, imagining her draped in an oversized curtain, a makeshift royal robe. "It's good to hear she's happy," I said, finding a small comfort in the thought. "It'll be good for Dakota to see her too."

"Exactly my thoughts," Joe agreed. "Lillie has a way of brightening every room she walks into."

Just as I was about to respond, another sharp pain hit,

followed by a deep inhale as I tried to steady the rhythm of my breathing.

"Tamara?" Joe's concern crackled through the speaker, "What's wrong?"

"I'm not sure. I've been having these sharp pains."

"Sharp pains?" His voice took on a panicked edge. "How long has this been going on?"

"Just since this morning," I admitted and rubbed my stomach, feeling the ache persisting beneath my fingers. "Mostly it's manageable, but every now and then there's a spike that catches me off-guard."

"Do you need me to come now?"

I hesitated for a moment, the pain slowly subsiding. "No, I think... I think I'm alright."

"Are you sure? I can be there in a couple minutes if you need me."

"I'm sure," I said, forcing a small laugh. "You just keep an eye on our little princess."

"Alright, T," he replied, though I could hear the unease still present in his voice. "Just call me if you need me."

"Will do." Hanging up, I slid my phone into my pocket and rested my hands on my belly once more. This time, though, it was not just out of habit or comfort—but with a sense of foreboding. My due date was still four and a half weeks away, but the persistent contractions were worrying me more than I wanted to admit.

I was about to go inside when Nathan's minivan pulled into the hospital parking lot. He noticed me and waved, but even across the parking lot, I could see the somber expression etched onto his face. He got out of the vehicle, he walked over to me, searching my face.

"Tamara." His voice was a hoarse whisper as he hugged me awkwardly, careful of my protruding belly. "I got here as soon as I could."

"I know. Thank you," I replied, pulling back slightly so I could observe his face better. His usually warm green eyes looked glassy and tired.

"How is she?" he asked, looking anxiously at the hospital's main entrance.

"She is stable. Mom and Dad are with her now. She's strong, you know? Like us—like our family."

Nathan let out a pained laugh, running a hand through his disheveled hair. "We've had our fair share of battles lately, haven't we?"

I sighed heavily, my mind shifting to him and Amanda. The emotional affair... the potential dissolving of their marriage. "How are you holding up?" I asked, reaching out to squeeze his arm in a show of support.

He shrugged but didn't pull away from my touch. "For now, I'm five days sober." He admitted, his gaze distant. "And Amanda and I are working through things."

"That's all you can do, Nathan," I said. I paused, searching for the right words, before adding, "One step—heck, one minute at a time."

"Right." He summoned a weak smirk. "Minute by minute."

We both knew it was easier said than done.

Suddenly, a spasm hit, more painful than before. I grimaced, gripping Nathan's arm tighter.

"Tamara?" He pulled away, his eyes wide. "What's wrong?"

"I'm okay," I managed to say, trying to steady my breathing. The contractions were coming closer together now, and stronger too. "It's just...." My mind spun, tendrils of fear unfurling with every heartbeat. It was too soon—weeks too soon.

"The baby?" Nathan interjected, his words a flurry of panic. "Is it the baby?"

I nodded, clutching my belly protectively. I had felt off all day, but I had blamed it the stress of Dakota's situation. But this was different. Thoughts of my unborn child, cocooned in safety up until now, swirled with nightmarish possibilities. Premature birth. Complications. Loss.

"We need to get you inside. Now," he said, urgency creeping into his tone.

As if in a daze, I found myself following Nathan's lead, my shaky hand gripping the cold edge of his shirt as he guided me into the hospital. My other arm was wrapped around my belly, each surge of pain from my abdomen causing me to draw in sharp breaths.

Nurses and doctors busted around the hospital as we entered. "We need help!" Nathan said, signaling to a nurse who was passing by.

"What seems to be the matter?"

Please God, please let my baby be safe.

"It's my sister," Nathan replied, his voice thick with concern. "I think she's in labor, but she's weeks early."

Just then warm fluid gushed down my legs and a sharp pain clenched my abdomen. A gasp of surprise escaped my lips, and Nathan's face paled as he understood the significance of what was happening.

Nathan quickly explained the situation to the nurse, who wasted no time in calling for a wheelchair.

"Call Joe. Tell him to come, now."

CHAPTER 61

March 10, 11:05 a.m.

DAKOTA

The door creaked open to my hospital room, and there they stood: Mom's soft eyes brimming with unshed tears, Dad's jaw set in a familiar, stoic line.

Their steps were hesitant as they stepped into the room. They stopped at the foot of my bed, glancing from me to the multitude of machines keeping me tethered.

"I'm so sorry," I whispered, the words barely escaping through the tightness in my throat. My hands trembled on the thin sheets as I spoke. "For all the pain... for everything I've done."

Tears brimmed in Dad's eyes, and Mom reached for my hand, her fingers a feather-light touch against my skin. "We're not here for apologies, Dakota." Her words hung in the air like a soft melody, soothing my aching heart. "We're here because we love you."

A choked sob escaped my lips before I could stop it. I blinked rapidly to clear the tears blurring my vision.

Dad rubbed the nape of his neck with a calloused hand. "We're just... we're just glad you're still here, Dakota. I couldn't—" He cut himself off, swallowing hard. "I couldn't stand the thought of losing another one."

His words, raw and edged with unspoken sorrow, hung in the

air, an echo of a pain so deep it stole the breath from my lungs. I nodded, not trusting my own voice. His gaze met mine, a mirror of the darkness that gnawed at my insides. The specter of Gabriel —my brother—their son—lost to us. But last night, when I had crossed over, he had been there.

Alive. More alive then one could imagine, in a place so full of love and light it was almost blinding. I wanted to tell them, to share the balm it had spread over my wounded soul. But would they believe me? Or would it be another cruel knife thrust into hearts already riddled with scars?

The silence in the room grew dense, a physical weight pressing on all of us. My focus darted between them, reading the quiet desperation in their expressions. A desperation I knew all too well. My fingers clenched around the bed sheets.

"Mom, Dad," I began again, steadier now. "When I was out, I saw Gabriel." The image of him, so vivid and gentle, flashed in my mind. "It was beautiful there, so full of love and peace. He was happy."

I could feel the weight of their stare, heavy with a mixture of hope and sorrow. As I described the serenity of that place, the tranquility that had embraced me like the softest blanket, their expressions shifted. Mom's hand found her mouth, stifling a sob, while Dad's eyes glistened, the dam behind them threatening to break.

Tears streamed down my face, unrestrained, as the memory clung to me—a haunting melody that refused to fade.

"Seeing him there... it made me realize," I continued, my voice catching on a hitched breath, "I could finally let go of the guilt of his passing. And I don't want you carrying it either," I added, my hands reaching out to grasp both of theirs. They were warm, a stark contrast against the cold of the hospital room. "I think... I think Gabriel wouldn't want us to live in perpetual grief."

Dad's eyes misted over, and he turned his face away, bowing his head. Mom squeezed my hand, her thumb sweeping over my knuckles in a rhythmic pattern. It was an unspoken comfort that she had shared with me since I was a child.

"Dakota." Dad's voice was coarse, heavy with emotion I'd rarely seen him display. "This is my fault. The silence of the hospital room and the hum of the machines seem to punctuate his self-blame. "I was a terrible father," he continued, avoiding my gaze. "Your addiction... Gabriel... if I hadn't..." A single tear broke free from the corner of his eye, carving a path through the weathered landscape of his face. "I was absent so much, and when I was there, I was too busy drowning in my own vices."

Dad's admission sent a chill through me, as if the shadows in the corners of the room were creeping closer, drawn by our shared pain. The fear that had always lived inside me, that I was alone in this fight, began to recede with his words.

"Paul." Mom reached out, laying a gentle hand on his knee. "We can't change the past, but we're here now. We're here for Dakota."

She turned to me then, her features brimming with a love so fierce it felt like it could chase away the darkness that threatened to engulf me. "Please," she whispered, her hand finding mine, her grip warm and unwavering, "keep fighting. Keep healing. We don't want to lose you too."

I nodded, too choked up to speak, the simple act requiring all the strength I could muster. In their eyes, I saw not just the reflection of my own fears, but also the glimmer of something else —hope, perhaps, or maybe the beginnings of forgiveness.

I lifted my arms, the motion slow and deliberate as if pushing through a viscous fog, reaching out to them. My parents leaned in, wrapping their arms around me, the contact tentative at first, as though I might shatter into a thousand irretrievable pieces. But then the embrace tightened, and the walls I had built around my heart crumbled under the weight of their love.

CHAPTER 62
March 10, 11:15 a.m.
TAMARA

Lying in the hospital bed, I prayed for the baby's safety as another contraction wrenched my stomach. Every muscle in my body tightened like a coiled spring. The pain was a roaring fire in my gut, overwhelming and undeniable. I breathed through, counting seconds in my head, letting each one melt away, slow and painstaking like the drip of an ancient glacier. One...two... three... four... five... until finally it passed.

Joe rushed through the door just as I let out a long sigh of relief. He hurried to my side, taking my hand and squeezing it reassuringly.

"I got here as soon as I could." He brushed a loose strand of hair from my face. "Nathan has Lillie."

I nodded with a soft smile, thankful that Nathan had been here to take care of her.

"How are you doing?" He searched my face, trying to read the lines of pain and exhaustion etched there.

"Better now that you're here," I replied, squeezing his hand as another contraction crushed through me like a vice.

"Breathe, Tamara," Joe said, his voice a steady anchor in the stormy sea of my agony. "You're doing great."

I clung to Joe's hand, my grip unyielding as I rode through the pain. I bit back the moan that threatened to escape.

The hospital room was abuzz with a silent kind of tension. Nurses in their starched uniforms moved in and out like wraiths, their faces masked but eyes revealing a studied professionalism flavored with empathy for my condition.

"You're so strong," he whispered gently, his voice dancing on the edge of tenderness and admiration.

I didn't feel strong. I felt worn, torn apart by the ceaseless waves of pain that kept ripping me. "Joe," my voice was a thread of sound, frayed and trembling. "The baby... it's too early."

"Only four weeks," he reassured me, tracing delicate circles on my hand with his thumb. "Our baby is just eager to meet us." Anticipation and excitement radiated from his face, dispelling some of my worries and filling me with hope for the future.

"But what if—"

"No what ifs, Tamara," he gently cut me off. "Our baby is going to be just fine."

His confidence comforted me. "You really think so?"

"I know so," he confirmed, his voice trembling slightly with suppressed emotion. "With all my heart and soul."

His assertion was followed by a quiet and stilled moment, our shared gaze holding the gravity of our love and fear, our strength and vulnerability. The silence was twined with the whispers of our unspoken prayers, each pulsing heartbeat echoing a plea for our baby's safety.

A lady dressed in a doctor's coat entered the room holding a chart. "My apologies for the interruption," she said, flipping open the chart with brisk efficiency. "I'm Dr. Alicia Smith. I'm the obstetrician on shift here at Jefferson General." She offered a reassuring smile. Her focus flitted between Joe and me before she moved further into the room, her white coat swishing gently around her. She set the chart down and studied the different monitors. "It looks like your blood pressure is a tad high, and so is your pulse." She walked across the room and washed her hands.

"We will monitor the blood pressure closely. If it rises too much, we may need to take the baby by c-section."

"Whatever is best for both Tamara and the baby," Joe said, his voice firm yet betraying a hint of fear.

"Absolutely," Dr. Smith responded. "We always prioritize the health and safety of both mother and child." She moved closer to my bed and began to examine me, pressing her cold stethoscope against my swollen belly. "You're in very good hands."

Another contraction surged through me, causing me to bite my lip. Beside me, Joe kept murmuring words of encouragement.

"I need to do a physical examination of your uterus, to see how far you're dilated. She informed us, her tone remaining professional. "This will be uncomfortable, but it's necessary."

I nodded, mentally bracing myself as she prepared to carry out the examination. Joe held on to me, his eyes locked on mine in a silent promise of support.

She worked efficiently and swiftly, her professional demeanor unbroken. "You're six centimeters dilated, Tamara. We're going to keep monitoring your blood pressure closely, to make sure everything is safe for you and the baby."

Dr. Smith left the room then, advising us that she'd return to check on me in an hour or sooner if needed.

"You okay?" Joe asked when we were alone again.

"I'm scared, Joe," I confessed over the hum of the monitors that filled the room, each beep a testament to the life within me straining to break free.

"I know," he admitted softly. "I am too. But we've faced scarier things before, haven't we?"

I thought of Dakota in a hospital bed upstairs, hooked to machines that beeped and whirred just like these ones. "Yeah, we have."

"And we survived." He leaned closer, his forehead resting gently against mine—our intimate bubble in the sterile hospital room. "We will get through this as well, Tamara. You, me... and so will our baby."

Emotions flooded through me at his words—words so filled with unwavering faith and undying love. His confidence washed over me once more.

"I love you." The words were heavy with raw emotion as I spoke them.

"I love you too." His hands cradled my face and his lips found mine in a kiss that was as much a promise as it was an act of love. His mouth was warm and comforting, the taste of him familiar and reassuring. As he pulled away, his forehead rested against mine again.

The contraction came then, tearing through my body like a tsunami. Joe held me as I gritted my teeth against the pain, his strong arms a welcome anchor in the storm. "Breathe, Tamara. I have you."

The contraction finally passed, leaving me panting and trembling. The room fell silent again except for the steady beeping of the heart monitor and the quiet whir of the ventilation system.

CHAPTER 63

March 10, 6:24 p.m.

TIM

I spent hours hunting through the sketchier parts of Chimacum, Hadlock and Port Townsend, determined to find Justin, Avery and Ricky. After checking in at the hospital, I drove towards Quilcene. The sun had set about a half an hour ago and the night was dark, the moon hidden behind thick clouds. The only light came from the headlights of my car, slicing through the darkness and casting long, eerie shadows on the empty road ahead.

As I turned onto Muncie Street, I spotted the Oldsmobile parked outside Ryan's old rental house. The house was a dilapidated thing, forgotten by time and forsaken by society. Its peeling paint and cracked shutters provided the perfect veil for the illicit activities within its walls.

I drove around the block and parked in a secluded spot away from the house. I took a deep breath, steeling myself for what was about to come. I had spent the last few years as a cop chasing men like Justin and Avery, trying to bring them to justice and protect people like Dakota. The thought of what they had done to her made me sick. It had to be stopped, now.

I got out of the car and moved stealthily toward the house. Every step I took was filled with dread, knowing all too well the kind of men who were inside. But underneath that dread was a burning resolve. The very thought of them hurting Dakota, exploiting her vulnerabilities for their gain...it caused a fire to ignite in my veins.

I moved with careful, silent steps, my feet barely making a sound as I crept closer. I noticed a light on and a slightly opened window.

As I approached, the faint hum of conversation and the acrid smell of chemicals wafted through the night air. I crouched near the semi-open window, straining to hear their voices. They were talking about the drugs, their plans to distribute them around town. I felt my blood boil. Those drugs had nearly killed Dakota, yet these men were laughing, celebrating as if they hadn't a care in the world. The breaking point came when I heard them joke about Dakota, their cruel laughter ringing through the night air.

"Little Dakota thought she could get clean." Justin's voice, venomous and vile, slithered through the opening. "Like we'd ever let her forget where she came from."

"Like she'd ever make it out alive," Avery chimed in, his chuckle a knife twisting in my gut.

Rage boiled within me, a torrential storm threatening to overcome my resolve to do this the right way. I drew in a deep breath, fighting to keep control. Now was not the time for impulsivity or revenge.

"Let's just finish up here," I heard Avery's voice over the harsh beats of Metallica. "Ricky will be back soon."

With that, my decision was made. I shot Ramirez a text, telling her where I was and what I was about to do, even though I knew it would take some time for backup to arrive.

I slipped around the side of the house and made my way to the door. My pulse pounded hard, pushing adrenaline through my veins.

With calculated precision, I positioned myself outside the door. This was it. My moment to strike—to catch them red-handed in their sordid trade. Adrenaline surged through me, a tidal wave that threatened to break free.

With my gun in hand, I kicked at the door and burst through the threshold, splintering wood and chaos erupting in my wake. Time slowed as I took in the scene: Justin and Avery hunched over a glass table, shards of crystal meth spread before them like a feast for the depraved. Their initial surprise quickly gave way to a rage that mirrored my own.

"What the hell are you doing here?" Avery snarled, hurling himself up from the couch with a speed that belied his size.

Justin, still in shock, could only manage a strangled gasp, his gaze darting between me and the mess on the table before him. I pointed my gun toward Avery's chest. "This is over." My voice echoed in the room, an unwavering pronouncement of war. "I'm here to end this."

Avery laughed, a sound as grating as grinding metal against asphalt. "Tim Moore, huh? Dakota's little toy soldier thinks he can take us alone?" Despite his bravado, I could see fear flickering in his expression. He was not used to being on the losing end, and he knew he had landed there.

"I'm not alone," I said, my voice steady. "Backup is on their way. You've gone too far. You've ruined too many lives."

Justin choked on his breath, his pallid face going even whiter. Avery's eyes widened then quickly narrowed into slits and then he lunged at me, knocking the gun out of my hands.

My heart pounded in my chest as I watched my gun slide across the floor, lost in the chaos. But I didn't back down; my resolve was stronger than any fear. The room became a blur of motion, a whirlwind of violence and fury. I dodged, parried, and struck with the precision of a man who had everything to lose. Sweat mingled with blood, the coppery tang sharp in my nostrils. In the fray, a fleeting thought of Dakota—her haunted eyes, her whispered pleas for forgiveness—propelled me forward. This fight was for her, for the future she yearned for, one untainted by the filth of her past.

A harsh blow sent me staggering back, but I held my ground. My fists connected with Avery's jaw, the crack echoing through the room. He toppled backwards into Justin, sending both of them sprawling onto the floor in an ungraceful heap. The sight of their shocked faces was satisfying, a small victory in this brutal battle.

As I lunged for my gun, Avery scrambled to his feet, a wild look on his face. He threw himself at me with full force, his momentum catching me off-guard. We tumbled onto the floor a few feet from the gun. His meaty hands clawed for my throat, but adrenaline and sheer determination kept me moving. My fingers slipped in the crimson pool around us as I grappled for control. As we rolled across the floor, a sharp pain seared through my side.

I gripped Avery's wrist, wrestling for control. His bloodshot eyes bore down into mine, a mirror of the desperation we both felt. But I wasn't just fighting for my life. I was fighting for Dakota's future.

A sharp glint caught my eye; a broken bottle beside the couch. Justin was finally coming out of his stupor and reached for it.

"No!" I roared, slamming my fist into Avery. The crack of his nose under my knuckles was drowned out by his sudden, pained howl. I rolled out from underneath him to see Justin coming at me.

Justin held the bottle over his head. "Avery!" he shrieked, waving the bottle around like a wild man. "I got him!"

Avery was on his feet again, his face a mask of fury. He turned towards Justin and me, his focus darting between the bottle in Justin's shaky grasp and the fierce determination etched onto my face.

"No, Justin. I got him," he growled, and with animalistic speed launched himself at me.

I braced myself, but it wasn't enough. Avery's massive form slammed into me like a freight train, knocking the wind from my lungs as we crashed onto the debris-strewn floor. Pain exploded in my side as my ribs protested the brutal fall, but I fought through it.

"Filthy pig!" Avery spat into my face, his hot breath fouling the air between us as we wrestled on the ground. "Thought you could take us down?"

I gritted my teeth against the pain. "Just getting started," I managed to grind out, despite the weight pressing plausibly on my chest.

Avery shifted his weight and forced himself around me in a tight hold. I flailed around but could not shake him. With massive strength, he forced my hands behind me, immobilizing me.

I looked to see Justin in front of me, holding my gun at my face.

Avery's laugh was hollow, a chilling echo that bounced off the apartment's grimy walls. "Finish him," he directed Justin. Justin smiled and cocked the gun. My life flashed before my eyes, Dakota. Sage. My parents. Was this how it was going to end?

Then, out of nowhere, a wooden chair came down hard against Justin's head.

"What the hell, Ricky?" Avery spat out.

Ricky?

I squinted through my haze of pain, and sure enough, it was Ricky. His face was a dark thundercloud, his jaw set in a hard line as he tossed aside the remnants of the chair.

"You traitor!" Justin shrieked from the floor, blood trickling from his forehead.

"I'm a traitor?" Ricky yelled. "You were about to kill a cop. I just saved you."

Fury tore across Avery's face, and he lunged at Ricky.

The sudden shift in Avery's focus gave me a crucial window of opportunity. With everything I had left, I swept my leg with a swift kick to his knees. He stumbled, his forward momentum halted, giving Ricky enough time to dodge his attack.

Avery roared in frustration—a primal cry that set my nerves

on edge. On instinct, he swung his meaty fist at me, but I was ready for him this time. I blocked the strike and countered with a punch of my own. His head snapped back from the force.

"I told you," I gritted out through clenched teeth, "this is over."

But Avery was relentless, a wounded animal with nothing left to lose. He charged at me again, his knuckles grazing my cheekbone before I could dodge. The pain soared through me, white-hot and blinding.

"No," Avery growled, "you're over."

His fist swung at me again, but Ricky had stepped in front of me, his palm absorbing the blow meant for me. He grunted against the impact but held firm, returning the favor with a punch of his own that landed square on Avery's jaw.

Avery staggered backwards, a hand pressed to his bleeding mouth. He seethed with unhinged rage, looking between Ricky and me, calculating his next move. But something had shifted in the room. The balance of power had tilted in our favor. The beast was cornered.

"Get out of here!" Ricky growled to me, never taking his eyes off Avery.

"No," I said firmly, straightening up as best I could. "We finish this together."

Ricky gave me a quick nod, a shadow of a smile flickering on his lips as he readied himself for Avery's next attack.

A frozen moment passed, charged with lethal tension. Then Avery lunged. He was rabid, relentless, determined to make his last stand. Ricky and I met him head-on, side by side. Avery swung wildly, lashing out in a desperate bid for survival.

He aimed for Ricky first, but Ricky danced out of range. Avery missed his mark and stumbled forward off-balance. Seizing the opportunity, I drove my fist into his abdomen, forcing the air from his lungs in a satisfying huff.

Sirens in the distance were a welcome noise.

Avery doubled over, wheezing and gasping as he tried to

regain his footing. But I didn't give him the chance to recover. With everything I had left, I grabbed his flailing arm and twisted it behind his back. A choked yelp escaped him as I forced him onto his knees, using my other hand to apply pressure on the back of his neck.

Ricky was moving too, crossing to where Justin lay sprawled on the floor, unconscious. "Tim, cuffs!" Ricky shouted, nodding towards my duty belt which had been knocked loose in the brawl. With a quick sidestep, I scooped them up and tossed a pair to Ricky, who secured Justin's wrists with efficiency. I mirrored the action, clamping the cold metal around Avery's wrists, who spat a venomous string of curses in response.

The room was filled with the wails of sirens growing closer, red and blue lights flashing through the grimy windows. Avery continued to struggle beneath me but his attempts were growing weaker. A bead of sweat trickled down my temple, the adrenaline still pumping through my veins. I didn't loosen my grip on him. I couldn't afford to.

The room was a wreckage of overturned furniture and scattered drugs, a testament to the battle fought within.

I met Ricky's gaze. In that prolonged moment, gratitude for his sacrifice and tension coexisted within me like oil on water, refusing to merge but impossible to separate. Here stood a man who'd saved Dakota, and now he laid his life on the line to save me. Yet, this same man was intertwined with the darkness we fought against—a paradox personified. "You need to get out of here."

This story was far from over, but Ricky wouldn't go down tonight. He had proven himself an ally in the chaos, but the lines between friend and foe remained dangerously blurred.

"I owe you," Ricky mouthed, watching the lights shimmer through the windows before slinking into the shadows.

I turned to the restrained men. The sirens were a deafening roar now, their flashes painting the room in an ominous light. It was only a matter of seconds before the cops would storm in.

"Checkmate," I whispered to Avery. His heavy breathing filled the room, his wild eyes still seething with anger and betrayal. He was cornered and captured—but he wasn't broken.

The front door crashed open then, and I spun around to face the officers bursting through the door. A sick realization hit as I took it all in. I had won the battle, but the war was far from over.

CHAPTER 64
March 10, 7:02 p.m.
TAMARA

Another contraction bore down on me, and the beeps of the monitors around me became more intense. Joe's hand tightened on mine, his soothing voice repeating a mantra of reassurance. "Breathe, Tamara."

As the contraction rolled over me like a tidal wave, I clung to his words, using them as an anchor in the storm of pain and uncertainty.

"You're doing great," Joe murmured when the contraction finally passed.

A nurse bustled into the room to check on me—a routine that had been happening every twenty minutes or so. She quickly checked the monitors, making careful notes on the chart. When she turned to me, her expression was professional, yet there was something in her eyes that caused my pulse to speed up.

"I think it may be time to call Dr. Smith back," she said, her voice calm, reaching for the phone on the wall.

The words hung heavily in the air, sinking into the silence of the room, before breaking against the steady rhythm of my heart. Joe met my gaze, his expression a mirror of my own—a cocktail of fear and anticipation.

The nurse spoke quietly into the phone about my blood

pressure growing worse and the contractions becoming more frequent. Her words were clipped and efficient, painting a picture of urgency that heightened my fear.

Beside me Joe tightened his grip on my hand even more, sensing my fear. "It's going to be alright, T."

"Promise?" I asked, turning to him as another wave of pain seized me.

"I promise," he replied, his voice steady despite the fear I knew was lurking beneath the surface.

Within minutes Dr. Smith was back in the room, her face composed but serious. "Tamara, your blood pressure is higher than we would like. It's a condition called preeclampsia and it's not uncommon in late pregnancy. We're going to have to perform a c-section immediately."

The words hung ominously in the room, causing my mind to race with all the potential complications; for me, for the baby.

"Everything will be alright," Joe said again, determination in his tone.

"Yes," I whispered.

"A room is being prepared now," Dr Smith informed us. "Your husband can join us once he has scrubbed in like the rest of us."

Joe gave a curt nod, his grip on my hand tightening for a moment before he was ushered out of the room. The nurse began to prep me, speaking in soft soothing tones about what to expect, but her words were like white noise against the pounding of my heart. They helped transfer me onto a stretcher, and then they wheeled me toward the surgical wing of the hospital, the harsh fluorescent lights flashing rhythmically overhead. The world around me became a blur as another contraction seized me, stealing my breath away. I exhaled a shuddering breath, clutching at the thin gown they'd draped across me as we moved swiftly down the corridor.

The scent of the operating room greeted me first; antiseptic with an undercurrent of something metallic.

The cold air pricked my skin as they transferred me onto the operating table. I could hear the rustle of starched scrubs, the metallic clink of surgical instruments being prepared. Yet, everything felt distant, as if I was a spectator in my own body.

Then Joe was at my side again, wearing blue scrubs and a face mask that only his familiar hazel eyes peered through. I reached out, my hand trembling, and he immediately took it, his grasp warm and firm. "I'm right here."

"I know," I replied, my voice but a whisper amid the bustle of the room. His presence, though, was the steadfast anchor I needed amidst the chaos.

"We're going to administer a spinal block," Dr. Smith said, drawing gloves over her hands. "This will numb your lower body and you'll be awake for the delivery." The cold steel of the medical tray gleamed under the harsh fluorescent lights as drapes were placed around me, creating a sterile barrier.

"Hey," Joe said, his voice soft, pushing through the clinical chatter around us. "Look at me, T."

I focused on him, looking into those familiar hazel depths, losing myself in the love radiating from them. This was our moment—a terrifying, beautiful moment that was a testament of our love and resilience. "I love you," he whispered, his voice barely audible over the hum of the machines and the clinical chatter of the medical team.

"You're going to feel some pressure," Dr. Smith interjected, her attention focused on the task at hand. "But you shouldn't feel any pain."

I nodded, my focus still locked on Joe's. Suddenly, it was as if the world had shifted on its axis. My senses refocused, zoned in on the pressure she'd mentioned. It was a peculiar sensation, detached and undeniably real all at once. Yet Joe's hand never left mine, his gaze never faltered. The room was filled with a flurry of activity, but all I could hear was the steady rhythm of his breath.

"There we go," Dr. Smith said, her expression intent.

The seconds stretched into minutes or perhaps hours—time

felt malleable, elusive. The hushed whispers of the medical staff became an incomprehensible murmur, fading into the background as I felt an unfamiliar lightness, a sense of release. A limbo of sorts between pain and relief. It was surreal, almost like floating in a dream.

And then the sound came. That tiny cry that pierced through the hushed whispers and the consistent beep of the monitors—it was a battle cry, a proclamation of life, a celebration of love. Everything else seemed to fade into insignificance.

"Our baby," Joe whispered, his voice hoarse with emotion. The moment was sacred, etched in the fabric of time, fated to be remembered and cherished indefinitely. The emotional roller coaster had reached its peak and it was miraculous.

The nurse picked up the little bundle, swaddled in soft cotton and approached us. "A beautiful baby boy," she said, her voice quivering with restrained delight.

Joe and I shared a look, a silent exchange that embodied a profound joy neither of us could articulate. A bubble of laughter escaped my lips, disbelief mingling with exhilaration as the nurse placed our son into Joe's arms. His hand, once my anchor against the pain, now cradled our baby with a gentleness that took my breath away. Tears streamed down his face as his gaze crinkled with an emotion that looked a lot like awe.

Our son looked at Joe, his tiny fingers clutching onto those of his father. His miniature mouth opened and closed in a silent yawn, causing my heart to swell even further with love. Each detail of his face seemed like a miracle—the sprinkle of soft hair on his head, the pouty lips that he'd inherited from me, the tiny eyebrow raised as if in perpetual curiosity.

Dr. Smith watched the scene unfold before her, a satisfied smile on her face. "Congratulations to both of you."

"He's perfect." He looked from our son to me, as if attempting to commit this moment to memory. "Welcome to the world, little man."

A surge of emotion washed over me as I watched Joe and our

newborn son engage in their first silent conversation—a silent bond already forming between them. I felt a tear trickle down my cheek, followed by another, and another. This was happiness in its purest form.

"Happy tears," a nurse said, handing me a tissue. "They're the best kind."

I gave her a shaky nod, my gaze never leaving the scene before me. Not for the comfort of the tissue or the assurance of her words. My world was condensed into this moment—etched in the innocence of our baby's face, in Joe's overwhelmed smile, and in the joyous exhaustion that hooked into my bones.

CHAPTER 65

March 10, 7:13 p.m.

TIM

"Tim!" Ramirez shouted as she busted through the door. "What the hell happened here? Are you okay?"

"Just another peaceful evening in the neighborhood," Pain shot through my head as I spoke, and I winced, reaching up to touch the tender welt that had formed.

Ramirez frowned, scanning the wreckage before finally landing on the restrained Avery and Justin. She signaled to the other officers to move in, pointing them towards the fallen men with a curt wave of her hand. As they descended on Avery and Justin, checking their restraints and reading off their rights, Ramirez approached me.

"Looks like you need stitches," Ramirez muttered, her face grave as she examined the wound.

"I'm fine," I reassured her before she could ask, wincing slightly as I gingerly prodded at my side, feeling the tenderness of the bruise that was sure to bloom there.

"Always full of bravado, aren't you, Moore?" She shook her head, her lips pursed in amused disapproval.

A scuffle drew our attention towards Avery and Justin as they were hauled onto their feet by the officers. Avery's eyes met mine, filled with defiance and raw hatred. The icy stare promised retribution, but I returned it steadily. After tonight, he would be behind bars, and that was a victory for me.

Ramirez squeezed my shoulder, pulling me to face her. "You did good, Tim. Hell of a mess, but you brought them in."

"Yeah," I agreed, unable to muster the energy for any more humor. My gaze drifted towards the door Ricky had disappeared through. Then my attention flicked to Avery who was now being escorted out of the room.

"We're gonna need a medic," Ramirez said into her radio.

"I said I was fine."

Ramirez ignored me, continuing her conversation with dispatch. I grumbled under my breath, but didn't protest further. I knew there was no use arguing with her once she'd made up her mind. Besides, I could feel the throbbing in my head escalating into a pounding hammer, and maybe stitches would be a good idea after all.

The scent of fear and perspiration lingered in the air, diffused with the metallic tang of blood, all a grim testament to the night's events.

The room now buzzed with activity as photos were taken and items were bagged as evidence.

"Looks like we've got a long night ahead," she muttered, scanning over the room.

"Just another day in paradise," I said with a crooked grin. She chuckled, the sound echoing hollowly in the cavernous room, swallowed by the shadows creeping along the walls.

"I just got one question for you, partner. Why is it that you get to have all the fun and glory, and I get stuck cleaning up the mess?"

"Those are the breaks, kid," I chuckled, causing my side to ache.

"You're insufferable," she muttered, shaking her head. I merely shrugged, my half-smile still in place despite the exhaustion creeping into my bones. "The medics should be here any moment; make sure they check for a concussion too."

I nodded in response, grimacing at the pain. As I limped toward the door Ramirez spoke once more. "Get some good rest tonight. Captain Simmons will want a full report on his desk tomorrow."

"That's if I survive the night," I said, attempting a weak jest.

"Not funny, Tim," she shot back, her voice sharp. "You have people who care about you, you know."

"I'll be fine, Ramirez. I always am." I forced a small grin, trying to take some of the worry off her face. But she only sighed, shaking her head.

As I stepped outside, the chilly night air wrapped around me like an icy shroud. My nerves felt raw and rubbed thin, the adrenaline from earlier starting to fade. I hobbled to the ambulance parked near the house and sat on the gurney with a groan, pain shooting up my side with the motion. The medic attending to me was a middle-aged man with kind eyes behind his glasses. He swiftly set to work, examining my wounds while I grappled with the stinging pain each of his movements provoked.

The medic finished patching me up with a grim expression on his face. "You need to take it easy for a while," he said, handing me a bottle of painkillers.

I took the bottle with a curt nod, but my thoughts were with Dakota. I needed to get to the hospital, to let her know I was okay. That Justin and Avery were dealt with, and I'd be going after Victor next. She needed to know that I would do whatever it took to make her safe again.

I sped home in order to clean-up. I couldn't go to the hospital looking like this. I flipped on my flashing lights and gunned the accelerator, pushing my car to its limits. The wind shrieked past the windows like a hollow ghost.

As soon as I arrived home, I exited my car and slammed the door shut and limped to Dakota's and my home, wishing she was here with me now. The night was still as a grave, the silence broken only by my own ragged breathing and the echoing slam of the car door. With painful motion, I hurried inside and went straight to the bathroom. Undressing quickly, I turned on the shower and climbed in.

The hot water beat against my skin, stinging the fresh wounds on my face and my side. I gingerly touched the bruises painting my ribs in violent hues of blue and purple.

Stepping out of the shower, I dried off and stared at my reflection in the fogged-up mirror. Despite the water and soap, my face was still a sight to behold. A deep purple bruise was beginning to form around my left eye, while my upper lip was noticeably swollen. Each mark told its own story of the fight I had just been in. I carefully placed a new butterfly bandage over the gash above my eye.

"You should see the other guy," I joked darkly to myself, thinking of Avery's mangled face. The laughter that escaped me was tinged with pain as my ribs throbbed. The medic on scene had assured me that nothing was broken, but each movement sent sharp jolts through my side, telling a different tale.

I quickly dressed and headed to the hospital to see Dakota, flinching at each jolt of pain that ping-ponged through my body as I drove.

The city lights were a blur as I sped down the empty streets, an ominous symphony of shadows playing out across the buildings.

A grim thought struck me—that Dakota would look at my battered face and see the world she was trying to escape from reflected back at her. The thought sickened me, but what could I do? I'd done what needed to be done to protect her.

Pulling up at the hospital, I took a moment to compose myself, my hands gripping the steering wheel so tightly that my knuckles went white. I had to be strong for Dakota, had to show her that, despite everything, we could fight this.

As I stepped out of the car, I felt a cold gust blow across my bruised face, making me wince involuntarily. I limped through the automatic doors, feeling like a gory spectacle in the sterile environment. Heading to the elevator, I hit the number four and waited impatiently for the metal doors to open. The fourth floor was immersed in an eerie, starched quietude punctuated only by the muted sounds of medical equipment doing their life-saving jobs.

I swallowed hard and walked past them, pushing through a set of double doors that led to Dakota's room. When I entered the room, Dakota was awake, staring out the window, expression pained as if she was in deep thought.

"Coda," I rasped, my voice sounding foreign to my ears. Her head slowly turned towards the sound of my voice.

Dakota drew in a sharp breath at the sight of me and beckoned me to come to her. I stepped in closer.

Her hand rose to my face, tentative at first, then with more purpose, as if she wanted to memorize the texture of my skin. The coolness of her fingertips traced the line of my jaw before alighting upon the gash above my right eye. I winced involuntarily, not from the sting of her touch, but from the tenderness behind it.

"Careful," I whispered.

"You look awful," she said, her voice laced with sadness.

"You should see the other guy." I tried using the same joke as earlier on myself, but it fell flat in the somber hospital room.

"I didn't want this." Her features were a mess of guilt and worry.

"Don't worry about me," I lied, because in that moment, her concern for me felt like a pair of warm hands cradling my beaten heart. "I'm tougher than I look."

She searched my face, always seeing through the bravado to the truth beneath. I knew she saw the shadows of pain in my eyes, the tightness around my mouth. But she didn't press, and for that, I was grateful. We both carried our scars—mine on the surface, hers etched deep within.

Her eyebrows furrowed and she turned to the window, her

gaze unfocused and lost once more in the mournful, moonlight sky. The room fell into a silence that was pregnant with unspoken words and half-finished sentences. A single tear slipped down her cheek, catching the soft light of the moon that streamed in through the glass pane.

Silently, I moved a chair to sit beside her, my body protesting every small movement. "Talk to me, Coda. Please."

The moments stretched out, long and aching, until finally she spoke. "I can't keep doing this."

A sudden fear struck me at her words. She couldn't keep doing what? Was she trying to end this? "Keep doing what, Dakota?"

The silence between us became its own entity, thick and expectant, as Dakota turned to me.

"I can't stay here, Tim," she whispered, her voice barely above the hum of the city beyond the window. "It was a mistake to come back here. I was stupid to think that I could build a future with you when my past was nipping at my heels at every turn."

Her words felt like a cold vice grip on my chest as I tried to process them. "But if you hadn't have come back, we wouldn't be together."

"I know, Tim. I don't regret us. I just know that I can't keep doing this. The shadow of my demons are too strong for me to fight against."

"Okay," was all I managed, my throat suddenly tight. It wasn't an agreement or a question, but an acknowledgment of her pain. My heart was a leaden weight in my chest, but I had to keep it together—for Dakota. I gave her hand a reassuring squeeze as I swallowed the lump that had formed in my throat.

"If there is ever going to be a chance for me, for us, I have to leave this place and never look back." She glanced at her hands, playing with the engagement ring on her left hand. The symbol of our love, reflecting the moonlight in its diamond.

I nodded, my eyes growing wet. I loved this woman with

everything in me. How could I have not seen how deep this struggle had been for her. She had been here fighting her demons with all of her strength, so that she could be with me. She had supported me as I went to school and pursued my dream, but it had cost her. And brought her to a place of relapse and brokenness. She deserved for me to do the same for her.

"Dakota, if what you need is a fresh start, then I'm with you. We'll find a place. Somewhere new. Somewhere safe. For both of us."

She searched my face, seeking the sincerity behind my words, weighing the truth of my commitment. And in that searching, I knew she found it—my unyielding dedication to her healing journey.

I watched as a slow smile spread across her face. It was like witnessing the sun rise over a long, arduous night. She brought her hand to my cheek, her touch gentle and cautious. "Are you sure? I mean, this changes the things you've dreamed about."

"Without you, Dakota, there isn't a future I want." There was no hesitation in my response, only the truth that filled the spaces between us.

"Okay," she whispered, her voice hoarse. "Okay ..."

"We're in this together," I told her as I looked at her with all the sincerity I could muster. "Wherever you go, I'll follow."

She looked at our intertwined hands then up at me. Her voice was soft when she spoke, yet it carried a weight that echoed around in the silence of our room. "Thank you."

"No thanks needed," I said. "I love you."

A small smile touched the corner of her mouth. "Timothy Moore, always the hero."

"Only for one person," I replied, leaning closer so our foreheads touched. A moment stretched out, filled with the unspoken fears of our uncertain future. "Dakota, I'd walk into hell itself if it meant you'd find peace."

She closed her eyes, a tear slipping down as she nestled into the crook of my arm. We stayed like that, wound together, the ghosts of our past fading into the periphery. In that dim room, with we faced the first night of the rest of our lives—two souls, intertwined, ready to step into the unknown. And as darkness embraced us, I welcomed it, for within its folds lay the promise of dawn, of new beginnings, and of redemption hard-won.

CHAPTER 66

March 11, 8:22 a.m.

TAMARA

As the morning light filtered into the hospital room, Joe sat next to me, holding my hand as we gazed at our newborn son. He was a perfect combination of both of us, and his delicate features stirred such intense love that it almost hurt.

"Look at him, Joe," I whispered, brushing a fingertip over the downy dark hair that crowned his head. "He's beautiful."

"Just like his mother." There was a reverence in his voice, a tender strength that made my insides weak and strong at the same time.

Every coo and sigh from our newborn son carved a deeper space for him in my heart—a heart that had known its share of fractures. Yet here, in this room, bathed in fluorescent light that seemed to soften just for him, hope flickered brighter. Maybe this time, joy would linger longer than fear.

"You did so good, T," Joe said, placing a tender kiss on my forehead. "He's perfect."

"What do you think of that middle name?" I asked, though the question felt weightless against the enormity of the life in my arms.

"I love it," Joe said.

The door creaked open, and Nathan stepped into the room,

Lillie perched on his hip. Her curly hair bobbed as she craned her neck to catch sight of what we were all fussing about.

Nathan approached us slowly, maintaining a reverential distance as his attention fell on the newborn. The lines of his face softened into a tender smile that reflected Joe's. There was an implicit understanding passing between them in that moment—an unspoken promise of camaraderie and joint fatherhood.

"Hey, little man," Nathan greeted, his usually commanding voice reduced to a soft whisper. Lillie reached for Joe, and he took her into his arms. Then she turned toward me bright eyes widened with curiosity as she caught sight of the baby.

"Mama, babay?" she asked, pointing her tiny finger towards the bundle in my arms.

"Yes, Lillie." I chuckled warmly. "That is your new little brother."

Her eyes sparkled with the kind of joy only seen in children, a purity that could melt the coldest hearts. She reached out her small hand, trying to touch him. We allowed her, watching as she lightly patted his blanket-swaddled form with a gentleness we hadn't known she possessed.

"Be gentle, sweetheart," Joe said softly with adoration in his voice as he watched his precious child meet her brother.

Lillie nodded solemnly, her touch remaining feather-light on the baby's blanket. "Babay," she repeated, her soft voice filled with a newfound reverence.

"Good girl," I said.

Nathan looked at his nephew and then at Joe. "I would have thought he would be smaller for being a month early."

"Seven pounds, three ounces," Joe said proudly.

"Wow, Tamara, it's a good thing he came early. He would have been close to ten pounds if he had stayed in there," Nathan joked with a grin.

I laughed lightly at Nathan's remark, deciding to ignore the temporary pang of discomfort it brought. "I suppose there's a silver lining to every cloud."

The baby stirred at the sound, his tiny features scrunching adorably as he squirmed in my arms.

"Is there room for a few more visitors?" The voice came from the door. Dakota, flanked by Tim, stood in the doorway. She wore her normal clothes, and color had returned to her face. From the outside looking in, you would have never known she had almost died of a drug overdose two days ago. It was amazing how the sadness of one day could be swallowed by the joy of another.

"Of course," I replied.

As they stepped forward, I noticed Tim's face. A gash lined his right eyebrow, and a bruise circled his left eye.

"Rough day at work, Tim?" Nathan joked, eyeing Tim's injuries.

"You could say that," he replied.

I thought of him asking me to pray for him yesterday when he left the hospital, that Dakota had been targeted by drug lords. Had he taken them down?

"It's a long story," Tim added, exchanging a look with Dakota. "And now is not the time." Tim managed a warm smile despite his bruised face.

"Fair enough," Nathan said, giving Tim a soft slap on the back. "We're just glad you're here."

Tim and Dakota made their way over to the hospital bed, their focus on the newest member of the family. "He's perfect, Tamara."

Dakota nodded in agreement and reached out to touch his tiny hand.

"Want to hold him?" I offered, shifting the baby slightly, readying myself to pass him to her.

Dakota hesitated, a brief flicker of uncertainty crossing her features, but then she nodded. Gently, I placed my son into her arms. Her hands cradled him with such care, it was as if she held her redemption wrapped in a hospital blanket.

"Hey there, little guy." Dakota met my gaze, a silent conversation passing between us. In that look, I saw the girl who had climbed trees and skinned knees, the teenager who had spiraled into shadows, and the woman who now stood before me, clinging to hope like a lifeline.

Tim's phone dinged, and a look of frustration crossed his face as he checked the message. "I gotta go take care of some things at work."

A look of fear crept over Dakota's face.

"It's okay," Tim said quietly. "Just my boss. He wants an account of what happened yesterday."

She nodded and held the baby closer. "Do you need me to come with you?" Dakota offered, her voice barely audible, but the concern was unmistakable.

Tim shook his head. "No, it's just paperwork stuff. Don't worry." His response seemed to alleviate her distress somewhat, but she still clung to our baby as if he were a shield against the harsh world outside. "I'll be back soon," he promised, bending to press a kiss to Dakota's forehead before he left. He limped out of the room, obviously in pain from whatever scuffle he got into yesterday.

The room fell quiet again; the only sound was the soft cooing of the baby. We watched as Dakota gently rocked him, her attiontion riveted to his tiny face. Nathan broke the silence first. "Look at you, Dakota; you're a natural," he said, his admiration evident in his voice. His compliment seemed to catch her off guard and she looked at him in surprise.

"Me?" She glanced at the baby in her arms before looking at Nathan. "I don't know about that."

Joe laughed, a low rumble that filled the quiet room. "He's right. I swear to you, in all the years I've known you, I've never seen you look more peaceful than you do now, holding that baby."

Dakota blushed, a charming shade of pink painting her cheeks. Her focus dropped to the bundle of joy cradled in her arms. "You think?" she asked softly, the tone of her voice suggesting that she was more talking to herself than anyone else.

"Yes, absolutely," Nathan affirmed, watching as her face

softened into a smile. "You know, you might consider having one of your own someday."

The shock on Dakota's face was something everyone noted but no one mentioned. A flicker of something—fear? longing?—twisted her expression before it smoothed away.

"Maybe someday..." she muttered, her voice holding a note of wistful longing. She brushed her fingers gently over the baby's soft cheek. "For now, I just need to take things one day at a time."

I looked at Nathan and Joe who were silently smiling at the scene unfolding before them.

The baby cooed, his tiny hand wrapped around Dakota's finger, drawing her attention back to him. "I've actually been thinking about what you said—about coming to stay with you and Joe for a while.

My gaze shifted from the baby's downy head to Dakota's uncertain face. "Really?"

"I think its the best place for me right now." She sounded resolved, but there was a vulnerability in her voice that couldn't be ignored.

"We'd love to have you, sis. It would be good for you... and for him," I said, nodding towards the baby.

She smiled, her expression glowing with gratitude. The room was then filled with an overwhelming warmth, easing the tension that had been present just minutes before.

Joe nodded a broad grin lighting his face. "There will always be a place for you in our home." His words added another layer of assurance that seemed to lighten the air around us.

"Nice," Nathan said with a fist pump, face lighting up. "Dakota is coming to Ocean Shores. That's only a half hour from where I live. It's high time our family spent more time together."

Dakota chuckled slightly, a lightness seeming to follow her laugh. "Looks like you're stuck with me then," she said, her gaze shifting from Nathan to me. She held the baby a bit closer as if to reassure herself of his existence.

Just then there was a light tap at the door. I looked toward the noise and a mix of surprise and joy filled my heart. Josiah, our brother who lived over a thousand miles away, stood in the doorway with the same mischievous grin that had been stamped on his face since we were all kids.

"Josiah?" I blurted out, unable to contain my shock.

"This family is impossible to keep up with." He chuckled, stepping into the room and glancing around at the faces of surprise. "I got on the plane for one sister," he said, motioning towards Dakota, "and the other one goes into labor a month early."

"Always trying to outdo each other, " Nathan chimed in, his laughter filling the room as he pointed between Dakota and me.

"And who is this little guy?" Josiah asked curiously, gently taking the baby from Dakota. He held the newborn, a look of pure affection painted on his face.

"One heck of a surprise, isn't he?" I asked proudly.

Josiah grinned at me, bouncing the baby lightly in his arms.

"He's perfect," he murmured, looking at the baby with a soft smile. "Welcome to the family, kiddo."

As Josiah cooed at the baby, our dad's booming voice came from down the hall. "I can't wait to meet my new grandson."

"Shhhh, you'll wake every baby in the maternity ward," Mom scolded.

Nathan, Dakota, Josiah and I looked at each other and laughed at my parents' banter. It was a vibrant, warm laugh that filled the room and for a while, drowned out the harsh reality of the world outside.

Mom and Dad appeared in the doorway, their faces beaming.

"Josiah?" Mom gasped, her face lighting with surprise.

Dad ran a hand over his short-cropped hair, disbelief playing on his weathered features. "Well, look what the cat dragged in," he muttered, but his eyes sparkled with delight. "It's so good to see you, son." Dad crossed the room as if drawn to the newborn in Josiah's arms. "Look at that little guy," Dad said, his voice brimming with pride.

Mom was right on his heels, her expression softening as she approached the bedside. Her hand fluttered to her mouth, and I knew she was swallowing tears of happiness. "And such a head of hair! He definitely has that strong Jensen gene," she said, her arms outstretched in anticipation.

Josiah handed the baby to my mom without hesitation. "Hello, little one," she cooed, and I felt a surge of love so potent it felt like my heart might break. "He's got your eyes, Joe," she said, looking toward him. "And look at that strong jawline."

"Think so?" Joe replied, as he cast a sidelong glance at me, a silent question in his features.

I nodded in agreement with my mom.

"What's his name?" Dad asked with tenderness and then looked at me expectantly. I shared a look with Joe and then told them.

"Joseph Paul Phillips." His name tasted like a promise on my tongue—a vow that he will know a life brimming with love—void of the shadows that have chased us through the years.

"Joseph Paul," Dad repeated, his voice a low rumble, his expression unreadable.

I studied him, searching for some sign that this meant as much to him as it did to me. The man before me was a patchwork of contradictions, frayed edges sewn together by the redemptive threads of time. His eyes, once wild and uncompromising, now teemed with regret and longing. His hands, calloused and stained, were still capable of the gentlest touch.

"Named after two good men," I added, not unaware of the contradiction. This man, who had loved me and abused me, overcome demons of anger, yet still wrestled demons of addiction.

Dad looked at me then, a hint of surprise in his weathered features. I wasn't sure what he had expected, but it wasn't this. Not his name being passed on to the next generation.

"Tamara," Dad began, his voice thick with unspoken emotions. It's then that I realized the strength it must have taken for him to be here, sober and present, when the pull of old demons never truly faded.

"Thank you," he said simply, but it was enough. Enough to acknowledge the weight of the name, the legacy we were entrusting to this tiny life.

My throat tightened as I leaned closer to Joe, our hands entwining, our gazes meeting in a moment of quiet understanding. He squeezed my hand reassuringly, his gaze moving from our son to me and back again.

"Okay, Mom. It's my turn," Nathan said, reaching for baby Joseph.

"Oh, alright," she said and reluctantly handed him to Nathan.

"Hey there, champ," Nathan murmured to the bundle in his embrace. "You're gonna be a tough one, aren't you? Just like your Uncle Nate."

I couldn't help but chuckle, though the sound was shaky with the remnants of tears. My brother, always the comedian, even when shadows lingered behind his grin.

My gaze flickered to Dakota as she watched from her seat, her eyes brimming with tears. She'd been through so much, yet here she was, showing up with all the strength she can muster. I was truly proud of her for that.

Dad was next in line to hold Joseph. He had regained his composure by then, his features softened in awe as he cradled his namesake, whispering words of wisdom only meant for Joseph's ears.

The room was filled with a profound sense of warmth and love as each of us took turns holding the little miracle that was Joseph. Somehow, despite the struggles we had been through, the disparity between our pasts and our present, we were a family. And for the moment, that was all that mattered.

CHAPTER 67

March 11, 9:24 a.m.

TIM

The brass doorknob was cold under my grip, but the dread pooling in my gut was colder as I pushed into Captain Simmons's office. The creak of the hinges seemed to resound like a warning siren, reverberating through the sparsely furnished room that smelled faintly of old coffee and printer ink.

Captain Simmon's grizzled face was cast in the harsh glow of a single desk lamp, shadows pooling beneath his furrowed brows. He looked up from a stack of papers, his expression as weary as I felt, the weight of justice pressing on us like a tombstone.

"Moore," he grunted, motioning me to the chair on the other side of his cluttered desk. As I sat, the leather let out a groan that echoed my unease. The usually comforting scent of worn paper and ink was now tinged with something bitter. He seemed to take in my battered appearance, the bruise above my eye, the way my upper lip had swollen in retaliation to a punch I'd taken last night.

"Do you mind telling me what in the hell happened yesterday?" I swallowed; the question hung in the room like a guillotine blade above my head. "How does an off-duty cop, already on thin ice, stumble upon the biggest drug bust Jefferson County has seen in years?"

His words landed like punches, knocking the wind out of me.

I was supposed to be the law, the virtuous one, but here I was in my captain's office, feeling like nothing more than a common thug. A bitter taste flooded my mouth. The irony wasn't lost on me.

I tried to stay calm and think, but my mind was a jumbled mess. I didn't know how to explain this. I reached for the most random thought in my brain and dove off the cliff, hoping I could bluff my way through this. "After we talked yesterday, I took a drive to Quilcene to get some oysters." What the hell was this garbage coming out of my mouth?

"Oysters?" He raised an incredulous eyebrow mirroring my thoughts.

"Yeah, oysters," I replied, trying to maintain an air of nonchalance.

The corner of the Captain's mouth twitched, and I couldn't decipher whether it was amusement or annoyance that sparked behind his eyes.

"And?"

"Well." My throat was dry, as if I'd swallowed a handful of sand, and I fought to keep my voice steady. "I saw something...odd."

Simmons settled in his chair, his denim shirt crinkling with the motion. The light of the single desk lamp cast his grizzled features into sharp relief, making him look more like some ancient carved figure than a man. There was a hard, granite-like quality to him that reminded me of the cold sea cliffs I used to dive off of when I was a kid. "Odd?" he repeated, folding his hands over his belly. "You'll have to do better than that, officer."

My grip tightened on the edge of the desk as my nerves threatened to get the better of me. "There were two guys sitting in the back of a rust bucket, lifting their hands like they were having a real passionate discussion. I got closer and realized it was Justin Williams and Avery Clark. I'd been keeping an eye on them because they used to run with Ryan Cooke."

"I see," Simmons said, his was unreadable. "And what were they discussing that held such passion?"

"I couldn't tell, sir, so when they left the spot, I discreetly followed them to the house. Then once they were inside, I snuck to the window and listened. I heard them talking about weighing out drugs and decided the best move was to let Ramirez know my move, and then I busted in on them."

"Dammit, Moore!" Simmons exploded, his calm demeanor switching to fury in an instant. His balled fists slammed onto the battered desk, shaking the loose papers that lay there. "You expect me to believe the excrement that's coming out of your mouth?"

"Yes, sir," I said, my voice steady, though my heart was pounding in my chest like a restless drum. "I know it sounds... improbable, but it's the truth."

Simmons ran a hand through his graying hair and sighed deeply. "Moore," he began, pinching the bridge of his nose with two fingers as if trying to alleviate a headache. "You're a good cop —one of the best we have. But damn. I'm not an idiot! None of this adds up. First the missing time on the tape, then you're just driving through Quilcene to get some 'oysters' and stumble on a bust this big. And to top it off, you were off duty and decided to act without backup." He paused for a second, to catch his breath, his face as red as a beet. "Do you have any idea how reckless you were?" he continued. His voice was now a low growl. "You could've been killed!"

"I know, sir," I managed to croak out. "But I couldn't just stand by and do nothing."

"The hell you couldn't have! There's procedures here— protocol we follow." Simmons spat the words at me, his face growing redder with each one. "You should've called for backup, not played hero."

"You're right, sir," I admitted, feeling the weight of his rebuke. "I messed up."

"You're damn right you did!" He continued to scrutinize me,

ELISHEBA HAXBY & JESSE VINCENT

his gaze unyielding. "I've been doing some digging, and I have a few hunches of my own."

My blood ran cold as ice at his words. I tried to speak, to say something to defend myself, but I had no words.

"After you left yesterday, I found out that your fiancée is in the hospital. Drug overdose." He let that hang in the air for a moment, as if he was waiting for my reaction. I felt like my whole body had turned to stone. If Simmons knew about Dakota, there was no way I could explain this away.

"My guess is that Justin and Avery had something to do with giving Dakota the drugs she overdosed on. You found them in a compromising situation, and instead of following protocol, you went rogue."

For a moment, all I could hear was the blood pulsing in my ears. It was a deafening, rhythmic throb that seemed to block out everything else. My hands instinctively curled into fists at my sides, my nails digging into the palms of my hands. This was it. Everything that I had worked for up in Victor's crack pipe. Simmons was only another inch from putting the rest of the puzzle together. That I had tampered with evidence. That I had been sucked into a criminal game because of the woman I loved and my fierce need to protect her.

My mind was running at full speed, trying to think of a convincing enough lie that would keep the noose from tightening further around my neck. But deep inside, I couldn't shake off the creeping dread that my truth was beginning to crack through the facade.

The silence stretched out, punctuated only by the muted sounds of the precinct outside the office—the soft murmur of voices, the distant clatter of a keyboard. It felt like an alternate reality, one where right and wrong hadn't blurred into indistinguishable shades of gray.

The knot in my stomach tightened until it felt like a lead weight. I looked into the eyes of the man who had shaped my career, who had taught me to uphold the law without compromise, and I understood that there could be no half-measures, no more evasion.

"Alright," I said, meeting his gaze. "You want the truth?"

Simmons' nodded, expression solemn. "The truth is the only thing that can help you now, Moore."

Captain Simmons's office felt like a shrinking cage, the walls closing in with each tick of the clock hanging precariously above his head. "Victor Mendez... he orchestrated everything," I began, my voice strangled by the truth clawing its way out. "He targeted Dakota. Used Justin and Avery as pawns in his sick game."

"And why would Mendez do that, Moore?" he asked, steepling his fingers together.

The words flowed out, like a dam breaking, all my pent-up fears and distress gushing forth. "Why does a man like Mendez do anything? It's about power, control."

"Go on," Simmons urged, his voice low and even, the sharp edge of authority cutting through the air.

"Justin and Avery, they enjoyed it, sir. Tormenting Dakota. They didn't just follow orders. They relished in them." The words spilled forth, staining the silence between us with their dark hues. It was as if speaking the truth aloud made it all the more real, more vile.

The captain's hands lay flat on the desk, his fingers drumming an impatient rhythm. "And Dakota?"

I swallowed hard, the acid taste of fear coating my tongue. "She overdosed, sir. Died, actually, for a brief moment. But Ricky —Ricky and I—we brought her back."

"Damn it, Tim! That's awful." His voice was a notch louder now, punching through the stifling atmosphere of the room, but kept my heart pounding—it was the memory of Dakota's pale face, lifeless yet hauntingly beautiful in her vulnerability.

I shook away the image and continued to speak. "When she woke, she confided in me that they had made her run several packages for them. They told her they would kill me if she didn't do what they told her."

My words hung over us like a guillotine, ready to fall and sever everything I had painstakingly built throughout my career. But there was no turning back now, and I knew it was time to lay the final piece of this grim jigsaw before him.

"The packages... drugs?" Simmons guessed, his face hardening at the thought.

"She didn't know what was in them, but each time they had her bring them to the Rodrigez house."

A quiet knowing shown in his features. "The missing time on the tapes."

I confirmed his suspicions with a nod, knowing it was a death blow to my career and potentially years in prison if Simmons saw fit to prosecute me. "Yes," I said, my voice barely a whisper in the tense silence. "I stopped it when I saw Dakota walking to the house with the package." The confession was like a knife, cutting through the last remnants of my deception. But oddly, there was a measure of relief in it as well.

Simmons frowned, studying me as if he was seeing me for the first time. "And the drugs? The one she overdosed on?"

"Fentanyl." I swallowed the bitter taste on my tongue.

The captain frowned as his eyes bore into mine, filled with a mixture of disappointment and sadness. "Damn, Moore," he finally said, his voice gravelly. "You've dug yourself a pretty deep hole here."

"I know, sir," I replied. "But I had to save her."

Simmons shook his head slowly. "You know we have procedures for this kind of situation. Protocols that could've protected her and you."

I clenched my jaw, the bitter taste of regret mingling with fear. "In theory, sir," I retorted softly. "But we both know how easily theory can crumble before the harsh realities of the world we live in. And because of those sick jerks Dakota almost died."

Simmons continued to stare at me, the weight of his gaze pushing on my resigned shoulders. After a moment's silence, he sighed heavily. "I understand your feelings, Moore," he said in a low, weary tone. "Believe me, I wish the world was a place where things like this didn't happen. But you're a cop. You swore to uphold the law, not break it."

His words lashed at me like a whip, leaving invisible welts on my conscience. I had broken the law, yes, but only because I had believed it was the only way to save Dakota from herself. "I know, sir," I muttered, my voice barely above a whisper. "But the law failed Dakota. She was just a kid when she got sucked into this mess. And people like Victor, they don't care about the law. They use it, twist it to their own advantage."

Simmons leaned forward, resting his elbows on the desk. His fingers steepled in front of him, hiding his mouth as he thought. His eyes still bore into me, but they were softer now, more understanding than accusing. "You're right," he admitted grudgingly. "The system is far from perfect. But that's no excuse for breaking the law."

"I did what I thought was right, sir."

Simmons stood abruptly, moving to the window. He looked out at the busy city below us, a world ignorant of the storm brewing within these four walls. "You were one of my best officers, Moore," he said quietly, his reflection in the glass a picture of contemplation.

"I'm still that officer, sir," I said, standing as well. "I didn't do it for thrill or personal gain. I did it to protect the woman I love. Please tell me what you would have done if this was your wife or daughter?"

Simmons stayed quiet for a long while, his gaze distant—lost in a horizon I couldn't see. "I don't know, Moore," he finally admitted. His reflection in the glass seemed smaller somehow, subdued by an unseen force. "I don't know."

We fell into silence again, the ticking of the clock once more echoing in the room. Time felt like it had stopped altogether—the world outside still bustling, moving on oblivious to the turmoil within.

Finally, Simmons broke the silence, his voice steady and

resolute. "Moore, you've made a mess of things—but I'll be damned if I don't see something of myself in you." He turned to face me then. "Love makes us do ungodly things."

I felt my heart lurch in my chest as I waited for his next words. The hope that had died now seemed to stir again like a phoenix from the ashes.

"I was going to suspend you without pay," he continued, pacing slowly to his desk. "But for now, why don't we call it a leave of absence. You're a good cop, Moore, and a good man. I don't want this mistake to tarnish your future. You take some time and get your head on straight."

I was stunned into silence. His words hung between us like a tangible thing, surprising me, giving me hope where moments before there had been none.

"Thank you, sir," I managed to say, my voice raspy from the relief flooding through me.

He waved away my thanks dismissively and sank into his chair, rubbing a hand over his visibly tired face. "Just don't make me regret this decision. This isn't a free pass. You've got some serious thinking to do."

I nodded, understanding that this was an opportunity— probably the only one I would get—to make things right. I had been prepared for the worst—jail time, disgrace, the end of the line. Instead, I was being given a second chance. "I actually was going to bring you my resignation today. Dakota and I are going to take some time with family to heal from all of this, and then figure out our next steps."

Simmons nodded, setting his mug back on the table with a deliberate thud. "That's a wise move. Maybe the wisest one you've made in a long time. It pains me to say so, but I accept your resignation.".

I felt a pang of gratitude and sorrow simultaneously. "Thank you for everything. You've been like a father to me, sir."

Simmons held my gaze for a moment longer before breaking the silence. "Make sure you make something of this second chance

I'm giving you," he said, his voice gruff but sincere. "Don't let that girl down." With that, he turned away, effectively dismissing me. I hesitated for a moment but then walked out of his office. As I gathered my things from my desk, I thought of the Restorative Justice class I was almost done with. This right here felt like my own personal version of it—I had broken the law, I had made huge mistakes, but now I had a chance to atone for my past mistakes, to right some wrongs, and to heal the wounds that had been created. I realized then that justice wasn't about punishing the guilty, or exacting revenge. It was about healing, about giving second chances to those who wanted to do better.

CHAPTER 68

April 2, 5:02 p.m.

DAKOTA

The refreshing touch of the ocean breeze calmed the anxious corners of my mind. I had been staying in Ocean Shores for several weeks now, but there were still times when memories from my last few weeks in Jefferson County would flood back, bringing with them a sense of impending danger and the belief that I was nothing more than a pawn in Victor's game to save Tim. Breathing in deeply, I filled my lungs with the salty air and exhaled slowly, scanning the horizon. The sand beneath me shifted with each gentle wave, reminding me of the days that seemed to slip through my fingers like grains of sand.

Tamara and Amanda sat with me, taking in the beautiful scenery before us. The brilliant sun overhead bathed us in a warm, comforting light—a beautiful contrast to the tormenting darkness that had been my life for so long. Their soft laughter joined with the rhythm of the crashing waves, a soothing symphony that nudged my weary heart towards thoughts of hope.

"Remember when we were kids?" Tamara leaned on her elbows, gazing at the canvas of blue above us. "We used to build sandcastles"—she gestured vaguely towards a patch of untouched beach—"as if we could create our own little kingdoms."

"Mine always crumbled," I said, recalling the impermanence of those sandy structures. "Yours stood tall until the tide came in."

"Maybe," she agreed. "But we built them together, Dakota. And when they washed away, we just started over the next day."

The simplicity of her words and the raw truth in her voice struck a chord within me. "Starting over..." My voice trailed off, and I grabbed a shell from the sand, its once vibrant colors now dulled by time and tides. "It's not as easy as it used to be."

"Nothing worthwhile ever is," Tamara replied, a soft yet resolute tone threading her words.

I nodded, a silent acknowledgment of her wisdom. The shell in my hand suddenly felt heavier, burdened with the weight of my past choices. I tossed it gently back to the sea, watching as it was swallowed by the foam.

"Think you can help me build a new one?" I asked after a moment, the question hanging in the air between us like a fragile promise.

Tamara's smile was warm as the sun on our backs. "I've got nowhere else I'd rather be."

"Me neither," I whispered, more to myself than to her, the ghost of conviction stirring somewhere deep inside. I drew my knees to my chest. The grains of sand stick to my damp skin. Beside me, Tamara shifted, her body still carrying the tender fullness of recent motherhood.

"We're here for you, Dakota. No matter how many time the tide rolls in."

Her words, full of unspoken assurances and unconditional support, hummed in the air around us. I sat there, staring at the hypnotic sway of the ocean waves, as if they held the answers to all my uncertainties. It wasn't just about survival or getting through another day. it was about living, truly living, and reclaiming the pieces of ourselves we thought lost.

"Can I tell you a secret?" I asked, more to the waves than to either of them.

"Always," Tamara answered instantly, her loyalty a steady beacon.

"I'm scared," I confessed. "Of starting over, of failing, of not knowing if I can be the person I want to be." The vulnerability of it made my insides quiver.

Amanda scooted closer, her hand coming to rest on mine. "Fear's just the flip side of hope, Dakota. You can't have one without the potential for the other."

"Deep," I said with a chuckle, though her words resonated with a truth I couldn't deny.

"Mom-level deep," Tamara agreed, her laughter mingling with ours.

They didn't know how their presence anchored me, how these moments were the life rafts I clung to in the turbulent sea of recovery.

Quiet settled over us like a veil, broken only by the lapping of the waves and the occasional shriek of a seagull. I looked at the ocean, its vastness so intimidating yet soothing at the same time.

In the distance, Joe, Tim, and Nathan formed a trio of guardians, silhouetted against the fiery streaks of sunset. Nathan's arms gestured animatedly as he shared a story with the kids, their giggles carried to us on the wind. Joe held Joseph Paul, swaddled and quiet in his arms, a picture of paternal serenity. And Tim was there, on the outskirts, his gaze finding mine across the expanse of sand.

"Good guys, those three," Amanda observed, drawing her knees up and wrapping her arms around them. "They've really stepped up."

"Especially with everything we've been through," I added, feeling the weight of my past struggles blend into the collective narrative of our resilience.

Tamara nodded, her eyes shadowed with the weight of shared hardships. "But we're standing strong, aren't we? One day at a time."

"One day at a time," I repeated. The words were both my

mantra and my promise. A promise not just to myself, but to the people who believed in me.

"Life's a wild ride, but I wouldn't want anyone else in my coaster car," Amanda quipped, and we erupted into laughter, the sound mingling with the symphony of the seaside night.

And in that instant, surrounded by the love of those who had seen me at my lowest and held me until I could stand again, I knew—I wasn't just recovering. I was rebuilding.

Joe brought Joseph Paul to Tamara then. "I think he's hungry," he said, his voice gentle and full of love for the tiny life he cradled.

Tamara took the bundle from him, smiling as she looked down into the tiny face of her son. I watched as she started to feed him with a delicacy reserved for precious things of this world.

The sight of them together, mother and child, stirred something deep within me. "Look at what love can do," I said, observing their bond, I saw the tangible evidence of new beginnings and promises kept.

I imagined Joseph Paul's tiny hands grasping onto the world with innocence and trust. The softness of his cheek, the curve of his fingers—every detail a marvel, every breath a whisper of potential. In this small being, I recognized the possibility for change, a chance to redefine my own existence.

A seagull cried overhead, its sound a lonely sound against the vast expanse of sky and sea, a continuous, unending rhythm that underscored the stillness of our moment.

Once Tamara had finished feeding Joseph Paul, she rested him on her shoulder and gently patted his back.

"Tamara," I murmured, my voice soft but clear above the symphony of waves, "he's absolutely adorable."

She turned to me, her eyes crinkling at the corners as she smiled, the pride evident in every line of her face. The baby—Joseph Paul—was a bundle of warmth in her arms, wrapped in a soft blue blanket.

"Thank you, Dakota." Her response was a gentle exhale as she held him close.

"Could I...?" My question trailed off, but my arms instinctively opened, an unspoken appeal hanging between us. I longed to feel the weight of his tiny body against mine, to share even a fraction of the joy that seemed to radiate from Tamara.

"Of course." She nodded, shifting Joseph carefully into my outstretched arms.

The transition was seamless, her trust in me palpable. As I cradled him close, feeling the softness of his cheek against my arm, Joseph Paul stirred slightly, nuzzling into the crook of my elbow as if he knew instinctively that he was safe. It was a small gesture, but it felt monumental.

"Hi there, little guy," I whispered, my voice barely above the sound of the surf. .

Tamara watched us, a contented sigh escaping her lips. In this moment, with her blessing and the acceptance in those big, innocent eyes, I sensed the fragile beginnings of hope weaving its way through the tapestry of my fractured life.

Peering into Joseph Paul's eyes felt like gazing into two tiny pools reflecting the infinite sky above. They were a startling blue, vivid and clear. He blinked, and with each flutter of his delicate eyelids, something primal and deep-rooted stirred within me. "You have the entire universe in your eyes, Joey," I murmured, my voice a reverent hush against the backdrop of the ocean's whispers.

Tamara leaned closer, perhaps recognizing the silent communion unfolding before her. "He does, doesn't he? Like he sees right through to the heart of things."

A lump formed in my throat as I nodded, unable to articulate the swell of emotions that threatened to breach my composure. Tears spilled over, trailing down my cheeks, warm and salty like the sea breeze. I brushed them away, laughing softly at my own vulnerability.

The weight of him in my arms was grounding, a tangible

reminder of life's relentless continuation. My fingers traced the soft curve of his cheek, marveling at the perfection of his tiny features. Tamara's past—our past—had been a chaotic storm of bad choices and darker days, yet here in my arms was a testament to the possibility of beauty born from turmoil.

How could something so perfect come out of all that we had been through? The thought played in my mind, an incredulous whisper that grew louder, bolder. Maybe... maybe it wasn't too late for me either. Hope, a fragile seed, began to sprout amidst the ruins of my self-inflicted desolation.

Tim approached then, his broad silhouette cutting through the warm crimson hues of the setting sun. His gaze met mine, and I could see a quiet longing in them as he watched me with Joseph Paul. A longing for us to start our own family someday.

I smiled at him and then turned my attention to Joseph Paul. "Hey, little man, you're gonna teach Auntie Dakota some important stuff, aren't you?" I asked, my voice tinged with a newfound resolve. "Like how to start fresh."

Joseph Paul cooed in response, a sound so pure and innocent that it seemed to slice through years of accumulated cynicism. In those tiny pools, I saw not only his future but the glimmer of a second chance for my own.

Tamara's voice broke through my reverie, her tone a mix of wonder and affection. "Look at you two. He knows you're family, Dakota."

Her words stirred something deep inside me—a conviction, a desire, a quiet certainty. I would not be the person I was. I would overcome. For him, for Tim, for Tamara...for myself. My heart pounded with the weight of this silent pledge, its rhythm aligning with the sea's eternal cadence.

A cool breeze swept over us, carrying the salty tang of the ocean. I closed my eyes, letting the serenity of the moment calm me. The tides of change pulled at the very core of who I was.

"Joe, would you look after Joseph Paul for a minute?" Tamara asked softly, her gaze fixed on me with a sister's understanding.

"Of course," he replied, taking the baby from my arms. I felt a pang of loss as the warmth left me, but it was quickly replaced by a sense of solidarity as Tamara reached for Amanda's hand.

"Can we pray for you, Dakota?" Tamara said, her voice choked with emotion as she stood, gently pulling Amanda up beside her.

I looked at Tim, who caught my gaze with a smile as he moved closer and put his hand on my back. I felt my heart squeeze, the uncertainty of what lay ahead pressing me. But there was comfort too, in the soothing rhythm of the ocean and the warmth of my sister's hand in mine. I nodded, unable to speak, my throat tight with emotion.

"Dear Lord," Tamara began. "We lift Dakota to you. Bless her with the strength to overcome, to heal, and to find peace."

I thought of Jesus then and the moment I had seen him during my near-death experience. His eyes were full of a piercing warmth, a depth of understanding that seemed to reach into the very marrow of my soul. He was filled with an incredible kindness, and though I was not worthy, he loved me nonetheless.

I had always been skeptical of religious beliefs, my past filled with too much hardship and betrayal to believe in the goodness of a divine entity. But that moment... it was as if all my doubt, all my fear, was stripped away. I felt an undeniable connection to something larger than myself, a palpable presence that filled every corner of my being. And then and there, I knew beyond a shadow of doubt that Jesus was a Higher Power worth surrendering to.

Tim's hand was on my back, strong and comforting. and I wondered if he could feel the same love and peace that was enveloping me. His gentle touch grounded me as I sat there, eyes closed and heart open.

"Guide her steps," Amanda whispered fervently. "Help her to see the beauty and potential in every new day."

I listened, the words enveloping me like a warm blanket, igniting a spark of hope in the cold recesses of my soul. My heart swelled with gratitude for these two women, standing sentinel, their prayers a beacon in the darkness I had known too well.

"Help her to know she is never alone," Tamara continued, "that we are here for her, always."

Their prayers became a mantra, a sacred promise that echoed deep within me. As they prayed, my vision blurred with tears, each one a release, a step away from the shadows of addiction and toward the light of possibility.

"Thank you," I managed, my voice barely above a whisper, my eyes lifted to the vast sky above. The horizon stretched before me, a line where sea met heaven, a reminder of infinite possibilities. I was ready, I affirmed silently, to walk towards that horizon. To get better. And as we stood there, united on the cusp of tomorrow, I knew—deep in the marrow of my bones—that I was already stepping into a new chapter of my life.

Epilogue: June 16

TAMARA

The golden sand cradled me as I sat with my back against the weathered canvas of my old beach chair. The rhythmic ebb and flow of the ocean's breath whispered against the shore, a lullaby for Joseph Paul, who lay nestled in my arms like a seashell swaddled in blue cotton.

"Look at them," I murmured, watching Lillie's dance across the sand. Beside her was Hope, the beautiful child of a messy past. They were sisters, bound by blood yet raised worlds apart, their bond an intricate tapestry woven from strands of love and sacrifice.

Levi watched the girls play, his eyes reflecting the pride of a father. "They're beautiful together."

Sarah, ever the gentle soul, sat beside him. "Like two pearls from the same ocean," Sarah said, a smile gracing her lips.

Dakota nodded, the corners of her mouth tilting with affection. She sat cross-legged on the sand, her toes working absentmindedly through the grains.

I watched them, my heart filling with a mixture of joy and wistfulness. It was a scene I'd replayed in my mind a thousand times.

"Mommy, look!" Lillie's voice called out, beckoning my attention to the moat she and Hope were digging around their fortress. The sun caught Hope's hair, turning it to spun gold, a halo around her face.

"Beautiful work, my love!" I called back. My baby stirred in my arms, his tiny fingers reaching toward the vastness of the sky.

Levi's fingers brushed over the leather-bound journal, weathered like driftwood, as he eased it from his canvas bag. He opened it to a fresh page, the crisp whiteness stark against the tan of his hands, marked by the passage of pens and years.

"Been working on another one of these," Levi said, his voice carrying the timbre of quiet reflection. "Not trying to capture everything... just the moments of Hope's life that feel important. I want to give this journal to Hope one day. A record of all that God has done in her life."

"She will love that," I said, glancing over at him. "Maybe as much as I did."

I watched him write as his pen danced with purpose across the paper thinking about how much his writings changed the course of my life. Perhaps it might do the same for Hope. Tears welled in my eyes and a lump formed in my throat, thick with emotion.

"Seeing them together... Lillie and Hope... It's like watching a love story that we wrote without knowing the ending." My voice trembled, words barely above a whisper. "It's so good to see that some things work out in the end."

The salt-laden air carried my confession, mingling it with the symphony of waves and seagulls. Sara reached out to mine, giving it a reassuring squeeze. Our shared understanding flowed between us, the invisible thread that connected our hearts.

"Life has a funny way of coming full circle, doesn't it?" Sarah mused, focusing on the children who were oblivious to the depth of the moment, immersed in their own world of castles and dreams.

"More like a spiral," I reflected, "each turn bringing us closer to the core, where all our stories begin and end." I breathed deeply, inhaling the briny scent of ocean and resilience.

Joseph Paul gurgled softly, a bubble of contentment forming on his lips as he nuzzled closer, anchoring me to the here and now.

"Indeed," Sarah affirmed, her voice echoing the sentiment with every beat. "A beautiful spiral."

My gaze drifted from the tender scene before me, the delicate balance of past and future playing out in the sand, to the boisterous energy unfolding at the edge of the beach. The sun cast long shadows that danced rhythmically to the cadence of the volleyball game. Joe leapt high, a silhouette against the amber sky, his hand smacking the ball over the net with a victorious thud as laughter and jeers erupted from the men.

"Nice spike, Joe!" shouted David, his voice cutting through the salt-tinged breeze as he readied himself for the next serve.

"Watch the comeback, boys!" Clay called out, his feet digging into the sand as he prepared to receive. He was all focused energy, coiled like a spring, waiting for the moment to unleash.

I watched their carefree abandon, a contrast to the quiet reflection I shared with Sarah. The men were completely immersed in their game, their shouts and competitive jabs.

"Hey, Levi, you're up next!" Tim hollered, a bead of sweat rolling down his temple as he rotated out of the game, chest heaving slightly from exertion.

Levi shook his head with a chuckle, brushing away grains of sand from the journal's leather cover. "I'll pass this time, Tim. You guys seem to have it covered."

"Come on, man," Tim persisted. "Don't make me look bad. I need someone to blame if we lose!"

"I'll swap in," Dakota announced, brushing a lock of her hair from her face as she stood up, stretching her limbs with a vitality that surprised.

"Are you sure?" Tim asked, concern etching his brow despite the smile tugging at her lips.

"Absolutely," Dakota replied, confidence surging in her voice. "I need to show these guys how it's done."

Tim laughed at her feigned bravado, a sound that warmed my heart. It had been a long road for Dakota, but now she was here, standing tall with a spark in her step that had been missing for too long. "Alright, go get 'em, champ."

As Dakota made her way to the makeshift net, Tim grabbed a water and collapsed next to us, wiping the sweat from his brow. His attention remained on Dakota, watching as she moved.

Joe picked up the volleyball and tossed it to Dakota. With a spring in her step, she joined the court, where the men were readying themselves for the next volley.

"Hey, Tamara," Levi murmured, observing the scene unfolding before him. "I just want to thank you so much for making my 40th so memorable. It may be the best birthday I've ever had."

Witnessing our lives intertwine in such a powerful way was an experience that transcended mere celebration; it was proof of our struggles and triumphs, and evidence of our healing and unity.

As if reading my thoughts, Levi added, "There's something about today... It's like every moment is a gift, a reminder of where we've come from and the peace we've found."

"Gifts worth recording," I mused, nodding toward his journal, the keeper of fleeting moments destined to become cherished memories.

"Exactly," Levi agreed. "Some things are too precious to let slip away."

"Levi, with all the changes lately, I've been meaning to ask... what are you up to now?"

Levi closed his journal and leaned back on his hands, the sand yielding beneath his weight, and glanced out at the horizon where the sea met the sky in an endless embrace. "Well, I am still doing pastoral counseling, but recently I started consulting for a non-profiy. We specialize in prison work and restorative justice.

"Restorative justice?" Tim asked, sounding curious, leaning towards Levi.

Levi turned. "Yeah, it's about breaking cycles, you know? Bringing healing where there's been hurt. It is quite rewarding."

Tim moved closer. "I just finished my degree in criminal justice and one of my last classes was on restorative justice. After everything that went down"—he paused, his eyes briefly clouding with the gravity of past events before clearing with newfound resolution—"I've been thinking about looking more into it."

"Really?" Levi perked up, interested, his face brightening at the shared connection.

"Yeah." Tim nodded, his gaze drifting towards Dakota. "Never thought I'd say it, but school's got me considering new paths. Who knows where it'll lead?"

"Portland is really blossoming in terms of community projects." He glanced at Tim. "If you ever find your way down there, we could definitely find a place for you. The non-profit's always on the lookout for passionate people with experience in criminal justice."

I watched Tim's reaction keenly, noting the flicker of intrigue that crossed his features. His gaze shifted to the sand, contemplating the grains that stuck stubbornly to his skin, embodying the potential of being part of something greater.

"Think about it," Levi encouraged.

Tim's hand raked through his damp hair. "Portland, huh?" he mused aloud.

"Levi's right," I chimed in, thinking it would be good for Dakota and Tim to get out of Washington after all they had been through. "There's a whole community there that could benefit from what you've learned, from who you are."

Tim chuckled, the sound mingling with the distant crash of waves. "We have been looking at a change of scenery," he conceded, looking at Dakota again. His posture relaxed as if the tension of uncertainty began to ease from his shoulders. "Thank you; I'll consider it."

I let out a contented sigh. There was a certain magic in the air, a sense that everything was aligning just as it should, and I clung to that feeling like a lifeline. With every cheer from the game, every giggle from Lillie and Hope playing in the sand, I felt the threads of all of our lives intertwining, creating a cord strong enough to withstand the tides of change.

About The Authors

Elisheba and Jesse met in Youth With A Mission in 2001. Elisheba was impressed by Jesse's creative mind and his dedication to story crafting. Jesse was impressed by Elisheba's deep walk with Jesus and her commitment to emotional authenticity. They became friends and years later decided to start writing together through a set of supernatural circumstances.

Jesse carried the idea for their first book, Ninety-Nine, since 1999. At the time he knew it was a download from God, but struggled to write from an emotionally raw woman's point of view. Throughout the years when bringing this frustration to God, God simply responded with "this is not your story." Then in 2010 Elisheba heard from God to start writing and that her stories would lead people into an encounter with the love of God. She brought this word to Jesse and it clicked for both of them to work together on this project. The idea was conceived and nine months later the first book was birthed.

The journey of writing and publishing was quite challenging, filled with many hurdles and mistakes. But every step of the way God met them, helped them, and healed them. Over the many years of writing together, learning the craft, and pursuing inner healing, they decided to start a business to help other authors do the same. They wanted to combine their belief that God wants to create through His people with the need to help creatives be healed enough to partner with God and produce this creativity. To do this, they founded Above The Sun, LLC.

For more writing by Elisheba Haxby, Jesse Vincent, and Above The Sun, please visit:

ElishebaHaxby.com
AboveTheSun.org

What's Your Story

Above The Sun is a community of hope-filled creators who believe the world can be transformed through authentic stories. Our mission is to develop authors who are committed to becoming whole in order to successfully bring their message to their unique areas of influence. If you have a book in you and you are willing to do the work to release it, we would love to connect.

Visit us at AboveTheSun.org